THREE NIGHTS
IN
HAVANA

Three Nights in Havana

Pierre Trudeau, Fidel Castro and the Cold War World

Robert Wright

HarperCollins*PublishersLtd*

Published by HarperCollins Publishers Ltd

First Edition

Grateful acknowledgement is given to the following for permission to reproduce photographs
and illustrations: p. 1, Jean-Marc Carisse; p. 23, Canadian Press; p. 53, Firstlight; p. 70,
Reidford/*Globe and Mail*; p. 87, Duncan Cameron/Library and Archives Canada;
p. 121, Library and Archives Canada; p. 146, Jean-Marc Carisse; p. 148, Macpherson/
Toronto Star; p. 161, Canadian Press; p. 184, Duncan Cameron/Library and Archives Canada;
p. 200 Roschkov/*Toronto Star*; p. 208, Canadian Press; p. 217, Canadian Press;
p. 232, Macpherson/*Toronto Star*; p. 250, Canadian Press; p. 267, Prime Minister's Office.

HarperCollins books may be purchased for educational, business,
or sales promotional use through our Special Markets Department.

HarperCollins Publishers Ltd
2 Bloor Street East, 20th Floor
Toronto, Ontario, Canada
M4W 1A8

www.harpercollins.ca

Library and Archives Canada Cataloguing in Publication

Wright, Robert A. (Robert Anthony), 1960–
Three nights in Havana : Pierre Trudeau, Fidel Castro
and the Cold War world / Robert Wright.

ISBN-13: 978-0-00-200626-2
ISBN-10: 0-00-200626-X

1. Canada—Foreign relations—Cuba.
2. Cuba—Foreign relations— Canada.
3. Canada—Politics and government—1968–1979.
4. Canada— Foreign relations—1945–. I. Title.

FC626.T7W75 2007   327.7107291'09047   C2006-905845-8

HC 9 8 7 6 5 4 3 2 1

Printed and bound in the United States
Set in Janson
Design by Sharon Kish

For Laura, Helena, Anna and Michael

Contents

Preface

When Fidel Castro appeared in Montreal in October 2000 for the state funeral of Pierre Trudeau, most Canadians were taken entirely by surprise. Few had any inkling of the depth of the two leaders' mutual affection. Trudeau had visited Cuba as a footloose thirty-year-old in 1949 and again in 1964, just before he joined the Pearson Liberals as justice minister. During the October Crisis of 1970, he secretly asked Castro to take five Front de libération du Québec (FLQ) terrorists off Canada's hands, and Castro obliged. Yet only in January 1976 did the two men meet face-to-face for the first time, and only in the 1990s, when Trudeau had retired from politics, did they place their friendship on a familiar footing. Margaret Trudeau famously called Castro one of the sexiest men in the world but, true to form, the intensely private Pierre said hardly a word about him. The result has been three decades' worth of speculation, sycophancy and smear.

Three Nights in Havana chronicles the origins of the friendship between Pierre Trudeau and Fidel Castro, two world leaders whose fates were intertwined well before the Canadian prime minister stepped off his Armed Forces Boeing 707 at José Martí Airport in 1976. The Cold War stand-off between the United States and the Soviet Union made formal enemies of Canada and Cuba, just as surely as history had made them colonies of rival European empires. But neither Trudeau nor Castro was ever comfortable in the role of compliant ally, and by the mid-twentieth century the same could be said of many of their contemporaries. Canadians and Cubans may have little in common but they do share one important national characteristic—a determined refusal to exist merely as the satellite of some other power. Pierre Trudeau and Fidel Castro personified this refusal. It was what brought them to power. It was also what drew them to each other. This is their story.

A word on terminology. Fidel Castro has been called, at different stages of his political career, Dr. Castro (because he holds an earned law degree from the University of Havana), premier, prime minister and "Maximum Leader." He is also first secretary of the Communist Party of Cuba, commander-in-chief of the Cuban armed forces, and, as of December 1976, president of the State Council. Ordinary Cubans call him *El Jefe* (the Chief) in casual conversation. In this book, I have opted for the more formal *El Comandante*, the term by which he is known to readers of *Granma*, the Communist Party newspaper, and other official publications. Of his many titles, this is the one in which he is said to take the greatest pride. It also has the practical advantage of distinguishing the Cuban leader both from (U.S.) presidents and (Canadian) prime ministers. I have adopted as well the Cuban convention of capitalizing the term *Revolution*.

This book could not have been written without the help of others. It gives me great pleasure to acknowledge them here. Research funding was provided by the Canada Council for the Arts and by the Symons Trust Fund for Canadian Studies, for which I am indebted. For putting themselves at my disposal early on in my research, I am grateful to Christian Lapointe, Kim Cowan, Ghislain Chaput and Greg Donaghy at Foreign Affairs Canada, and to Paul Gibbard at the Canadian Embassy in Havana. For their willingness to be interviewed for this book, I am indebted to Juan Antonio Blanco, Carlos Fernandez de Cossío, Tom Delworth, Mark Entwistle and William D. Rogers. James Hyndman took a keen interest in the project at every stage, sitting for long interviews, agreeing to an extensive e-mail correspondence and reading an early draft of the book in its entirety. For his unstinting generosity, I am deeply grateful. My thanks go out as well to Paulette Dozois at Library and Archives Canada, Jo-Anne Valentine and Ted Kelly at the Foreign Affairs Library in Ottawa, Paul Losch of the Smathers Library at the University of Florida, Trish Johns-Wilson and Pam Conley of the Bata Library at Trent University, and Karen Benacquista, Heather Gildner and Charlie Ewing of the Toronto Public Library. I am also grateful to Ann Louise Bardach, Curtis Fahey, John Kirk, Max and Monique Nemni, Andrew Potter, James Ron, David Sheinin, Tim Stapleton, Craig Walker, Dan Wright, R. K. Wright and Lana Wylie. Special thanks to my research assistants, Louise Taylor, Kyle Branch and especially Christine McLaughlin, and to my editor at HarperCollins Canada, Jim Gifford.

The standard author's caveat, that the views expressed in his work are his alone, must apply tenfold to any book on Pierre Trudeau and Fidel Castro, so intensely have both men been deified and demonized over the years. I have tried to bring a historian's balance and objectivity to this story, but where I have failed I have done so single-handedly.

As always, my greatest debt is to my wife, Laura, and my children, Helena, Anna and Michael. And as always, words cannot begin to express this debt. This book is for them.

Funeral for a Friend

"*Viva Fidel!*"

So shouted the crowd as Fidel Castro arrived at Montreal's Notre-Dame Basilica for the funeral of Pierre Elliott Trudeau in October 2000.

Jimmy Carter was there. So were Prime Minister Jean Chrétien, poet Leonard Cohen, Prince Andrew and the Aga Khan. But it was Castro, clad in a sombre grey suit and maintaining a stoical silence, who captivated the fifteen thousand or so Canadians who had come to pay their respects to the late prime minister. In cheering for Castro—and in invoking the "*¡Viva!*" cheer with which Trudeau had endeared himself to the Cuban people a quarter-century earlier—Montrealers were paying tribute not only to the Cuban *Comandante* but also to the memory of a beloved Canadian prime minister. Castro's presence at the funeral, an exceptional gesture of respect for a world leader who seldom travels outside his home country, symbolized the very qualities that Trudeau's Canadian devotees had come to love in him: loyalty, fierce independence, the courage of his convictions.

Castro was one of only two sitting heads of state to attend the service. He had come not as a statesman but as a long-time friend of the late prime minister's family. "The regard I felt toward [Pierre] was like that toward a member of the family," he later reflected. "I didn't just like him, I was very fond of him and his family."

As perplexing as it had been to their Cold War allies, Fidel Castro and Pierre Trudeau had enjoyed a warm personal relationship since the prime minister's historic state visit to Cuba in 1976. The two leaders discovered early on that they were, as former Canadian ambassador to Cuba Mark Entwistle puts it, "intellectual soulmates." Both were educated by Jesuits and trained in the law; both were men of formidable intellect whose political idealism had inspired millions of their compatriots, infuriated millions of others and changed the course of their nations' history. There were also traits in their larger-than-life personalities that set them apart, qualities that each man recognized and respected in the other: an indomitable passion for politics, an adventurous lust for life combined with an almost ascetic self-discipline, a shy demeanour paired with a notoriously stubborn will.

With the passing of Pierre Trudeau, Castro knew that he had lost a true comrade. He expressed his condolences to the Trudeau family in the warmest of terms. "I have come to Canada, in time of deep grief for the Canadian people," said Castro, "to pay tribute to the undying memory of Pierre Trudeau, a world class statesman who was a close personal friend and one for whom I felt great admiration. I always considered him a serious political leader, sincerely interested in the world problems [sic] and the situation in the Third World countries as well as a consistent politician who made a transcendental contribution to the modern history of Canada. He was an upright and brave man who, regardless of difficult circumstances, fostered his country's relations with Cuba."

2

Until the last years of his life, Trudeau had been an honoured guest in Castro's house and a valued confidante. The two discussed everything from current events to their children's milestones, snorkelling together whenever they got the chance. In marked contrast with Trudeau's reputation in Canada as an aloof and dispassionate man, Castro revered him as "one of the most sincere men I have ever known, friendly and modest in his treatment of people." Pierre Trudeau may have been "the representative of an important, large and rapidly developing country," the *Comandante* insisted, "but he never believed himself superior, and it was this humility—his ideas and his personality always cheerful, always optimistic—that won us over." When news of Trudeau's death reached Cuba, Fidel Castro decreed a three-day period of mourning across the island, ordering all flags to fly at half-mast.

Because of Castro's fondness for Pierre Trudeau—and because of the extraordinary splash Margaret, Pierre and their son Michel had made in Havana in 1976—the former prime minister enjoyed a degree of celebrity and influence in Cuba that few Westerners could boast. A good word from Pierre Trudeau could go a long way toward inking a business deal between Canadians and Cubans, if only because he so rarely traded on his reputation.

As an ally of the Soviet Union and as an adversary of the United States, by contrast, it is fair to say that Fidel Castro had always been a political liability for Trudeau. Castro knew this, and so his debt to the former prime minister was that of a statesman as well as a friend. Trudeau's 1976 state visit was the first by the leader of a NATO country since 1960, the year the United States imposed its crippling economic embargo against Cuba. Trudeau had intended the trip to signal an end to Cuba's political isolation, but it did far more. When he arrived at José Martí Airport outside Havana, he was greeted by a thirty-foot poster of himself and then driven into the city in a motorcade flanked by 250,000 cheering Cubans. During his famous speech at the port city of Cienfuegos, delivered in Spanish to a crowd of 25,000, Trudeau cheered, "¡*Viva Cuba y el pueblo cubano! ¡Viva el Primer Ministro Fidel Castro! ¡Viva la amistad cubano-canadiense!"*[1] Such exuberance was a far cry from the quiet diplomacy for which Canada was famous, and it had pleased Castro greatly. A photograph of the two leaders made the cover of *Time* magazine. For a moment it looked as though Castro the communist pariah was on his way toward rehabilitation in the West.

As it turned out, Pierre Trudeau's state visit to Cuba was never reciprocated. As improbable as it seems for a man who has been a head of state for almost fifty years, Fidel Castro has never visited Canada officially. By the time of Trudeau's funeral in 2000, other than occasional refuelling stops at Gander or Vancouver, the *Comandante* had been to Canada only once, in 1959. This, in fact, was one of the reasons his presence in Montreal for the Trudeau funeral caused such a stir. It was the closest Fidel Castro has ever come to enjoying the pomp and ceremony of a state visit to Canada. It also marked his first meeting with a Canadian prime minister on Canadian soil.

———

Pierre Trudeau died on 28 September 2000. The official cause of death was prostate cancer but the former prime minister was also known to be suffering from Parkinson's disease and pneumonia. Since retiring from politics in 1984, Trudeau had maintained an extremely low public profile, practising law at Heenan Blaikie in Montreal and devoting himself to the raising of his sons, Justin, Sacha and Michel. The only exception to his vow of political silence had been his angry pronouncements against Brian Mulroney's constitutional accords in the late 1980s and early 1990s. Always a master of the political *coup de grâce*, Trudeau's bold accusation that Mulroney was "ready to trade Canada's soul for an electoral victory" had done a good deal to torpedo both the Charlottetown Accord and the Progressive Conservative Party. Afterwards, as unexpectedly as he had reappeared on the political

---

1. "Long live Cuba and the Cuban people! Long live Prime Minister Fidel Castro! Long live Cuban-Canadian friendship!"

scene, Trudeau again vanished into the shadows. Apart from his *Memoirs* project, which took the form of a CBC-TV documentary and later a book, he avoided the spotlight altogether in the Chrétien years.

The last time Canadians saw Pierre Trudeau on the public stage was in November 1998, and under the cruellest of circumstances. That month his son Michel was swept to his death in an avalanche. A seasoned outdoorsman like his father, the twenty-three-year-old had been returning from a ski trip in Kokanee Glacier Park in British Columbia. He was carried by the avalanche into the icy waters of Kokanee Lake, where, according to those who had been with him, he struggled for several minutes under the weight of his backpack and skiing gear, and then disappeared. Margaret later tried to put a brave face on the circumstances of Michel's death, telling the press that he had not suffered. "Micha just actually put his head on his shoulder and fell asleep," she said, using his family nickname. In truth, the situation was far more macabre. "We could see him," one eyewitness recalled. "We knew it was going to be a slow and painful death. But we couldn't reach him. He was in the middle of the lake." Some observers romanticized the wilderness death of Michel Trudeau, calling it a uniquely Canadian tragedy. For most Canadians, however, the loss was one of unmitigated sorrow.

Pierre Trudeau was visibly shattered by the death of his son. At the memorial service for Michel, he looked gaunt, almost ghostly, a man consumed with grief. As prime minister, Trudeau's implacable will had been as much a political liability as a strength, leading to charges that he was arrogant and pitiless. But here, frail and inconsolable, was a Trudeau Canadians had never seen. Even the most hard-bitten of his adversaries shared in the outpouring of grief with which the nation mourned the loss of his son. There is no question that the death of Michel cast a pall over Pierre's last years. Friends observed following the tragedy that he had grown even closer to his remaining children and also that he had become increasingly disillusioned with the world. Some said that his politics had drifted to the left, putting him ideologically closer to his friend Fidel

Castro than ever. The prospect of a new international order dominated by corporations was said to be especially loathsome to Trudeau, hardly surprising for a man who spent the better part of a lifetime trying to advance social justice.

Michel's death reunited Pierre Trudeau with Margaret, for whom the loss of a beloved son was equally cruel. Margaret had been subjected in the 1970s to a torrent of abuse from Canadians. And because she was, by her own admission, extremely thin-skinned, she suffered it only with great difficulty. With the death of Michel, however, Margaret, along with Pierre, elicited Canadians' deepest sympathy. Those who could recall her sensitive temperament pitied her grievously. Few images from the memorial service for Michel Trudeau, held at Saint-Viateur Church in Outremont, were as searing for Canadians as that of Pierre and Margaret standing hand in hand and sharing a grief the depth of which only they and their surviving sons could fathom. Six months after Michel's death, Margaret separated from her second husband, Fried Kemper. At about the same time, she broke the family silence on Michel's death to offer her public support for the cause of avalanche awareness. "When you have such a horrific death of your beautiful child," she reflected, "your sons' brother, your husband's son, it's just so outrageously painful that in the healing process it's so important to make the life you've lost live on in our hearts and make a difference. Micha would have loved that."

Fidel Castro was one of many sympathetic observers to lament that the deaths of Michel and Pierre Trudeau had come in quick succession. "Presently," he said, in a short statement released prior to his arrival in Montreal in October 2000, "I share in the grief and sorrow of Pierre Trudeau's family and of all Canadians. I cannot help but remember that only two years ago this family suffered another terrible tragedy with the passing of Michel Trudeau whom I had met at a very early stage of his life when as a four-month old baby his father took him on a visit to Cuba and I held him in my arms more than once." He added solemnly, "I have brought with me some photos of those dearly cherished days, to leave to the family as mementos."

Castro's sympathy for the Trudeau family was heartfelt. In a CBC-TV interview taped after the funeral, the *Comandante* reminisced about the many times Michel had accompanied his father on visits to Cuba after his trip as a newborn. "I met that little baby when he came here when he wasn't even four months old," Castro recalled, "and he won everyone's heart, he went to the sea with us, because I invited [Pierre] to a key in the south of Cuba, south of the Zapata Swamp, at the edge of the really deep water—he really liked sports, he liked fishing—and it never crossed my mind that he would bring the baby, but he brought his family." Pulling out photographs of himself with the teenaged Michel, Castro thumbed through them with CBC journalist Paule Robitaille. "Look," he said, "I told you about this. Look at him here when he was already as tall as I am. How many years after? Fifteen years after, that was in 1991. Look, [Michel] is taller than I am. Next I am going to show you this one. He's here, look, he's here as well. He came to Cuba three times, Trudeau came four."

———

During Pierre Trudeau's final days, it was Margaret who stayed by his side day and night. Riddled with cancer but still as lucid as ever, Pierre spent his last hours in bed, surrounded by his family and listening to Beethoven and Barbra Streisand records. He was, Margaret later recalled, at peace with the prospect of his own imminent death but still overcome with emotion at the end. "He was sad the last morning when he woke up and I was there, of course, on his pillow and he had tears rolling down his face, and that's all right. We just cheered him up. I said, 'You can cry all you want, I'm so glad you're giving us another day.'" That it was Margaret by his side at the end spoke volumes, not only about the depth of their mutual affection but also about her strength of character—something for which far too few Canadians had ever given her credit. At the deathbed and again at the funeral of the former prime minister, Margaret at long last redeemed herself for the many faux pas and flights of fancy in which she had indulged as his "flower child" bride.

There was an irony in the fact that Margaret had found herself again drawn to Pierre, and he to her. But it was an irony not lost on Fidel Castro. By January 1976, when the Trudeaus embarked on their state visit to Cuba, their five-year-old marriage was already disintegrating. Divided by their dramatically different ages and temperaments, and increasingly isolated from each other by the compartmentalization of life at 24 Sussex, Pierre and especially Margaret sensed that the status quo could not hold. Their 1976 visit to Cuba thus proved bittersweet. On the one hand, it brought them close together for one last time in an exotic locale and under circumstances that were unexpectedly exhilarating for both of them personally. Yet, on the other hand, it catalyzed Margaret's inchoate yearnings for independence into a full-blown rebellion, after which any return to the lonely, scripted life of a prime minister's wife would be impossible. Within months of their return from Cuba, Pierre and Margaret would separate. They would divorce in 1984.

Fidel Castro's presence at the funeral of Pierre Trudeau cast this irony into sharp relief. His being there signified not only his abiding respect for the late prime minister but also his warmest condolences for Margaret, hearkening back to a pivotal time in her life, when friends were few, when allies were even fewer, and when Fidel Castro, of all people, had treated her with a tenderness and respect she had come to expect from no one. To this groundswell of nostalgia was added the equally touching fact that Castro had come to Montreal bearing the promised photos, which he presented as a gift to Margaret just hours before the funeral. Some of them showed Castro himself holding Michel as a baby—images certain to rekindle in Margaret the best and worst of memories. In 1976 Castro had unknowingly tapped some of Margaret's deepest emotions and desires. He did so again at the funeral of Pierre.

Fidel Castro is a loquacious man, given to long formal speeches and elaborate monologues even in casual conversation. Two things were therefore striking about his role at the funeral of Pierre Trudeau. The first was that he did not speak publicly at all—a measure of respect for Trudeau that arose out of the certain knowledge that anything other than solemn silence would diminish the gravity of the situation. The second was that his public expression of condolence to the Trudeau family took the form not of words but of gestures. The press followed Castro's every move because every move seemed so poignant.

Castro's sentiments were not the only ones that mattered, of course, nor were they the most important. For the five days between Pierre Trudeau's death and his funeral, Canadians from all walks of life, many of whom had had no great love for the former prime minister, were caught up in the high drama of his passing. Most agreed that the loss to Canada was enormous. To the generation of Canadians whose political loyalties had literally been forged in the crucible of his leadership, his death was epochal.

National media coverage the week before the funeral captured the solemnity with which Canadians first reacted to the news of Trudeau's death and then, by the thousands, paid their last respects. An estimated seventy-five thousand people filed past the body of the former prime minister as it lay in state in Parliament's Hall of Honour and later in Montreal's City Hall. Thousands more lined the railway route between the two cities over which the casket was carried, accompanied by Justin and Sacha and Trudeau's old friends Roy Heenan, Jacques Hébert, Roméo LeBlanc and Marc Lalonde. Fidel Castro made what Canadian officials later called a "surprise appearance" at Montreal City Hall the night before the funeral to pay his respects. It was the first of many spontaneous acts of homage to Trudeau's memory that took the *Comandante* off his official itinerary and sent Canadian and Cuban security officials scrambling.

The day of the funeral, Trudeau's casket was taken by hearse from Montreal City Hall to Notre-Dame Basilica in a ceremonial procession of such emotional intensity that even the normally reticent Mounties were choked up. The crowds were thick on Rue Notre-Dame and in Place d'Armes, the open square between the basilica and the stately old Bank of Montreal building to the north. Some onlookers burst spontaneously into choruses of "O Canada" as the cortège passed by. "The applause, the anthem—it was very hard not to cry," said Sylvain L'Heureux, one of the Mounties to walk beside the hearse. Elsewhere RCMP officers not lucky enough to be selected for the ceremonial procession were entrusted with the task of securing City Hall, the basilica and the two-block route between them. For days before the funeral, they had been supervising city workers as they welded down manhole covers, erected metal barricades and secured the church inside and out. A giant television screen had been erected outside the basilica for the thousands of people who were expected to show up, complicating security further. Sniffer dogs scoured the entire procession route the morning of the service. Armed Mounties stood watch on street corners and in front of the shops and restaurants along the street. Sharpshooters took positions on the roof of the art deco Aldred Building northeast of the basilica, where they could survey the crowds in front of the church's main entrance. Along with the five hundred official guests of the Trudeau family, roughly fifteen hundred members of the public were carefully screened before being admitted through the west tower doors and into the church's second balcony for the service.

As any visitor to Montreal knows, Notre-Dame is one of the most imposing architectural structures in Canada, and certainly its most historic. Designed by Irish-American architect James O'Donnell in 1823 and constructed between 1824 and 1841, the church was conceived on a grand scale. Capable of holding up to ten thousand worshippers, it could lay claim in the mid-nineteenth century to being the largest religious edifice in North America. Originally planned as a classical structure, to the casual observer today the main church seems Gothic in the extreme—cavernous, ornate yet austere, eerily dark even at high noon. The overall effect is to exaggerate the ethereal glow of blue light that frames the sanctuary and the pulpit, and to enhance the impact of the thirty-five hundred candles that flicker throughout the massive chamber.

It was fitting that Trudeau's funeral proceedings took the form of a full-blown funeral Mass at Notre-Dame. As unlikely as it may have seemed for such a dyed-in-the-wool liberal, Pierre Trudeau had always remained the most devout of Catholics. Margaret later recalled that, when she met him, his faith was so profound that she decided to convert. "Pierre loves ritual," she wrote in her 1979 memoir. "To this day not a Sunday goes by when he does not assemble the children solemnly around him, and read aloud to them from his leather-bound family bible, handed down from generation to generation of Trudeau sons."

Security at the funeral service had to be tight. The ceremony had inevitably drawn a great number of the world's powerful and famous. Prime Minister Jean Chrétien remained in the forefront of the proceedings from the moment the casket arrived in Montreal, his normally bon vivant face frozen with grief over the death of his political mentor. "Pierre Trudeau was what we wanted to be in Québec," Chrétien said solemnly. "I am very, very privileged to have worked with him and to be his successor." The Liberal Party of Canada, past and present, was well represented at the funeral. Governor General Adrienne Clarkson was in attendance, as were former Canadian prime ministers Joe Clark, Brian Mulroney, John Turner and Kim Campbell. Quebec premier Lucien Bouchard, the nationalist who had helped orchestrate Mulroney's twin majorities in 1984 and 1988 before deserting the federal Conservatives to form the separatist Bloc Québécois, was there, but he steered well clear of his erstwhile federalist allies. Former U.S. president Jimmy Carter had come at the request of President Bill Clinton to head up the sizeable American delegation. Along with Castro, poet Leonard Cohen, Marc Lalonde and Jacques Hébert, Carter had been asked by the Trudeau family to serve as an honorary pallbearer.

Representing the United Kingdom was Prince Andrew, who had attended Ontario's Lakefield College School in the 1970s and had been a great admirer of Pierre Trudeau's outdoorsmanship, the British defence secretary, Geoffrey Hoon, the high commissioner to Canada, Sir Andrew Burns, and several lesser officials. The question of who would represent the queen ignited a minor controversy in the Canadian press, though not in England. The *Globe and Mail* ran an unusually combative editorial the day of the funeral, in which Queen Elizabeth II and her son Charles were accused of snubbing Canada by opting out of the funeral in favour of some minor ceremonial tasks in the United Kingdom. The *National Post*, taking the monarchist position on the issue, noted that the queen was not in attendance only because the government of Canada—and the prime minister in particular, from whom she is obligated to take instruction—did not invite her.

Among the best-represented regions of the world was the Caribbean. Pierre Trudeau's concern for the developing world and his initiatives to modernize the Commonwealth had earned him great respect there. Edwin Carrington, secretary general of the Caribbean Community (Caricom) attended, as did Seymour Mullings, deputy prime minister of Jamaica, and Sir John Compton, a one-time prime minister of St. Lucia. Rounding out the Caribbean contingent was Castro himself. He arrived by limousine, surrounded by over a dozen bodyguards and Cuban officials—the usual entourage for a leader against whom death threats are continuous. To the crowd chanting "*¡Viva Fidel!*" he simply waved and moved quietly into the church.

For Margaret, the funeral was heartbreaking. She sobbed openly in the limousine that carried her and her sons to the basilica. Inside the church, she sat with Justin and Sacha, occasionally holding hands with her sons and hugging them for support. Of the two, Justin was the more visibly grieved, weeping occasionally alongside his mother. Sacha sat motionless for the most part.

Seated on the same bench as the Trudeaus was nine-year-old Sarah Coyne, Pierre Trudeau's only daughter. Her mother, Deborah Coyne, a constitutional lawyer, sat beside her. Sarah, a pretty girl with her blond hair and blue velvet dress, was said to have been the apple of Pierre Trudeau's eye in his later years. (It is surely a credit to Canadian journalism that she and her mother had until then been spared the media circus that often preys on the love lives of politicians.) In the row immediately behind the Trudeau families sat the honorary pallbearers. At one point during Communion, Margaret turned around to exchange a greeting with Jimmy Carter, who held her hand and, southern gentleman that he is, kissed it gently. Behind Castro sat a translator, who whispered into his ear during the spoken portions of the service. Some of the seats in the front row pews at Notre-Dame were empty, apparently causing a certain amount of confusion among Canadians watching the proceedings on television. The vacancies arose out of the arcane protocol of rank at state functions. By long-standing tradition, the governor general and the prime minister must occupy a pew to themselves, symbolizing their unequalled status. Even Prince Andrew, seated alone in the third row, held lower rank, since only the governor general may represent the queen in Canada.

Outside the basilica, thousands of Canadians watched the funeral ceremony on the giant screen, handkerchiefs at the ready.

———

The first ninety minutes of the two-hour service were taken up with the funeral Mass. Trudeau's old friend and political ally Jacques Hébert then gave a moving tribute, stressing Trudeau's personal virtues and his love for his children—a speech to which both Margaret and Justin reacted with audible sobbing. Prime Minister Jean Chrétien was visibly moved as well, his lip quivering and his eyes tearing.

Following Hébert's remarks, Justin Trudeau regained his bearing and rose to offer his own eulogy. On his way to the microphone, he paused to rest his head on his father's casket, causing yet another wave of raw emotion to course through the basilica, and through the nation via television. The casket, resting between the two main rows of dignitaries, was draped with the Canadian flag and so brilliantly lit from above that it seemed to glow from within. Justin then took his place before the crowd and delivered what was probably the most extraordinary eulogy in Canadian political history. In twelve scant minutes—the full text of the speech is but two pages long—he conveyed more about the deep humanity of his father than the former prime minister had ever revealed of himself. "There were certain basic principles that could never be compromised," Justin recalled his father saying, including the importance of disagreeing with somebody's position on something without "denigrating them" personally. For Fidel Castro, listening attentively in the audience, Justin's words must have had a deeply personal resonance. "This simple tolerance, and recognition of, the real and profound dimensions of each human being, regardless of beliefs, origins, or values—that's what he expected of his children and that's what he expected of our country." Justin concluded his eulogy with the beautiful, haunting farewell by which many Canadians will always recall the passing of their late prime minister. "Je t'aime, Papa."

With these words, Justin Trudeau fell into tears. So did many of those listening to him in person, outside the basilica and in their cars, offices and living rooms—wherever they may have been listening. Leaving the dais, Justin again placed his head on his father's casket, and then embraced Margaret and Sacha.

———

After the service, the Trudeau family emerged from the church accompanied by Pierre Trudeau's casket, to the applause of the crowd waiting outside. Fidel Castro, along with the other honorary pallbearers, was among the first to exit behind them. To the visible anxiety of his own security forces and the RCMP, the *Comandante* was in no hurry to be ushered into his waiting limousine. He chatted amicably on the step of the basilica with other dignitaries, including Jimmy Carter and Roméo LeBlanc. He gave Justin and Sacha hearty bear hugs, and Margaret—obviously drained from the two-hour ceremony—an especially long and close embrace. Here was evidence, if any were needed, that Margaret had made a far deeper connection with Fidel Castro than reports of their 1976 flirtation had suggested. The *Comandante* also embraced Pierre Trudeau's sister, Suzette Rouleau, on the steps of the church.

Jimmy Carter, also deeply moved by the service, gave Margaret and her sons a warm embrace. He was equally attentive to Trudeau's daughter, Sarah. With tears in his eyes, he gave her a gentle hug. "You're a brave girl," he said. From the basilica steps he spoke of his high regard for Pierre Trudeau. "He was the first person I invited to the White House after I was elected," Carter recalled. "He gave me some good advice. He was not only a good leader for Canada but of the whole hemisphere. He was my counselor and my adviser and my personal friend."

The public portion of the funeral ended with the family following behind the cortège as it made its journey from the basilica en route to Saint-Rémi-de-Napierville for a private burial ceremony. Justin and Sacha walked behind the casket, carrying a single rose each. Margaret did the same, plucking petals along the route. They were accompanied behind the coffin by Deborah and Sarah Coyne.

The body of Pierre Trudeau was buried next to that of his mother, Grace, witnessed only by his family, well away from the glare of the media.

———

The funeral and the private burial ceremony over, many of the assembled dignitaries retired to private quarters. Governor General Adrienne Clarkson hosted a gathering for twelve hundred at the Intercontinental Hotel, officially accepting the condolences of the many high-ranking Canadians who could not be accommodated at the funeral. Fidel Castro, who had a floor of the Intercontinental to himself, held private talks with Clarkson and Prime Minister Jean Chrétien. He later received the Trudeau family as well.

Despite Castro's subdued demeanour, politics inevitably followed him to Montreal. What he and Jean Chrétien said to each other during their brief, unofficial tête-à-tête is not a matter of the public record, but the meeting was later described by Canadian and Cuban officials as unexpectedly warm.

That Chrétien had agreed to meet Castro at all was surprising, a measure perhaps of his own sense of obligation to Pierre Trudeau. He was the only Canadian prime minister other than Trudeau to visit Cuba officially, in 1998, and it cost him a good deal of political capital. Chrétien had maintained that a policy of "constructive engagement" vis-à-vis Cuba was preferable to the hardline approach of the United States, especially when it came to influencing the regime's human rights record. In practice this meant walking a razor's edge. During his state visit, Chrétien had been assured by Castro that Cuban authorities would release four dissidents who had been arrested the previous year. But in March 1999 all four were found guilty of "counterrevolutionary activities" in a closed court and sentenced to prison terms of between three and a half and five years. Chrétien responded with a formal condemnation of the sentences, later suspending high-level contact with the regime. "Cuba sends an unfortunate signal to her friends in the international community when people are jailed for peaceful protest," he said dejectedly.

Jean Chrétien had taken an enormous political gamble and lost. The damage to his reputation was substantial. By the time of the funeral, Chrétien openly acknowledged that neither his policies nor even his personal interventions had had any effect upon Castro. Human rights organizations reproached the prime minister, claiming that if anything Cuba's suppression of political dissent had worsened since his state visit. His Canadian critics gloated. In the United States, anti-Castro hard-liners congratulated themselves yet again on their refusal to do business in "Castro's gulag." Shortly after his appointment as George W. Bush's secretary of state, Colin Powell would affirm his government's commitment to economic sanctions against Cuba, noting smugly that other countries in the western hemisphere had taken a conciliatory approach and had been "burned."

Such sanctimony from Chrétien's critics would not have surprised Jimmy Carter. Beleaguered by foreign policy crises that included the Soviet invasion of Afghanistan and the taking of U.S. hostages in Iran, Carter had lost the 1980 presidential election to Ronald Reagan in large measure because his conservative critics persuaded the American people that his foreign policy was weak, naive and harmful to national security. Like his friend Pierre Trudeau, Carter believed that peace between nations was better served by dialogue than confrontation, a conviction that produced both the historic Camp David Accords between Israel and Egypt and the SALT II nuclear-arms treaty with the USSR. Carter did more than any president before or since to normalize diplomatic relations between the United States and Castro's Cuba. Trudeau's 1976 state visit had in fact helped to make this possible. In 1977 Carter lifted restrictions on travel to Cuba and opened a U.S. "interests section" (a de facto embassy) in Havana. Cuba opened its own interests section in Washington the same year.

While he was in Montreal for the funeral of Pierre Trudeau, the soft-spoken Carter told reporters that he thought the great majority of Americans opposed sanctions against the Cuban regime. Castro was delighted. "Of all the presidents that have held executive power in the U.S. since 1959 until the present day," he said, "the person that most deserves my respect, for his ethics and his decency, is Carter." In May 2002, facing obstruction from the Bush White House and the venom of the anti-Castro right in the United States, Carter would become the first American president since the 1920s to visit Cuba. The same year he would win the Nobel Peace Prize for his efforts to advance peace, democracy and human rights. Had he lived to see his friend so honoured, Pierre Trudeau would have been elated.

———

Three Nights in Havana tells four interrelated stories. First and foremost, it recounts the story of Pierre Trudeau and Fidel Castro, two world leaders who discovered each other in 1976, and despite their significant ideological differences, became close friends. In the background is the story of Canada and Cuba, two nations that in 2005 quietly celebrated sixty years of uninterrupted diplomatic relations and a trading relationship that stretches back into the nineteenth century. The other two threads that wind through this narrative are perhaps less obvious but no less important or fascinating. The first is the epic drama of the Cold War and of Canada's and Cuba's place in a world dominated by two hostile and nuclear-armed superpowers. The second is the story of the rise to power of the Cuban-American émigré community, which has always served as the wellspring of anti-Castro passion in the United States. Were it not for the exiles, it is likely that the U.S. embargo against Cuba would have been dismantled on Henry Kissinger's watch. And were it not for the extremists within that community, who have conducted a non-stop campaign of terror against the Castro regime since the Eisenhower era, the history of Cuba's relations with the United States and Canada would be vastly different.

Interweaving the story of Cuba and Canada together with the story of Trudeau and Castro makes for a good fit. Both the high and the low points in Canada's relationship with revolutionary Cuba occurred in Trudeau's third term, and represented the culmination of Canadians' long and complex history with the Cuban people. The zenith came in 1976 with the prime ministerial visit, the nadir only two years later when, for the first and only time, the government of Canada imposed economic penalties against the Castro regime for its decision to send troops to Angola and other African hot spots. When Trudeau lost interest in Cuba, for most of the 1980s, most Canadians did too. And when Trudeau the private citizen rekindled his old friendship with Fidel Castro in the 1990s, he did so as part of a wave of Canadian investment, technology and tourism that deluged Cuba after the collapse of the Soviet Union.

Pierre Trudeau and Fidel Castro became friends despite their differences. They agreed to disagree. The same is true of Canada and Cuba. And it all began on a tiny coral key off Cuba's southern shore in 1976, with the cheer heard round the world. "*¡Viva el Primer Ministro Fidel Castro!*"

PART ONE

FRIENDS AND ENEMIES

1

¡Viva Fidel!
Castro in Montreal

On Sunday, April 26, 1959, less than four months after he had stunned the world by overthrowing Cuban dictator Fulgencio Batista, Fidel Castro made his first and only formal visit to Canada. He was en route from a ten-day tour of the eastern United States. Although he spent less than twenty-four hours on Canadian soil and never left Montreal, his presence galvanized the special kinship many Canadians had come to feel for him and his ragtag band of *barbudos* (bearded ones). Pierre Trudeau did not meet Castro on this occasion but he may well have been among the thousands of Montrealers who turned out in person to see him. In those days, when Trudeau was not off on one of his many trips abroad, he could usually be found squatting in his mother's stately house at the foot of Mount Royal, or camped out in his office on Rue Saint-Denis. Even if he did not take the opportunity to observe the famous rebel leader in the flesh, he could hardly have missed the media frenzy that was surging through his hometown. It is a virtual certainty that Trudeau was among the many Quebeckers who tuned into Castro's interview with popular Radio-Canada television host René Lévesque.

The Montreal that played host to Fidel Castro and his *Fidelistas* in 1959 was a study in contrasts, part Old World conservatism, part New World cosmopolitanism. Quebec premier Maurice Duplessis remained the unrivalled *chef* of provincial politics, backed by a Catholic establishment whose authority in the lives of ordinary Quebeckers was also unmatched. Expo '67 and the 1976 Olympics still lay in the future, as did Montreal's transformation into the modern metropolis it is today. Yet this most Catholic of cities also boasted a famously racy alter ego even in the Duplessis era. Despite the dogged efforts of Mayor Jean Drapeau to clean up Montreal's mob-controlled vice, the city was one of the few in North America that could rival Havana as a haven of illicit pleasure. Prostitution, gambling and the heroin trade thrived alongside the city's celebrated nightlife. Montreal was also the home of *Cité libre*, a journal founded in 1950 by Pierre Trudeau and other French-Canadian intellectuals to critique Duplessis's policies and set Quebec on the road to modernization. With the death of the *chef* in September 1959, this social and intellectual ferment would launch a political earthquake the likes of which Canada had never seen, making Montreal the epicentre of Quebec's own "quiet" revolution.

Castro's original three-day Canadian itinerary was to have brought him first to Montreal and then on to Ottawa and Toronto. In the nation's capital he was scheduled to meet Prime Minister John Diefenbaker, where, among other things, he was expected to make a formal request that RCMP officers train Cuba's rural guard. The Mounties, who had recently provided law-enforcement training in Jamaica and Chile, were said to be enthusiastic about helping the Cubans establish a professional police force. The irony could not have been lost on Fidel Castro even then. Canada's zealously anti-communist RCMP was responsible not only for the surveillance of Cuban nationals in Canada but for assisting the Central Intelligence Agency (CIA) in its intelligence-gathering operations throughout North America. Nonetheless, Castro played it straight for his Canadian hosts. "The Mounties, they're wonderful," he exclaimed. "I never saw them before except in pictures. Now when I see them, I'm especially pleased. Their uniforms"—here he harkened back to his early revolution days—"are the colour of our July the 26th Movement!"

Castro had also planned to throw out the ceremonial first pitch at Maple Leaf Stadium, where the Toronto Maple Leafs were scheduled to play their home opener against the famed Havana Sugar Kings of the International Baseball League. (Two weeks earlier, he had tossed the first pitch in the Kings' home opener against the Leafs in Havana.) Toronto officials were irked that they had not received a formal request from the Cubans to play host to the travelling entourage, and so had done nothing to organize a reception for Castro or even to mobilize the city police for his protection. In the end, it mattered little. A week before he landed in Montreal, Cuban officials announced that the "revolutionary hero"—as Castro was known in the Canadian press—would have to postpone his visits to Ottawa and Toronto. The Cuban consul general in Ottawa, Ramón Osuna, made Castro's apologies for him, telling Canadians that his boss faced many pressing problems back in Cuba and assuring them that he wished "no possible insult" to Canada by his change of plans. Castro's most immediate crisis was rumoured to be the counterrevolutionary insurgency that was brewing in the mountains of eastern Cuba, but Osuna dismissed the idea. (Castro himself would be queried in Montreal about the unrest. His reply: "That's silly. Everyone is with us. Who would create the unrest?") Asked in the House of Commons about the cancellation of Castro's visit to the nation's capital, Prime Minister Diefenbaker confirmed that the rebel leader had requested an audience with him but that "unfortunately it was impossible for me to find a mutually convenient time." Diefenbaker extended a public invitation to see Castro for a meeting on his return visit, promising "a full discussion on matters of interest to Cuba and Canada." The postponed meeting would never take place.

Whether John Diefenbaker had any genuine interest in meeting Fidel Castro remains an open question. His friend U.S. President Dwight D. Eisenhower had snubbed the Cuban leader during the American leg of the tour because, as he told Army General Vernon A. Walters, the television coverage of Cuban firing squads killing Batista loyalists had made him sick to his stomach. The five days Castro was in Washington, D.C., Ike was out of town golfing. In his place, Vice-President Richard Nixon agreed to meet with the Cuban leader. Their scheduled fifteen-minute appointment turned into a two-and-a-half-hour tête-à-tête in Nixon's living room, after which the vice-president penned a prescient memorandum. "My own appraisal of him as a man," Nixon wrote, "is somewhat mixed. The one fact we can be sure of is that he had those indefinable qualities which make him a leader of men. Whatever we may think of him, he is going to be a great factor in the development of Cuba and very possibly Latin American affairs generally. He seems to be sincere, he is either incredibly naïve about Communism or under Communist discipline—my guess is the former and I have already implied [that] his ideas as to how to run a government or an economy are less developed than those of almost any world figure I have met."

Other Cold Warriors in the United States, including Eisenhower's secretary of state, Christian Herter, had drawn similar conclusions during Castro's stay. All agreed that the thirty-two-year-old revolutionary was a gifted political actor, able to turn on the charm whenever it was advantageous to do so. But, despite his repeated assurances that he would restore what he called "representative democracy" in Cuba, Castro was visibly anxious any time he was asked about communist influence in his regime. He claimed that he had no intention of confiscating American assets—even though, in fiery speeches before the Cuban people, he had already threatened to nationalize U.S.-owned sugar refineries on the island. His regime was also known to be scrutinizing American corporate interests in Cuba, including the hated United Fruit Company. Castro said he wanted to maintain good trade relations with the United States, which was ostensibly the raison d'être of the tour, yet he refused to allow members of his entourage, including the president of the Banco Nacional de Cuba, to discuss foreign aid with the World Bank or the International Monetary Fund (IMF). As for his own politics, he insisted that he was no "Red" and that he took no orders from Moscow. Yet he equivocated when asked what side he would choose in a war between the United States and the Soviet Union.

Castro had been much more successful in ingratiating himself with ordinary Americans during the 1959 tour, many of whom had come to sympathize with the underdog *barbudos* during their two-year struggle against Batista. Everywhere they went in the United States, he and his one-hundred-person delegation were treated like a travelling carnival. The rebel leader visited Princeton, Yale and Harvard, where he was received with varying degrees of adulation by America's Ivy League youth. He spoke at luncheons and dinner banquets practically daily, and toured local attractions in the hours in between. The tour was not all fun and games, however. When Castro spoke before a crowd of thirty thousand in Central Park, the New York Police Department was placed on full alert because of an anonymous tip that seven men were in the city to kill him. It later came to light that the assassins were associates of mobster Meyer Lansky, and were not even in New York during Castro's visit. In an unrelated incident, a twenty-three-year-old former U.S. army sergeant was arrested for planting a pipe bomb behind the bandstand where Castro was speaking. When asked about such plots on his life, Castro replied with the plucky bravado for which he was already famous. "In Cuba they had tanks, planes and guns," he said, "and they ran away, so what can they do here? I sleep very well and don't worry at all."

Castro's star power was in full force when he finally showed up in Canada. The Cuban leader arrived from Boston, three hours late, on an Air Britannia turboprop, obviously thrilled to be among the seven hundred cheering Montrealers who turned out to greet him at Dorval Airport (now P.E. Trudeau Airport). "I feel as if I am in Havana!" he exclaimed. It took him fifteen minutes to make his way through the crowd to his waiting motorcade. Clad in his olive-green fatigues and combat cap, fully bearded and smoking a cigar, Castro had already perfected the public persona for which he is still instantly recognizable. Other *Fidelistas* on the tour were similarly decked out in the fatigues and beards they had worn as guerrillas but before long they would abandon the trademark look to Castro alone. When a Canadian reporter asked him about his combat attire, Castro replied that it served as a symbol that united him with the Cuban people. "Figure it out for yourself," he said dryly, noting that some Canadian men in the crowd looked much like him and his comrades. "They're Beatniks," someone told him. "Beatniks? What's that?" he replied.

From Dorval, Castro and his entourage were escorted by their official host, Montreal mayor Sarto Fournier, into the city. The honking and hooting of the Cuban motorcade was so exuberant, according to one report, that it had "visitors from other parts of Canada marvelling at Montreal's Latin abandon." At the airport and along the parade route, rooftop sharpshooters surveyed the crowded streets for assassination threats. As they would four decades later at the funeral for Pierre Trudeau, Montrealers turned out in the thousands to offer Castro hugs and handshakes. "Women and teenagers fought to be close to the Cuban leader," said one report. Any time his motorcade stopped—recognizable because it was flying the flag of Cuba—Montrealers cheered "*¡Viva, Castro!*" and "Hurray, Fidel!" In the populist style that would become a Castro trademark, the Cuban leader repeatedly alarmed his Canadian police escort and his own bodyguards by wading into the crowds to "talk to my people," as he put it. "He could have been killed three dozen times the way he ignored us," said one exasperated Montreal police officer. Castro was obviously charmed by Montreal, correctly noting that the colourful city resembled Havana in many ways. "There's a Latin atmosphere here that I sort of missed in the United States," he mused.

Some journalists had openly mocked Castro's heavily accented efforts to converse in English during the U.S. leg of his tour. A Castro speech is a "frightful massacre of the English language," wrote one of them. His statements were sometimes transcribed phonetically in the U.S. press, as in "I was pee-cher when I playing baseball, not catcher." Yet from the taped interviews that have survived from the era—his chat on network TV with the veteran journalist Edward R. Murrow, for example—it is evident that Castro acquitted himself remarkably well in English. He took great care to express himself clearly during his many interviews, consulting both his aides and a dictionary whenever he foundered. More to the point, he put himself entirely at the disposal of the press at every stop on the tour, sometimes fielding questions in English for hours on end.

Castro has always been highly sensitive to the manner in which he is treated in the U.S. media. It is likely that the condescension he met in 1959 cemented his resolve to speak English only when the political advantage of doing so was extraordinary. Not until 1977 would he again offer an American journalist an interview in English, and when he did so he chose ABC's Barbara Walters, someone whom he knew could carry his message of conciliation directly into the living rooms of the American people. The diplomatic damage that has arisen from Castro's refusal to speak English has been incalculable, since his speeches are seldom translated or covered by the media outside Cuba. For non-Spanish-speaking North Americans, Castro has thus always been something of a demagogue, shouting himself hoarse in huge rallies, gesticulating wildly and moving crowds of admirers to mass adulation. What has been lost is not only unmediated access to one of the great orators of the twentieth century. Also forgotten is the fact, unchanged since 1959, that although he has had many differences with the U.S. government, he has never had anything but the utmost respect for the American people. By refusing to speak English, in short, Fidel Castro has made it easy for his enemies in North America to demonize him.

———

Among Castro's scheduled stops during his motorcade tour of Montreal was the children's ward at Montreal's Sainte-Justine Hospital. There he cuddled some of the infant patients, cigar in hand, demonstrating the personal magnetism for which he is renowned among his own people. Like all politicians, of course, Castro is well aware of the public-relations value of being photographed in the embrace of children, something he missed no opportunity to exploit during his North American tour. But he also genuinely enjoys the company of young people, and his solicitousness around them is a key element of the unceremonious personal style for which he is also well known. While he was in Washington, D.C., for example, the Cuban leader snuck out of his hotel room, eluding even his own bodyguards, and spent four hours in a Chinese-food restaurant debating politics with a group of college students he encountered there.

Castro's evening itinerary was a whirlwind of speech-making and glad-handing. It began with a reception at the Queen Elizabeth Hotel, where he and his aides had taken suites. During the fete, the Cuban leader astonished his Canadian hosts by crashing the First Communion party of seven-year-old Louise Bruneau, which was also being held in the hotel. (Photographs of him and the child were splashed over the front pages of the Montreal newspapers the next day.) Castro's next stop was a banquet sponsored by Montreal's Jeune chambre de commerce, where, as guest of honour, he spoke before forty of the city's leading business people. There he received a warm embrace from Chambre president Claude Dupras and accepted the organization's gift of twenty thousand toys donated by Montrealers. The toys were earmarked for the Cuban government's "counter-bombing" campaign in Oriente province. For two years the children of the Sierra Maestra region had been bombed along with rebel targets, Castro himself explained during his forty-five-minute speech. "It has reached the point where now they are even afraid of the commercial planes that fly over them. We sent planes loaded with toys over the bombed towns." Castro's gratefulness was genuine. At midnight, by which time he was exhausted and virtually hoarse, he ventured out to a Chambre-sponsored "Toy Dance" at the Craig Street Armoury. "I came to this dance because I felt I had to show you my gratitude and the gratitude of all Cuba for what you are doing for our children," he told the crowd of four thousand in English. "And I promise you that when I return, I will have learned how to thank you properly in French, too!" When he returned to the hotel, he exchanged greetings with yet another crowd of two hundred well-wishers.

In the hours between the evening banquet and the midnight toy dance, Castro held court in his suite at the Queen Elizabeth. There he met officials of the RCMP to discuss the training of his rural guard. He saw Hal C. Banks, the controversial head of the Seafarers International Union (SIU), in order to hammer out an agreement regarding eight ships that had been sold to Cuba by Canadian National Steamships during an SIU strike. He also met Andy McNaughton in person for the first time, and thanked him warmly for his clandestine activities during the war against Batista. McNaughton was the son of the famous Canadian general and diplomat A. G. L. McNaughton. Code-named *Esquimal* (meaning "Man from the North"), the younger McNaughton had worked for Castro as a double agent during the guerrilla war—an extremely risky undertaking for which he had been named an honorary citizen of Cuba. Officially employed as an arms buyer for Batista, McNaughton had purchased weapons abroad with the regime's money and then funnelled them to the *Fidelistas*. He had also gathered intelligence for Castro, a subterfuge that, if discovered, might well have resulted in a grim fate at the hands of Batista's security forces. McNaughton was later asked why he had taken such risks for Castro. "I have friends in Cuba," he said. "I got to know their problems.

You can't close your eyes to some things. You have to make your decision and I made mine—to help the cause of freedom in Cuba."

Accustomed to impromptu speech-making among adoring crowds, Castro improvised speeches at Dorval and in the lobby of the Queen Elizabeth. His "rare gift for self-revelation" was beguiling, as one journalist put it, and his message was by now well rehearsed. The policy of the Cuban Revolution was "humanism, not communism," said Castro. "Anyone who says we are Communists knows nothing about political culture." When asked why he was delaying the long-promised general election in Cuba, he replied that the country needed time to allow for the creation of real political parties. He emphasized, no doubt accurately, that the most opportunistic strategy would be to call an election before any opposition to the *Fidelistas* could become established. "Right now, 94 per cent of the people are with us," Castro observed. "The longer we delay calling an election, the less support we will have. But an election today would be a Hitler or a Mussolini plebiscite because we are the only party." When asked about communist influence in his government—the question on which the U.S. media had badgered him relentlessly—he was visibly testy. "Do we have to kill the Communists in Cuba, or persecute them, because of their political ideas?" he demanded. "If we don't kill them or persecute them, does that make us Communists? The whole thing, it's absurd." Castro's message to Canadians was simple: Cuba was hungry and poor after Batista's flight. The dictator had left only $70 million from pre-revolutionary national bank reserves of $400 million, he told reporters. His country therefore had to start from scratch, and it was looking to Canada as a model of economic development.

At 9:15 on the morning of Monday, April 27, 1959, Fidel Castro flew out of Dorval Airport. His frantic tour of Montreal over, Castro departed much as he had arrived, amid a constellation of flashbulbs and throngs of well-wishers. En route back to Cuba, the rebel leader stopped first in Houston, Texas, and then in Buenos Aires, Argentina, where he was scheduled to speak before the Organization of American States (OAS).

There he made the sensational proposal that the U.S. government provide $30 billion in capital to solve Latin America's chronic problems of underdevelopment. It was a bold and brazen suggestion coming after almost two weeks of pressing the flesh in the United States, during which he had resolutely refused to talk about money. It did, however, illuminate Castro's sense of his own political destiny. Here was a new breed of leader for Latin America, he was signalling. The era of the banana republic was over. Fidel Castro was not a man to go begging for American assistance, cap in hand. Cuba's relationship with the United States would be one of equals or there would be no relationship at all.

———

In one sense, Fidel Castro's rise to power had been meteoric: it had taken the *Fidelista* guerrillas just two years to prevail against Batista militarily. Yet, in another sense, Castro had been preparing since his teens for the triumph of his revolutionary vision. While at the University of Havana in the late 1940s, where he earned a doctor of laws degree (hence the salutation "Dr. Castro"), he established his reputation as an exceptionally courageous nationalist firebrand. From the day of Batista's bloodless *coup d'état* in March 1952, Castro began to foment rebellion across the island. On July 26, 1953, he led an ill-fated attack on the Moncada army base in Santiago de Cuba, for which he served less than two years of a fifteen-year sentence before being amnestied by Batista himself. Acting as his own legal counsel, Castro exploited the national publicity of his Moncada trial by delivering the speech that would become the blueprint of the Cuban Revolution, immortalized by its brash concluding challenge to the court. "Condemn me," he pronounced. "It does not matter. History will absolve me."

Within twenty-four hours of his release from the Isle of Pines prison in 1955, Castro defiantly released to the Cuban press a "Manifesto of the People of Cuba." Calling this new phase of the struggle the 26th of July Movement, he plunged into the chaotic and violent Havana political scene, making speeches, publishing pamphlets and haranguing Batista on the radio. By summer, there was so much heat on him from the regime's security forces that he knew he had to leave Cuba. In July, Castro flew to Mexico, where he, his brother Raúl, the young Argentinean doctor Che Guevara and other exiled rebels dedicated themselves to training and equipping an army capable of launching a guerrilla war in the mountains of eastern Cuba. Eighteen months later, in December 1956, Castro and his eighty-one-man army, with all the guns they could carry, made their way from Mexico to Cuba's Oriente province aboard the leaky cabin-cruiser *Granma*. Batista issued a $100,000 bounty on Castro—dead or alive—and launched a merciless terror campaign against the peasant farmers thought to be abetting the rebels. Yet the people of the Sierra Maestra remained overwhelmingly loyal to Castro. His concern for the welfare of ordinary Cuban folk and his promise to make their problems a top priority of the Revolution became legendary. During the guerrilla war, the rebel leaders listened intently to the concerns of local people, providing them with medical aid and literacy instruction. Castro and his top commanders took the same risks in battle as their men and brooked no special comforts or rations. This inclusive, egalitarian ethos greatly impressed the Cuban people, drawing new recruits—men and women—to the rebel army practically daily.

On January 17, 1957, Castro had his first taste of military victory, taking a military outpost at La Plata by surprise and hauling its plentiful arms and munitions back into the mountains. In a gesture of magnanimity designed to win the sympathy of the Cuban people, the enemy wounded were treated (mainly by Che Guevara) and then released. The *Fidelistas* would treat all wounded soldiers the same way for the remainder of the war. It was a brilliant strategy, for it sewed doubts among rank-and-file soldiers and ultimately undermined their willingness to fight for Batista.

After La Plata, Batista knew he had a serious problem and he escalated his attacks on the rebels accordingly. He purchased sixteen B-26 bombers from the United States and deployed them against the *Fidelistas'* mountain camp to devastating effect. The next three months became, in Che Guevara's words, "the bitter days, the most painful stage in the war." The 26th of July Movement suffered some of its worst losses, particularly among its clandestine operatives in Havana. Yet these were also the months in which the rebel army managed to consolidate its forces in the Sierra Maestra, a process that continued throughout 1957 and into early 1958. By the end of their first year of armed struggle, the *Fidelistas* had achieved what even Batista conceded was a stalemate. This stand-off served to tip the balance in the rebels' favour, for, as Castro and Batista both knew, every day the regime failed to contain the insurgency its political legitimacy grew weaker.

In June 1958, when a massive army assault against the vastly outnumbered rebels was beaten back, it became clear that Castro's forces were now in the ascendant. With every battlefield advance, the rebel leader insisted that officers and soldiers alike be treated with respect and civility. "I think highly of you," Castro wrote in a letter to General Eulogio Cantillo, head of Batista's forces in the mountains. "My opinion is not incompatible with my having the honor of recognizing you as an adversary. I appreciate your noble feelings toward us, who are, after all, your compatriots, not your enemies, because we are not at war against the armed forces but against the dictatorship. Perhaps when the offensive is over, if we are still alive, I will write you again to clarify my thinking and to tell you what I think of you, the army, and what we can do for the benefit of Cuba."

In December 1958, Batista began preparing his own flight from Cuba. In Havana and other areas not yet controlled by Castro, his grip on power had weakened to the point that the Cuban people were now openly defying his regime. Over the week between Christmas and New Year's 1958, the rebels' successes came at a speed that surprised even themselves. Led by Che Guevara, the *Fidelistas* marched forcefully out of the Sierra Maestra westward to Havana. Santa Clara fell on December 30, a decisive victory. In the early morning hours of New Year's Day 1959, Batista and his family boarded a plane and fled to the Dominican Republic. A junta was proclaimed by one of Batista's generals in Havana, but, using rebel radio to great effect, Castro told the Cuban people to oppose it. The junta collapsed within a day. Fidel Castro was victorious.

———

Fulgencio Batista had known from early on that Castro's 26th of July Movement was a serious threat to his regime. But just about everybody else, including Washington, completely underestimated Castro. Being underrated had been part of the rebel leader's broader strategy for taking power. It was a master stroke.

To some extent, the Americans' underestimation of Fidel Castro reflected their underestimation of the Cuban people. Since the 1890s, Cubans had made great sacrifices to transform themselves and their nation from a second-class banana republic into the modern democracy idealized by the nationalist José Martí. Yet on the eve of Fidel Castro's Revolution the best-known Cuban in the United States was not José Martí or even Fulgencio Batista. He was Ricky Ricardo, the leading man on *I Love Lucy* played by Cuban émigré Desi Arnaz. This show had been launched on American television in 1951 and by the mid-1950s was reaching fifty-million viewers per week—possibly the largest regular television audience ever. Ricky Ricardo was pure Cuban stereotype—and virtually the only source of information about Cuba for the first generation of Americans weaned on network TV. "He easily reinforced the dominant images" of Cuba, observes historian Louis A. Pérez, "rumba band leader, heavily accented English, excitable, always seeming to be slightly out of place and hence slightly vulnerable, perhaps even childlike and nonthreatening." By the late 1950s, Ricky Ricardo had come to symbolize for many Cubans the condescension and contempt in which their country appeared to be held by the United States.

Exacerbating Cubans' sense of disillusionment was the demoralizing fact that the United States had not only given Batista's coup its blessing but had also shown indifference to his dictatorial style, his heavy-handed suspension of civil liberties, and his use of informants and secret police to stifle dissent. From the American vantage point, of course, Batista's uncompromising anti-communism and his commitment to the protection of U.S. business interests in Cuba made him a great asset. By 1959, American investment in Cuba was second only to that of Venezuela, with U.S. investors controlling 40 per cent of the sugar industry, 50 per cent of the Cuban railway system and 90 per cent of Cuban utilities. American foreign policy was thus designed to reinforce Cuba's status as a political and commercial satellite of the United States. But, from the Cuban point of view, the fact that the world's leading liberal democracy should arm and even train Batista's thugs was repugnant.

If most of the Americans who tuned into *I Love Lucy* every week were oblivious to the mounting turmoil in Cuban politics in the 1950s, most Canadians were even further removed from it. Every bit as enamoured of Ricky Ricardo as their U.S. allies, Canadians had almost no sources of information about Cuba that did not originate in the United States. Canada had no thriving Cuban émigré communities like those that had sprung up in New York and Miami, nor was there anything comparable in Canadian tourism to the roughly 350,000 Americans who were visiting Cuba annually by the mid-1950s. Roughly 5,000 U.S. citizens had become permanent residents of Cuba by the time of Castro's Revolution. Only 250 Canadians had done so.

In contrast with the Americans' extensive involvement in the Cuban economy, moreover, the Canadian presence was negligible. Canadian exporters faced high transportation and communication costs, which limited Cuban-Canadian trade in goods to those for which there were no major American competitors. (Cod was one such staple. Havana's first diplomatic posting to Canada was a trade official sent to Yarmouth, Nova Scotia, in 1903 to liaise with Maritime salt-cod producers.) The only sector of the Cuban economy in which Canadians predominated was financial services, and only because, prior to the First World War,

U.S. law forbade federally chartered banks from having foreign branches. In 1899, the Merchant's Bank of Halifax (renamed the Royal Bank in 1902) set up shop in Havana. By the 1920s, it boasted sixty-five branches across the island, a seven-storey office building in Havana and a client list that included the nation's leading business and political lights. By the mid-twentieth century the Royal and other Canadian banks had become a mainstay of commercial life on the island, commanding 28 per cent of total deposits in commercial banks. The same was true for the insurance industry, with Canadian firms like Sun Life, Manufacturer's Trust, Imperial Life and Confederation Life underwriting three-quarters of Cuba's life-insurance policies by the late 1950s. But financial services were the exceptions that proved the rule. For both Canada and Cuba, trade with the United States remained pre-eminent.

Canada's diplomatic presence in Cuba lagged as well. Until 1945, Canada lacked its own diplomatic representation in Havana, preferring to remain represented by the British legation. During the Second World War, when it was obvious that the sun was setting on the British Empire, Canada embraced its North American destiny and began to work toward an independent foreign policy in the western hemisphere. This goal would be greatly complicated before long with the emergence of the Cold War and the strategic necessity of a continental alliance with the United States. But as it was, Canada took the initiative, appointing ambassadors to Latin American countries for the first time. Cuba established formal diplomatic relations with Canada in 1942. Three years later, Canada reciprocated, establishing its own legation in Havana. Thus began the sixty years of uninterrupted diplomatic relations that Canadians and Cubans quietly celebrated in March 2005.

As for ordinary Canadians, most who saw pre-revolutionary Cuba first-hand did so as they still do, as tourists. But, whereas Canadians today often marvel at the near-absence of American influence under Castro, the story in the Batista era was quite the opposite. Havana was an American city. Canadian travel writer Douglas Blanchard noted in 1958 that he could not go anywhere in Havana without bumping into big-name American TV stars like Steve Allan. American-styled hotels, nightclubs and casinos, Blanchard reported, were only too happy to provide Canadian tourists "with every facility and device for losing money." As for the "real" Cubans—those not employed in the tourist industries—they were seen as friendly, courteous and distinctive. Cuban streets were clean, the Cuban outlook modern. The new super hotels in the Vedado area of Havana were "more modern than anything in Canada," wrote another travel writer in 1958. And they could be had for less than $350 a week.

One reason Fidel Castro's rebellion had been underestimated in North America was that the view from Havana was myopic. With the exception of occasional acts of sabotage, the insurgency in distant Oriente province had little impact on daily life in this most cosmopolitan of cities. That the *Fidelistas* were not perceived as especially threatening was evident in the way their cloak-and-dagger activities were rolled into the city's celebrated carnival atmosphere. "Havana is now the one completely wide open city in the world with unlimited gambling, organized vice, political graft and revolutionary bombs," noted one Canadian observer. Until late in 1958, it remained almost inconceivable to North Americans in Havana that the rebel army should be able to hold the eastern territory and advance the whole breadth of the island into the capital.

Among those who failed to gauge the seriousness of Cuban opposition to Batista were Canada's diplomats in Havana. Canada's official position on the insurgency was neutrality, which meant not taking sides within Cuba and not allowing Canada to be used as a staging ground for either side. (In April 1959, when Castro had the Cuban ambassador to Canada arrested on charges that he had acted as an agent for Batista's arms dealers, the Canadian government released a statement saying that it had no knowledge of arms being shipped to Cuba on either side of the conflict.) Canadian Embassy staff were not blind to Batista's corruption and his appalling human rights violations, but they saw no alternative to the status quo. They also accepted the official American position on Cuba. It seemed self-evident to everyone in Havana that any erosion of American influence on the island would be bad for the economy and therefore bad for the Cuban people. In 1957, the newly appointed Canadian ambassador to Cuba, Hector Allard, conveyed his mixed feelings about Batista to his superiors in Ottawa. "We have been occasionally in [*sic*] two minds about this," he wrote, "since there are many manifestations of a strongman government which are repulsive to minds raised in the atmosphere of Canadian democracy." Yet Batista also stood for the social and economic stability that Allard, his predecessors and Canadian investors had come to value on the island. The ambassador concluded that, on balance, the dictator represented "the best hope for the future."

As for Fidel Castro, Canadian Embassy personnel underestimated him completely. "Castro is not a military genius," wrote Chargé d'Affaires G. A. Browne in December 1956, "and as for his overall strategy, the only reasonable speculation is that he is either mad or that he has been badly let down by his supporters. It seems likely that these two alternatives may be interdependent, with megalomania in the driving seat." Seven months before the Batista regime collapsed, Ambassador Allard would himself report to his superiors at External Affairs that Castro was a spent force. "Concerning Batista's position, it seems to be as strong, if not stronger than ever. Many observers feel that Castro has shot his bolt. He has obviously committed a number of very bad psychological mistakes which clearly show a complete lack of political sense."

The Canadian diplomatic corps may have misread Fidel Castro's rising popularity in the 1950s, but for other Canadians in Cuba, particularly those who ventured outside Havana, there was no mistaking it. The two advantages Batista had brought foreign governments and investors—economic stability and impeccable anti-communist credentials—meant little to ordinary Cubans. Batista's iron-fisted rule and especially the terror of his not-so-secret police had eroded what little popular support he might have enjoyed at the time of the coup. Castro himself deserved much of the credit for exposing him as a tyrant. Starting with Moncada, the rebel leader had spared no effort in criticizing Batista's unconstitutional seizure of power and in making his notorious crimes known to the world. With memories of Hitler and Stalin fresh in their minds—tyrants against whom the world's democracies had been asked to make great sacrifices—Canadians were naturally sympathetic to the *Fidelistas'* struggle against despotism. Thus, in contrast with the Canadian chargé d'affaires who speculated around the time of the *Granma* landing that Castro was a deranged megalomaniac, Canadian reporters routinely referred to Castro in the most respectful of terms, calling him "a lawyer and former student leader" and often expressing admiration for the fact that he was still only in his twenties.

Fidel Castro has always known the political value of international sympathy. Even in the earliest days of the guerrilla struggle, when his rebel army numbered less than one hundred, he was adamant that the propaganda war remain a top priority. No sooner had he encamped in the Sierra Maestra than he sent one of his most trusted comrades, Faustino Pérez, to Havana to invite foreign journalists back to the mountains. In February 1957 veteran *New York Times* reporter Herbert J. Matthews was escorted secretly to Castro's base, where he interviewed the rebel leader and brought him for the first time to the attention of the outside world. Aged fifty-seven at the time, Matthews had been demoralized by the Republican defeat in the Spanish Civil War in the 1930s, and he now saw in Castro's struggle against Batista a similar idealism worth supporting. Castro knew the value of a sympathetic American voice, and also how to appeal to American readers' sympathies. "We have been fighting for 79 days now and we are stronger than ever," he told Matthews. "The soldiers are fighting badly; their morale is low and ours could not be higher. We are killing many, but when we take prisoners they are never shot. We question them, talk kindly to them, take their arms and equipment, and then set them free." Castro later revealed that he had his men parade in circles around Matthews to convey the impression that his rebel army was much larger than it actually was.

In the wake of the Matthews interview, Castro became a media darling. A CBS-TV crew lived with the rebel army for two months in the spring of 1957, filming the *Fidelistas'* every move and providing Castro with the kind of publicity that Batista could only dream of. That May, Canadian and American viewers tuned in to watch the CBS prime-time documentary *Rebels of the Sierra Maestra: The Story of Cuba's Jungle Fighters*. Again Castro was treated with the adulation due a patriot, his enemies characterized as ruthless bullies. At about the same time, United Press dispatches from Cuba began to implicate the American government directly in Batista's campaign against the guerrillas. "Cuba's crack U.S.-equipped First Infantry division," said one report, was being deployed against the rebels in a "government extermination campaign." *Extermination* was a powerful word in 1957, as it is today. As Castro well knew, such reportage from within the mainstream U.S. media did more to cement his status as a freedom fighter than anything he might have said on his own behalf. The occasional publicity stunt within the United States also heightened Americans' awareness of the rebel cause. In the sixth game of the 1957 World Series, for example, play had to be stopped because the field at Yankee Stadium was strewn with pro-Castro leaflets. An unidentified man was arrested by New York police. It was never confirmed with certainty whether the rebel leader had had anything to do with the incident.

It is evident that Castro's manipulation of North American public opinion extended to outright duplicity, especially when it came to his plans for post-revolutionary Cuba. In February 1958, the American magazine *Look* published an article written by the rebel leader in which he stated that Batista's defeat would be followed by liberal democracy and free enterprise. He made the same claim in his twenty-two-point "Manifesto" of March 1958. The manifesto—said to be supported by forty-two Cuban cultural, professional and religious organizations—called for a military junta to be established immediately upon Batista's resignation, followed by a provisional government and free elections. As Castro biographer Tad Szulc observes, such promises bordered on "intellectual dishonesty." The truth is that by this time the rebel leader was envisioning a full-blown social revolution, which he almost certainly knew was incompatible with liberal democracy. Castro's promise not to nationalize or expropriate foreign holdings in Cuba was especially questionable. Where his ideas about social reform were nominally compatible with democracy—ending corruption and promoting literacy training, employment, industrialization and health care, for example—he made the most of what he knew would have the greatest impact among sympathetic American readers. He also spoke of the need to fight communism, a statement completely at odds with his later admission that he "already had deep socialist and communist convictions" at the time of Moncada.

———

The extent to which Castro had managed to ingratiate himself with the Canadian press, and by extension the Canadian people, came to light during a hostage-taking incident in the spring of 1958. In June, as the "total war" between Castro and Batista was entering one of its most brutal phases, two Canadians were kidnapped by the rebels, along with ten Americans. All twelve of the hostages were engineers employed by the U.S. firm Moa Bay Mining, which operated in Oriente province. One of the two Canadians, thirty-seven-year-old Otto Kristjanson, had already been abducted and released three months earlier in a separate incident.

For days, the fate of the Canadian hostages made the front pages. Then, while the original twelve remained in captivity, an additional Canadian and twenty-nine Americans were abducted. The stated purpose of the kidnappings was to retaliate for the refuelling of Cuban fighter jets at the U.S. base at Guantánamo. But, despite the deadly seriousness of the guerrillas' threat to use hostages as human shields, Canadian press coverage of the kidnappings remained strikingly sympathetic to the rebels.

Canadian Embassy staff worked doggedly to negotiate the release of the Canadian hostages, but at no time does there appear to have been any real concern for their safety. When the Canadians were finally released, on July 2, 1958, one of the hostages, fifty-two-year-old Edward Cannon of Cornwall, Ontario, held a press conference. He said that, if Castro's Revolution was to be as "nice" as his own stay with the *barbudos*, the rebel leader would be making many new friends. "Castro doesn't kick your pants off or jeer at you when he has you over a barrel," said Cannon. "Instead he is pretty reasonable if he believes that you are in a mood to listen to what he has to say. Kind treatment under those conditions is something you will remember for the rest of your life. I know I will." Cannon added with a laugh, "Don't put all your money on Batista."

In subsequent interviews, Cannon elaborated on the details of his captivity. Castro told him that he and the others were abducted because Batista's planes were dropping "U.S.-made bombs" on the homes and villages of local farmers. It had made no difference to the rebel leader that Cannon was a Canadian. "This action was against North Americans, they told me, and it didn't matter what part I came from." During their stay at a rebel camp, they were so well supplied with food, drink and cigars that they offered to pay for them. "Your money is no good here," one of the *barbudos* told them. At one point the hostages were driven in cars to the areas that Batista's planes had left in ruins. The rebels "insisted that we take a look at that and ask ourselves any questions we wanted to," Cannon recalled. They were then taken to "a swimming party" where they met Fidel Castro. When asked why he did not stay with Castro, Cannon replied, "Come to think of it, I might have. But you see, Castro got a tip-off that Batista's bombers were on the way. He wanted us out of the way before they could hurt us. Anyway, I am not a rebel. Or am I?"

As such reports of Castro's magnanimity made their way back to Canada, various media outlets began to probe for Canadian connections to the rebel heroes. CBC cameraman Erik Durschmied spent the last month of the war at Castro's mountain hideaway, for example, reporting on the rebels' day-to-day routines. He discovered that they lived on a staple diet of fried beans, bananas and Canadian cod. The fish were smuggled into Cuba from a secret rendezvous point somewhere on the southern coast. By this time, the CBC's coverage of Castro had become so one-sided that it prompted an official protest from Cuban Ambassador Carlos Carrillo, who resented the network's portrayal of the rebel leader as a "Robin Hood."

Every once in a while, Batista got the opportunity to air his views in the Canadian press, but seldom was the spin sympathetic. In October 1958, the *Toronto Star*'s reporter in Havana, Lloyd Lockhart, interviewed "the strong man" to see how he felt about Fidel Castro. "First, I want it known that I am not a dictator," Batista told him, "although my political enemies call me one time and again." As for his opinion of Castro, he was predictably dismissive. "Nature is on his side," Batista told Lockhart. "He hides in rugged country, emerging to ambush soldiers or terrify citizens. I met him once face to face, and I knew then he was a trouble-maker. Now I know he is a case for psychiatrists. His greatest achievement in life was graduating from juvenile delinquency to adult murder. He is an egocentric with delusions of grandeur. He has never won the confidence of Cubans. He is a nuisance."

All of this favourable publicity, much of it stage-managed by Castro personally, had precisely the desired impact in Canada. Editorials and letters in the Canadian dailies throughout 1958 were overwhelmingly supportive of the guerrillas. "There is a tendency," wrote one Canadian observer in July, "to regard rebels as always being in the wrong. For years the Cuban people have been trying to rid themselves of corrupt government at the polls, only to find their new representative to be as corrupt as his predecessor. Perhaps in Castro they have found an honest man, who, if given the opportunity, could form a responsible government." Another wrote in October, "I have recently returned from Cuba, and whereas in North America police brutality and perverted sadism is [*sic*] the rare exception (thanks to a free press and alert judiciary), in Cuba, under Batista, it is a daily occurrence. I am certain that anyone who was in Cuba in the winter of 1956 will never forget the photograph appearing in all the controlled Cuban press. A proud, triumphant Batista leered happily while the bodies of young patriot students lay on the sidewalks and their lives' blood flowed down the gutter."

In the immediate aftermath of the rebel victory in January 1959, Canadians' views of Fidel Castro were little changed. He remained an endearing and respectable Cuban patriot. Canadian journalists were shown the many victims of Batista's torturers and they were justifiably horrified. As Castro was making his triumphal journey into Havana, he offered the Canadian journalist William Kinmond an exclusive interview. In the exuberant language typical of those heady days after the triumph of the rebels, Kinmond referred to Castro as "the swashbuckling, bearded, weaponed rebel leader." The interview, conducted in English, turned at one point to the question on many Canadians' minds: What was to become of Canada's business interests in Cuba? "We will not interfere with legitimate business," Castro said, "but every arrangement made with Batista will be investigated. If they are within the law your Canadian friends have nothing to worry about." The rebel leader paused for a moment. "You tell Canada that I am very fond of Canadians," he said. "We want to be friends with your country." This gesture of goodwill did not go unnoticed back in Canada. Canadians would be exempt, Castro seemed to be saying, from the Americans' complicity in Batista's crimes.

In Ottawa, meanwhile, there was little question about formally recognizing Castro's regime. External Affairs estimated that there were only forty-five Canadian students and tourists seeking safe passage out of Havana, and the rebels were insistent that they would be protected. Canada established diplomatic relations with the new Cuban regime on January 8, 1959, one day after both the United States and the United Kingdom had done so. Castro's Foreign Office assured Ambassador Allard that the new regime would respect all previous treaty obligations. Allard in turn confirmed "the desire of the Canadian government to have friendly relations" with the new government of Cuba. Canadian officials in Havana recognized that the regime's desire to wrest control of the economy from the hands of Americans might well play to Canada's benefit. Castro himself made the same point in his usual boisterous fashion. "Tell the Canadian businessmen to come," he exclaimed. "We need the money!"

———

Although he had courted world opinion masterfully from the Sierra Maestra, Fidel Castro lost the ability to control events almost as soon as he took power.

One problem was Che Guevara. Following Castro's lead, Guevara took pains in the early days of the rebel victory to maintain the appearance that he was a moderate. "I am a leftist," he told a Canadian journalist in early January 1959. "I am a believer in social renovations. I am an inter-American, a lover of Latin Americans." But dissembling was not one of Guevara's strengths. Within weeks, he could hardly contain his exasperation at being asked whether he was a communist. "Every correspondent asks that," he railed. "Isn't anyone interested in schools or hospitals?" Anti-Castro Cubans in Miami led by one-time Castro supporter Rafael Del Pino charged that Castro was blind to the communist "menace" in his own ranks. Guevara was named explicitly. So was Raúl Castro, who had been a communist before serving with his brother as a rebel commander and remained an admirer of the Soviet Union. When the head of Castro's air force, Pedro Luis Díaz Lanz, fled to the United States in June 1959 claiming that the communists were taking charge of the Revolution, anti-communists throughout North America rallied behind the anti-Castro exiles. Fidel Castro continued to deny that he had any Red leanings, but he could no longer counter the perception that radicals in his own camp were trying to hijack the Revolution.

Equally damaging to Fidel Castro's international standing were the summary executions and show trials that came in the wake of the rebel victory. Even before his triumphant arrival in Havana, Castro's rebel army had rounded up over a thousand "Batista cronies," many of them officers in the hated national police or the army. The number of people in jail and awaiting trial in revolutionary courts ranged upwards of six thousand. Fifty prisoners had already been executed, and summary executions in the countryside were rumoured to be widespread. In Castro's home province of Oriente, there were reports of "a widespread purge of Cubans accused of crimes against the people." In an especially tragic development, University of Havana professor Rafael Escalona—a man later eulogized by Castro's interior minister as an "outstanding, militant revolutionary"—was mistaken for one of Batista's thugs and shot several times. Just one week after the rebel victory, roughly two hundred and fifty Cubans had been executed by firing squad. By mid-January, many North Americans agreed that bloodlust and vengeance threatened to undermine everything Castro had fought so hard to achieve. "Fidel Castro's uprising earned wide sympathy and support," said one Canadian editorial. "It would be a shame if this were dissipated by off-hand killings, blood baths or revolutionary terrorism."

Western observers were highly critical of "rebel justice" but so, too, were many Cubans. On January 12, for example, a crowd of three thousand showed up at the public execution of six Batista men in Mauzanillo, protesting that such a spectacle was inconsistent with Cuban culture. Castro himself seemed to be ambivalent about the executions. Some days, obviously frustrated by the badgering of the North American press, he was unyielding. "We have given orders to shoot every one of those murderers," he said on January 15, referring to the almost six thousand Batista followers he had in jail and another five thousand who were at large. "If we have to battle world opinion to mete out justice, we are prepared to do it." A week later, in a calmer moment, he convened a press conference to downplay the issue, telling the press that the bloodshed would end "as soon as possible—and the sooner the better." He added that Cubans were not a bloodthirsty people, and he reminded his audience that they were "the same people who speak out against bullfights and the killing of dogs."

Even Castro himself would later admit that he miscalculated when he decided to allow a show trial to be held in Havana on January 23, 1959. On that day a three-person tribunal tried ex-Batista army officer Major Jesús Sosa Blanco in front of thirty thousand Cubans at the city's Sports Palace. Thousands more listened to the radio broadcast of the trial. After eight hours the defendant was convicted on five counts of murder and a number of lesser charges (though he was commonly believed to be responsible for over one hundred murders). To the pleasure of the jeering crowd, he was sentenced to death. The world press was so uniformly appalled by the "Roman circus atmosphere of the trial," however, that Castro cancelled two other high-profile trials slated for the Sports Palace and had the officers in question tried in a Havana courtroom. He had learned another valuable public-relations lesson: placing even the most vicious criminal in a kangaroo court raises the possibility that the criminal and not his victims may elicit world sympathy. It was a lesson he needed to learn only once.

Fidel Castro has said that, of all of the revolutions of the twentieth century, his was one of the least bloody. He is correct about this. There was nothing in Cuba on the scale of the carnage produced by either Lenin's Russian Revolution or Mao's Chinese Revolution. And in stark contrast with those closed communist regimes, Castro has, albeit inconsistently, allowed Cubans to leave the island if they do not care for his Revolution. None of this amounts to a defence of the terror in the Revolution's early days, however, or of the increasingly "Orwellian" pall that his regime was then casting over Cuba. From the Sierra Maestra, Castro had for two years promised democracy and the rule of law, yet within days of taking power he had trampled Cubans' civil rights, abandoned due process and sanctioned summary execution. "*Al Paredón*—to the wall" became the *Fidelistas*' vengeful rallying cry. Estimates of the number of people imprisoned in this first phase of the Revolution run as high as forty thousand. There was no strategic rationale for such heavy-handed measures, for at no point was the Revolution in serious jeopardy. On the contrary, the only power capable of undermining the Revolution in its earliest stages was the United States, and if anything the terror increased the prospect of American intervention rather than diminishing it.

The impetus to the reign of terror was vengeance, plain and simple. After the heinous crimes of the Batista era, when an estimated twenty thousand Cubans were murdered, it is hardly surprising that Cubans wanted revenge, nor that they cheered when the worst of the dictator's torturers were made to pay with their own blood. Nor, perhaps, is it surprising that Fidel Castro, a man whose comrades had for years been mangled and killed by Batista's thugs, was only too happy to "mete out justice," as he put it. But many North Americans had hoped that Fidel Castro was a Mahatma Gandhi, somebody who would use his moral authority to quell the bloodshed. They were sorely disappointed. Castro could have stopped the terror, with very little damage either to his Revolution or his reputation, and he did not. It was an enormous gamble. It remained to be seen how great the long-term cost would be to his reputation.

———

By the time Fidel Castro appeared in Montreal in April 1959, Canadian and American opinions of him and his Revolution had already begun to diverge. In the United States, his tough talk on American foreign policy, his willingness to work with Cuban communists and his harsh treatment of those he called "cronies" of Fulgencio Batista had already alienated elite American opinion from the corporate boardroom to the White House. Many Americans believed that their nation had enjoyed a long and intimate history with Cuba, one that included the sacrifices of the Spanish-American War, the mutual benefits of trade and cultural exchange, and the countless personal loyalties this history had inspired. According to Cold War mythology, the Unites States had lost China to the communists in 1949. They were not about to lose Cuba, a country whose sentimental grip on the American imagination was incalculably greater.

Many Canadians, by contrast, had come to feel some kinship with Castro and his rebels but there was little in the way of shared history or hard national interest to anchor this attachment. Canada had relatively few economic interests in Cuba, and the most important of these—banking and insurance—were favoured by the Castro regime. Almost no Canadians lived in Cuba, and relatively few even travelled there. As Cold War allies of the United States, Canadians acknowledged the communist threat to the West, but this sentiment was mitigated by the fact that socialists enjoyed a legitimacy in Canadian politics for which there was no equal stateside. Far from subscribing to the Monroe Doctrine, which held that the western hemisphere was an American sphere of influence, Canadians tended to view it with suspicion, predisposing some nationalists in Canada to identify with Fidel Castro's anti-imperialist views. Most Canadians, however, including Prime Minister John Diefenbaker, opted simply to reserve judgment, giving Fidel Castro the benefit of the doubt at least until he could restore stability to the island and navigate a peaceful path toward the post-Batista future.

After his 1976 state visit to Havana, Pierre Trudeau was accused of cuddling up to Castro either because he was a communist sympathizer himself or because he liked to tweak American noses. His cheer of "*¡Viva el Primer Ministro Fidel Castro!*" is today more infamous than famous—evidence, say his detractors, that he was a closet Red who as prime minister led Canada by stealth toward socialism, pacifism and anti-Americanism. By the time Trudeau left office in 1984, fumed columnist Barbara Amiel, "most Canadians had got accustomed to a world in which Pierre Trudeau skinny-dipped with Fidel and shouted '*Viva Castro.*'"

Such claims are baseless. As his 1959 visit to Montreal demonstrated, Fidel Castro was widely regarded as a revolutionary hero in Canada well before Pierre Trudeau entered politics. Canadians' sympathy for the Cuban Revolution was not hatched in the backrooms of the Prime Minister's Office or the Liberal Party, nor was Fidel Castro cheered by Montrealers in 1959 and again in October 2000 because he was thought a tyrant. He was cheered because he personifies a mystique that has resonated for many Canadians since he was camped out in the Sierra Maestra.

At the heart of this mystique is the epic story of Castro's rise to power—how, with the backing of the poorest Cuban peasants, he led his band of scruffy but incorruptible guerrillas out of the wilderness to defeat a ruthless dictator and assert Cuba's independence. For many Canadians watching from the sidelines, this drama held a special salience. As one-time European colonies, Canada and Cuba each won political independence in the late nineteenth century, only to end up as cultural and economic satellites of the United States by the middle of the twentieth. Cuba watchers agreed that, in its rush to throw off the last vestiges of Spanish colonialism, the island nation had become one of the most American places in the world. Cubans had discarded Old World pastimes like bullfighting and adopted baseball as their national sport; they had embraced Hollywood movies as a national passion; they had opened their doors to massive U.S. investment. The same trends were transforming Canada, as Canadians cut themselves loose from the crumbling British Empire and rushed to embrace the new continentalism of the Cold War era. Like Cuba, Canada had become an outpost of American mass culture, American investment and American values. And like the Cubans, many Canadians were deeply uneasy about it. To this day, despite their many obvious differences, Canadians and Cubans share an obsession with national identity arising directly out of their love-hate relationship with the United States.

Pierre Trudeau's "*¡Viva el Primer Ministro Fidel Castro!*" marked the high point in Cuban-Canadian relations in the Castro era but it did not signal a radical change in the Canadian sensibility. On the contrary, it grew directly out of Canadians' infatuation with the rebel leader in the years when his struggle against Batista was one of the most newsworthy dramas of its day.

The Castro mystique did not originate with Pierre Trudeau. He inherited it.

2

Paddling to Havana

Canada and the Cuban-American Stand-Off

On the first day of May 1960, just a year after Fidel Castro's visit to Montreal, two forty-something Canadian millionaires and a thirty-something friend set out to paddle a homemade canoe from Key West to Havana. The inspiration for the voyage was the same mix of boredom and hubris that has long drawn the idle rich to mountain climbing, hot-air ballooning and other expressions of derring-do. One of the men had designed and built the special craft himself. Though it looked much like the familiar coureur-de-bois canoe, it had oarlocks like a rowboat and could be propelled with the legs as well as the arms. No one had ever crossed the Straits of Florida in a canoe but, really, how hard could it be? The distance between the United States and Cuba, as Senator John

F. Kennedy had taken to reminding North Americans, was "only 90 miles." And as for the three adventurers, were they not seasoned veterans of Canada's most daunting waterways and men of impeccable physical conditioning? "If we get there without too much difficulty," one of them casually told the press before leaving Canada, "it's possible that we will stay on the water and cross to Mexico."

As mariners have known for hundreds of years, the Straits of Florida are a channel of powerful currents, pounding waves and blistering sun. These days it is infamous as the escape route for desperate Cuban *balseros* (rafters) who seek their freedom in the United States, an estimated seventy-seven thousand of whom have perished in the attempt. Midway through their second day on the water, having covered only fifty miles, the three exhausted Canadians agreed to abandon the crossing. They were plucked out of the surging waters by a CBC cameraman who was tagging alongside them in a rented shrimp boat and filming the adventure. One of the ill-fated paddlers, wearing a white turban and looking more than a little green around the gills, headed immediately for the stern and proceeded to vomit over the side of the boat. His name was Pierre Trudeau.

———

This vignette speaks volumes about the kind of man Canada's fifteenth prime minister had become in the years before he vaulted onto the national political scene. He had turned forty the previous October—advanced middle age by the standards of 1960—but he was no grey-flannel conformist. He was rich, unmarried, adventurous, worldly, fiercely independent and utterly self-absorbed. He was a man to whom everything had come easily—school, athletics, friendship, romance—and for whom mastery of the world was its own reward, whether this meant backpacking through war-torn Asia, learning a new language, confronting Quebec's elites or crossing the Gulf of Mexico in a homemade canoe. He was a man who adopted as his personal mantra the Enlightenment credo "reason over passion," making him something of an enigma even to some of his friends. When he was fished out of the Straits of Florida on that balmy spring day in 1960, he betrayed no disappointment about the failed crossing. "That would call for a demonstration of emotion," recalled Don Newlands, the cameraman in the shrimp boat, "and that was not in him."

Though independently wealthy and as cosmopolitan as any Canadian of his era, Pierre Trudeau was only one generation removed from the small, insular world of the French-Canadian habitant. His entrepreneurial father, "Charlie" Trudeau, had died in 1935 at the age of forty-seven, leaving fifteen-year-old Pierre as the family patriarch and heir to a $3-million fortune that he would manage for the rest of his life with a frugality bordering on stinginess. Trudeau spent his adolescent years at the Jesuit-run Collège Jean-de-Brébeuf in Montreal, where he developed the intellectual agility for which he would become famous. From Brébeuf he went on to study law at the Université de Montréal, political economy at Harvard and a smattering of graduate courses at the École libre des sciences politiques in Paris and the London School of Economics.

Although Trudeau developed a taste for Marxist theory while studying in Europe, he always said that it was his training at Harvard that cemented his lifelong "beliefs about individual freedom." Like many twentieth-century liberals, Trudeau sought wherever possible to reconcile liberalism's emphasis on individual liberty with socialism's concern for collective reform. Yet, as Trudeau well knew, the two ideologies are not fundamentally compatible. When faced with a conflict between individual and collective rights, the true liberal will rally to the defence of the individual. So it was with Pierre Trudeau. He had been attracted to fascism as a student of the Jesuits, but as he broke free of Quebec's insular intellectual climate in the 1940s, he revolted against the extremes of collectivist thinking. He became especially critical of nationalism—the worst of the collectivist fantasies in his view because it privileged one group over others and was therefore fundamentally unjust. Although he would occasionally write as a democratic socialist, Pierre Trudeau's deepest political convictions would remain resolutely those of a near-classic liberal. "The view that every human must be free to shape his own destiny," he later recalled of his Harvard training, "became for me a certainty."

In 1948 Trudeau embarked on a year-long spiritual quest that took him to Asia via Eastern Europe and the Middle East. He intended the trip not as an intellectual exercise but as one in which he could immerse himself in the language, dress and labour of local people. "This trip was basically a challenge I set myself," he later recalled, "as I had done with sports, with canoeing expeditions, and with intellectual explorations. I wanted to know, for instance, whether I could survive in a Chinese province without knowing a word of Chinese, or would be able to travel across a war-torn country (there was no shortage of regional conflicts at this time) without ever succumbing to panic." He got his wish, experiencing jail in Jerusalem and Belgrade, an attack by the Viet Cong on the way to Saigon, myriad death threats and deportation from at least one communist-bloc country.

One of Trudeau's last stops was Cuba. He ventured to the island in 1949 to cut sugarcane—a back-breaking task he wanted to confront as yet another personal challenge. Trudeau arrived just in time to see Cuban democracy at its zenith, something that almost no Canadians outside the diplomatic corps would get the opportunity to witness first-hand. A new Cuban constitution had been introduced in 1940, wartime demand for sugar had restored economic prosperity, and the ruling Auténico party had not yet fallen into the corruption and scandal that would demoralize the Cuban people and inspire Batista's 1952 coup. Trudeau did not mention his two-week cane-cutting adventure in his *Memoirs*, but it must have left more than a passing impression on him. When officials at External Affairs were organizing his 1976 state visit to Havana, they attempted to schedule an excursion to the very fields where he had laboured as a footloose young man. The prime minister himself took a hand in this planning, directing them to the places where he had stayed. As it happened, the outing could not be accommodated on his official schedule. Still, Fidel Castro was briefed about Trudeau's cane-cutting adventure in advance of their first meeting and he was impressed. The prime minister had shown solidarity with the Cuban people, said the *Comandante*, and he had demonstrated that he was not afraid of hard work.

His world travels at an end, the thirty-year-old Trudeau returned to Montreal in 1949. With his friend Gérard Pelletier, he launched the journal *Cité libre*, positioning himself as a leading critic of Maurice Duplessis's Union Nationale government. "We wanted to unite all the opposition parties around their principal shared objective," said Trudeau, "making Québec a genuine democracy, and getting rid of the government machinations that were endangering people's freedoms." With the death of *le chef* in 1959, and the advent of the reformist Liberals under Jean Lesage in 1960, Trudeau was appointed associate professor of law at the Université de Montréal, a position he had coveted throughout the 1950s. Professor Trudeau was, in at least one sense, just in time to be late. The end of the Duplessis era made the world view of *Cité libre* passé. The new breed of French-Canadian activists was strongly nationalist and in many cases both socialist and separatist. Trudeau thus found himself suddenly on the trailing edge of Quebec politics, defending a constitutional and federalist idea of Canada that many Québécois—as they now called themselves—found anathema.

———

Journalist Peter C. Newman recalled recently that, as prime minister, Pierre Trudeau carried a personal grudge against John Diefenbaker. Perhaps, but he also had a genuine soft spot for him. Trudeau said nothing of consequence about the former prime minister in his *Memoirs* but he did include an extraordinary photograph, which shows him wiping his eyes at Diefenbaker's 1979 state funeral. In the 1970s, Trudeau and Diefenbaker would be the toughest of political adversaries. Yet this did not prevent the Liberal prime minister from acknowledging the old Tory's lifelong contribution to Canada. In December 1975, just weeks before his state visit to Havana, Trudeau recommended that Queen Elizabeth confer upon Diefenbaker the prestigious Companion of Honour in recognition of "conspicuous national service." Diefenbaker later told the press that the tribute had come entirely at Trudeau's initiative and only after the two men had discussed it confidentially.

John Diefenbaker's tenure as prime minister (1957–63) coincided with the most tumultuous years of the Cold War including its denouement, the Cuban Missile Crisis of October 1962. In the two-and-a-half-year period that followed Fidel Castro's 1959 North American tour, tensions between Cuba and the United States escalated with a fury that surprised even the *Comandante* and culminated in a stand-off of such intensity that it has persisted to this day. To many outside observers, the wrath with which presidents Eisenhower and, especially, Kennedy went after the Cuban leader in these years was completely out of proportion to the threat he represented. Some critics of U.S. foreign policy would later argue that American pressure in these years actually radicalized Castro and drove him into the arms of the Soviets. But the historical record does not bear this out. In truth, Castro and American policy makers were on a collision course from the outset, which means that some sort of breach was probably inevitable. What is certain is that, by 1963, the official U.S. position on Castro had hardened into the most resolute of antagonisms, while the considerably less strident position of America's allies in Europe and Canada had altered very little.

Diefenbaker would lose the election of 1963 for his reputed dithering, but it was his principled defence of an independent foreign policy for Canada that in the early 1960s endeared him to Pierre Trudeau and others (including the philosopher George Grant, author of *Lament for a Nation*). Trudeau was especially impressed by Diefenbaker's courage in resisting American pressure while he was prime minister—his insistence that Canada maintain diplomatic relations with Cuba and particularly his refusal to deploy nuclear weapons on Canadian soil. Carlos Fernández de Cossío, Cuban ambassador to Canada between 1999 and 2004, has recalled that during a meeting with Cuban officials in 1995, Trudeau was thanked for placing the Cuban-Canadian relationship on a firm footing while he was prime minister. Pierre immediately corrected the record, said the ambassador, assigning the credit to Diefenbaker in the early 1960s. This was not false modesty. The contours of the Cuban-Canadian relationship that Trudeau inherited when he became prime minister in 1968 were forged in the Eisenhower and Kennedy years, when it had fallen to Diefenbaker to react, blow by blow, to the downward spiral of Cuban-American relations.

The irony was thick. More than any other individual it was John Diefenbaker, Canada's most famously anti-communist prime minister, who laid the groundwork for Pierre Trudeau's friendship with Fidel Castro. It was a paradox that thoroughly delighted Trudeau.

———

Less than a month after Fidel Castro returned home from his 1959 tour of North America, his government passed the Agrarian Reform Act, setting in motion the train of economic measures and counter-measures that led a year and a half later to the imposition of the U.S. embargo against Cuba. Agrarian reform was intended to put land into the hands of the Sierra Maestra "peasants" who had "suffered the most in the war," as Castro himself put it. But because foreigners owned 70 per cent of Cuba's arable land, the brunt of the law was borne by them, and particularly by large American corporations like the United Fruit Company. In October 1959, the U.S. Congress went on an "anti-Cuban rampage" and threatened Cuba with termination of its preferential sugar imports if it did not improve its expropriation terms. Such threats did not surprise Fidel Castro. "Our Agrarian Reform went against the interests of the big U.S. companies," he later recalled. "They made war against us because of our Agrarian Reform." Seeing that economic war with the United States was imminent, Castro appointed Che Guevara as the head of the Banco Nacional de Cuba in November 1959 and ordered him to sell off all of Cuba's gold reserves in the United States—a hedge against possible reprisals for the expropriation of agrarian lands. The bulk of these assets, amounting to over $60 million, were quietly deposited in Canadian banks in Havana.

The reports of communist involvement in the Revolution, which had followed Fidel Castro to Montreal, persisted throughout 1959. By the end of the year, Russian officers were rumoured to be indoctrinating the Cuban armed forces, in accordance with Raúl Castro's wishes, and Russian ships were said to be anchored in Cuban waters. Yet not until February 1960, when Soviet Deputy Premier Anastas Mikoyan visited Havana, did Washington concede publicly that Castro himself was drifting toward communism. For their part, the Soviets left little doubt about Cuba's new strategic importance in the Cold War. "Those who talk of war," Mikoyan boasted while he was in Havana, "know that if we can send a rocket to the moon with such precision we can send a rocket with the same precision to any point on earth." From New Delhi, India, Soviet Premier Nikita Khrushchev promised "friendly and self-less assistance" to Castro and scolded the West for "plundering" the resources of Latin America, Asia and Africa. Before Mikoyan left Cuba, the USSR announced that it would buy five-million tons of Cuban sugar over five years, extend Castro $100 million in credit over twelve years and sell him the fighter aircraft he had been unable to procure from the West. To add insult to injury, Mikoyan met with American novelist Ernest Hemingway in Havana and agreed to have *For Whom the Bell Tolls* translated into Russian for the first time.

Officially, the Eisenhower administration continued to assume what Secretary of State Christian Herter called a "take it easy" attitude toward Cuba. "I don't think anyone could say affirmatively that Cuba is Communist at the present time," Herter remarked in a televised interview in March 1960. On the contrary, he said, the United States was "very sympathetic to the aims of the revolution. We've never objected to the land reform law, as such. We've insisted, however, that American citizens, like all foreigners and Cubans, should be paid prompt and adequate and effective compensations for properties taken from them." As part of its take it easy approach, the Eisenhower administration announced that it would not tolerate the use of Miami and south Florida as a base for counterrevolutionaries. The U.S. immigration service was to be enhanced, surveillance at Florida airports increased, the FBI empowered to aid U.S. customs in interdicting gun-running, pilots with a history of anti-Castro activities blacklisted, and anyone providing information about illegal flights over Cuba offered a $5,000 reward.

All of this—the entire posture of restraint toward Cuba—turned out to be a smokescreen. Virtually the entire time that President Eisenhower was instructing the State Department and the U.S. diplomatic corps to take the high road in public, the White House was quietly mobilizing the American intelligence establishment—and with it, the Cuban émigré community—against Fidel Castro. In June 1959, the administration ordered the CIA to begin destabilizing the regime. A National Security Council memo later recalled of that decision, "Our objective was to adjust all our actions in such a way as to accelerate the development of an opposition in Cuba which would bring about a new government favourable to U.S. interests." Raids by émigrés on Cuba, backed by the CIA and launched from bases in the United States, began at roughly the same time. Six months later, the White House decided to collaborate with anti-Castro groups within Cuba in their efforts to overthrow Castro. This meant backing counterrevolutionaries in the little-known civil war that raged in eastern Cuba until 1966, a conflict that resulted in thousands of deaths.

The rebel leader had not been in power a year before assassination plans were being hatched against him in Washington. In December 1959, CIA Director Allen Dulles approved a draft document suggesting that "thorough consideration be given to the elimination of Fidel Castro." A month later, Dulles approached President Eisenhower with a plan for the sabotage of sugar refineries in Cuba. Eisenhower liked what he saw but believed the plan too modest. The president told Dulles that the time had come to increase the covert pressure on Castro from mere "harass-ment" to something "much more ambitious," and sent him away to work on "an enlarged program." That same month, the CIA convened its first "Special Group" meeting with the State Department to discuss the over-throw of the Castro regime. In March 1960, the same month Secretary of State Herter told Americans that "we are very sympathetic to the aims of the revolution," Allen Dulles returned to the White House with the "enlarged plan" President Eisenhower had requested. The centrepiece of the new plan was the assassination of Fidel Castro, an initiative that put in motion a five-year murder conspiracy that would become one of the CIA's most infamous (and fruitless) debacles.

With the agency's secret war on Castro shifting into high gear in the spring and summer of 1960, the diplomatic feud between the Eisenhower administration and the Castro regime could no longer be contained. At the urging of the United States government, the American petroleum companies Esso and Texaco refused a request from Castro to refine crude oil that had been imported to Cuba from the Soviet Union. Calling the U.S. subsidiaries' defiance a "challenge to the sovereignty of the revolu-tionary government," Castro seized U.S.-owned refineries in Santiago de Cuba and threatened to nationalize every investment Americans had in the country, "down to the nails in their shoes." On July 7, President Eisenhower announced that he was slashing 846,000 tons of sugar imports from Cuba—a $70-million hit on the Cuban economy that even Castro found unexpectedly harsh. Appealing for world sympathy, the Cuban leader railed against the Americans, who "in a frenzy of hate want to sink a people in hunger and ruin." From Vienna, Nikita Khrushchev sounded an ominous warning. "On our part," said the Soviet leader, "we will use everything to support Cuba in her just struggle for freedom and liberty won by the Cuban people under the leadership of the national hero, Fidel Castro." The next day, Eisenhower offered this blunt response to Khrushchev: "Hands off Cuba." The United States would not be intimi-dated by Soviet threats, the president said, nor would it "permit the establishment of a regime dominated by international communism in the western hemisphere."

The feud escalated. In August 1960, Castro nationalized virtually all major U.S.-owned industrial and agricultural firms in Cuba, estimated to be worth between $750 million and $1 billion. They included the Cuban Electric Company, Esso and Texaco, Moa Bay Mining and all thirty-six U.S.-owned sugar mills on the island. In mid-September he had all American banks seized. Then on October 19, 1960, to the surprise of no one, the United States ran out of patience with Fidel Castro and imposed a full-blown trade embargo on Cuba. Only food and medicine were to be exempted. The Cubans retaliated by nationalizing all U.S.-owned wholesale and retail firms, and all remaining industrial and agricultural concerns. On October 29, the U.S. ambassador to Cuba was recalled.

Fidel Castro had been expecting the embargo announcement for weeks, frantically stockpiling spare parts for Cuba's factories, mills, refineries and automobiles from North American suppliers. He knew that his new friends in the Soviet bloc countries would take up the slack in imports. But he knew as well that retooling the entire national economy along Soviet lines would be painful. Just how long the embargo would last, and just how painful the transition from American to Soviet technologies would be, no one in Cuba could have anticipated in 1960. Yet there can be no mistaking the cataclysm in retrospect. North American visitors to Cuba today have the eerie sensation of bearing witness to the shock effect of the embargo as it rolled over the island in 1960. The most visible symbols of this dislocation are the vintage American cars that have been chugging around Havana for forty-five years or more, their windshields cracked, their tires bald, their instrument panels dysfunctional. Decrepit American-styled factories, hotels and infrastructure tell the same story, evoking a dynamic and modern North American culture flash-frozen half a century ago. The remnants of the later Soviet era are also on display, of course—the ubiquitous Ladas, the Russian-built tractors and buses, the gloomy architecture of Soviet office buildings and row houses. As even

Castro himself has conceded from time to time, usually in moments of pique, Soviet technology was always second-best.

———

Prime Minister John Diefenbaker's role in setting out a distinctive Canadian position on revolutionary Cuba has been almost as wilfully misconstrued as Pierre Trudeau's. Conventional wisdom has it that Diefenbaker's contempt for John F. Kennedy drove him to adopt a pro-Castro position just to spite the United States. His patriotism, it is said, got the better of him. Thus, where Trudeau has been rebuked for loving freedom too little, Diefenbaker has been pilloried for loving Canada too much. Both claims are specious.

Well before he became prime minister, "Dief the Chief" was best known as one of Canada's coldest Cold Warriors. Like many Tories of his generation, he agreed with Winston Churchill's blunt estimation of the Soviets: they were intent on world conquest, and they could not be trusted. Diefenbaker's anti-communism never waned. In September 1960, just weeks before the American embargo was imposed on Cuba, he stood up at the United Nations and accused Nikita Khrushchev of hypocrisy in calling for the elimination of Western colonialism. "I think it would be gener-ally agreed," said Diefenbaker, "that whatever the experience of the past, there can no longer be a relationship of master and servant anywhere in the world. [Khrushchev] has spoken of colonial bondage, of exploitation and foreign yokes. Those views [were] uttered by the master of the major colo-nial power in the world today." It was a speech in which Diefenbaker took enormous pride. A decade later, when even the likes of Richard Nixon and Henry Kissinger were singing the praises of détente, Diefenbaker was still assailing the naïveté of Western leaders who believed that "the USSR is going to exchange its aggression for love and affection." Pierre Trudeau was among those Canadians whom he accused of such naïveté. When Trudeau went to Havana in 1976, Diefenbaker was one of his fiercest critics.

Diefenbaker had no love for Fidel Castro. "Castroism," he believed, "was at worst a symptom and the most radical manifestation of the social and economic tensions existing in Latin America. One treats an illness by getting rid of its causes, not by erasing its symptoms." In truth, Diefenbaker's personal feelings toward John Kennedy had nothing whatsoever to do with Canada's decision not to fall in behind the U.S. embargo. The American sanctions were imposed in mid-October 1960, one month before Kennedy defeated Richard Nixon in the U.S. presidential race and three months before he entered the White House. Far from being driven by anti-Americanism, Diefenbaker's approach to the crisis was marked at every turn by his sensitivity to the U.S. position, and by his deep respect for his friend President Eisenhower, whom he always said had a great "appreciation of Canada and Canadians."

Diefenbaker's sentiments were reciprocated. Acting on Eisenhower's instructions, the U.S. State Department had consulted Ottawa in secret prior to the embargo announcement. According to Canadian officials, the Americans "at no time requested Canada, formally or informally, to impose an embargo of its own." They simply wanted Canada's assurance that Canadian trade with Cuba would not undermine the intent of the United States sanctions. This assurance they got. In an "unwritten understanding" concluded just prior to the embargo announcement, Canadian officials agreed to "prevent Canada from being used as a back door for the export of an extensive list of industrial supplies, equipment and machinery from the United States to Cuba." Recently declassified State Department documents have revealed that, far from encouraging Canada to support the embargo, the United States secretly urged Diefenbaker to maintain normal relations because it was thought that Canada would be well positioned to gather intelligence on the island. In short, Prime Minister Diefenbaker was confident about Canada's Cuba policy not because he had stubbornly crossed the Americans but precisely because he had earned their confidence. As he said in the House of Commons on December 12, 1960, "we respect the views of other nations in their relations with Cuba, just as we expect that they respect our views in our relations."

Contrary to the myth that Diefenbaker's refusal to impose a Canadian embargo on Cuba was out of step with the Cold War loyalties of Canadians, the prime minister actually found himself in the hot seat for conceding too much to the United States. The business-oriented *Globe and Mail* challenged him immediately, arguing that the "unwritten understanding" with Washington made Canada complicit in enforcing the embargo. "The effect on our reputation abroad will be disastrous," observed the paper. "The Cubans and other Latin Americans—and also the Asians and the Africans—are quite astute enough to draw their own conclusions. They will conclude when it is a question of pleasing Washington or making our own independent decision on a contentious issue, we prefer to please Washington."

The Eisenhower administration had not expected Canada to fall in behind its embargo, and for good reason. For one thing, the quarrel with Fidel Castro was highly contentious in the United States. It had moved to centre stage in the 1960 election race, prompting a national debate about Republican foreign policy and putting presidential hopeful Richard Nixon on the defensive. His challenger, Democrat John F. Kennedy, adopted an anti-Castro position but was also critical of the embargo, accusing the Eisenhower administration of merely reacting to events. "I am not satisfied," said Kennedy in a September campaign speech, "to have the deadly hand of communism extend its frontier from East Berlin, more than 3,000 miles away, to our former good neighbor in Cuba, only 90 miles from Florida, only eight minutes by jet." In addition, no other NATO country—indeed, no other country at all—proved willing to follow the American lead and impose sanctions on Cuba in October 1960. Castro's nationalization measures were not seen as a threat to the western alliance, nor had his visits with communist leaders seemed especially worrisome to America's allies. Isolated and mindful of the risks of being seen to act unilaterally in the world, Eisenhower could not afford the perception that he had tried to dictate Canadian policy. He got as much out of Diefenbaker as he had any reason to expect, and he knew it.

Diefenbaker's insistence on an independent Cuba policy for Canada was founded on his belief that a hardline policy would drive Castro even further into the arms of the Soviets, a view shared by his secretary of state for external affairs, Howard Green, and Green's undersecretary, Norman Robertson. On Diefenbaker's instructions, Canada's diplomats in Havana informed the Castro regime that, while Canadians respected Cuba as a sovereign state, they were not overly sympathetic to the Revolution. The maintenance of trade relations, they said, should in no way be understood to compromise either Canada's friendship with the United States or its defence commitments within NATO. Never did Diefenbaker or External Affairs cease to express their hope that Cuba would remove itself from the Soviet sphere of influence.

When he sat down to write his memoirs in the mid-1970s, Diefenbaker knew that his decision not to back the embargo had already been grossly distorted, its historical context eclipsed by later controversies. Much water had by then flowed under the Canadian-American bridge. Cuba had acquired enormous symbolic value on both sides of the 49th parallel. And as for Diefenbaker himself, he had been deposed in 1967 as the leader of the Progressive Conservative Party amid accusations that he was indecisive and out of touch. To set the record on Cuba straight, Diefenbaker painstakingly recounted his original rationale for refusing to fall in behind the U.S. sanctions. Canada had a duty, he said, to maintain cordial relations with the recognized governments of other nations, even when their "philosophical outlook" varied with Canadians'. The Monroe Doctrine was neither recognized by international law nor binding on Canada. Cuba had done nothing to warrant any "departure from normal diplomatic conduct." And ostracizing Cuba would only drive it into the Soviet orbit, foreclosing on the possibility that Canada might "influence the course of Cuban events."

The last of Diefenbaker's points was the most significant of all. "Canadian policy toward Cuba," he recalled, "had the overwhelming support of Canadian public opinion and of Canada's press." On this point, he was exactly right. The prime minister had done exactly what Canadians would have had him do.

———

President Eisenhower severed diplomatic relations with Cuba on January 3, 1961. It was one of his last acts as president, and coming as it did on the second anniversary of the triumph of the Revolution, it was loaded with symbolism. Eisenhower claimed that he had no choice in the matter. The previous day, Fidel Castro had ordered all but eleven U.S. embassy officials off the island, claiming that some had been directing counter-revolutionary terrorism under the cover of diplomatic immunity. This reduction in U.S. representation, said Eisenhower, made it impossible to conduct normal diplomatic relations with Cuba. "There is a limit to what the United States in self-respect can endure," he added. "That limit has now been reached."

Prime Minister Diefenbaker had been briefed by the State Department about the American decision to break off diplomatic relations with Cuba, but he made no formal comment. Instead, an official at External Affairs told the Canadian press that Canada had no "diplomatic difficulties" with the Castro regime and that its relationship with Cuba would continue uninterrupted. Editorial opinion in Canada supported the government position, with the dominant view still being that "it is only for Ottawa to say with whom Canada will or will not associate." The *Globe and Mail* reiterated its earlier stance. "This country has no quarrel with Cuba," observed the paper. "It is proper, therefore, that diplomatic relations should be maintained between Ottawa and Havana."

By this time, Canada's position on Cuba had begun to raise eyebrows in Washington—but not because of anything Diefenbaker had said or done. At issue was evidence that Canadian businesses were shamelessly exploiting the American exodus from the Cuban market. Fidel Castro had himself contributed to this perception. He had exempted Canadian firms from his Agrarian Reform Act, and later from his expropriation policies.

When Castro nationalized the American banks in September 1960, he not only left the Royal Bank and the Bank of Nova Scotia alone but quietly deposited confiscated American assets into their vaults. And when he did finally nationalize the Canadian banks three months later, he was only too happy to compensate them—a striking contrast to his seizure of the American banks, which took the form of an armed occupation by Cuban militia. When asked about his preferential treatment of the Canadian banks, Castro explained that they were helping to shore up the Revolution. The irony was rich. The big banks of Bay Street have always been the foremost symbols of Canadian capitalism. That they were admired by the world's leading guerrilla revolutionary and complicit in his moves on American assets did not go unnoticed in the United States.

Some Canadian politicians and business leaders were unabashed in their enthusiasm for the sudden vacuum in the Cuban market. In November 1960, a U.S. news service reported that Canadian businessmen were pouring into Havana, striking deals and hobnobbing with Fidel Castro. The following month, a Cuban delegation led by the minister of economic affairs, Regino Boti, arrived in Canada to discuss trade now that the Americans were on the sidelines. Diefenbaker's minister of trade and commerce, George Hees, was so taken with the Cubans that he told the press he could imagine Canada doing $150-million worth of business with Cuba annually. "You can't do business with better businessmen anywhere," he beamed. "They're wonderful customers." Canadian exports to Cuba had received little notice when they were part and parcel of hemispheric trade, but after the break in Cuban-American relations they came under intense scrutiny. Cuba's purchase of five hundred thousand Canadian chickens and turkeys, several hundred pigs and 500 cows, for example, made headlines on January 7, 1961, just four days after the announcement that the United States had severed diplomatic relations. Canadian officials in Washington did their best to placate American criticism. Canada was shipping newsprint, cod and seed potatoes to Cuba, they said, and not "bootlegging U.S. goods." But such hair-splitting did little

good. In U.S. diplomatic circles, Canadian opportunism seemed genuinely incomprehensible.

Within days of Canada's announcement that it would not follow the United States and sever diplomatic relations with Cuba, the Canadian Embassy in Havana and the Department of External Affairs in Ottawa began receiving threats. A group calling itself the People's Revolutionary Alliance threatened to destroy Canadian interests in Cuba once Castro was overthrown. Another group threatened reprisals against Embassy personnel in Havana. Pickets were organized in front of the Canadian Embassy in Washington and the consulate in New York City. American tourists were urged not to vacation in Canada. John Diefenbaker and his wife had planned to vacation in Florida over the winter of 1961, but the Canadian ambassador in Washington, Arnold Heeney, advised them against it. Anti-Castro Cubans in the Sunshine State, he said, might make things "uncomfortable" for the prime minister and his wife.

Ten days after the United States severed diplomatic relations with Cuba, Fidel Castro offered to begin a new dialogue of peace with incoming president John F. Kennedy. He told the Cuban people that the new president appeared to be somebody who could usher in a new enlightened era in Cuban-American relations. "We really have no points of friction with the United States," said Castro, "since all industries, all mines and all banks are ours. The only problem is Guantánamo and we are in no hurry about that base." On January 20, following Kennedy's inaugural address, the Cuban leader again offered to "bury the hatchet." It was not to be. Kennedy and his advisers were intent on reforming U.S. foreign policy but, like their Republican predecessors, they were committed Cold Warriors. Their policy for Latin America envisaged liberal reforms that would undermine the appeal of revolution, whether "Castroist" or communist. The Peace Corps and the Alliance for Progress, both launched in March 1961, came out of this vision. So did Kennedy's $600-million aid plan for Latin America.

At a now-famous press conference held on April 12, 1961, the president was asked for his personal opinion of Castro. "Well, he has indicated his admiration on many occasions for the Communist revolution," Kennedy responded. He was then queried on "how far [the United States] would be willing to go in helping an anti-Castro uprising or invasion in Cuba." The president's reply was carefully worded. "Well, first I want to say that there will not, under any conditions, be an intervention in Cuba by United States armed forces," he said, "and this government will do everything it possibly can, and I think it can meet its responsibilities, to make sure that there are no Americans involved in any actions inside Cuba." Three days later, B-26s piloted by Cuban exiles began bombing Cuban airfields. Two days after that, at 5 a.m. local time on April 17, 1961, exile Brigade 2506—trained and bankrolled by the CIA—landed at Playa Girón, the Bay of Pigs. What followed over the next two days was the worst blunder of Kennedy's presidency.

The Cubans had been so certain that an American-backed invasion was imminent that they put the issue before the UN Security Council.

Castro had as many as one hundred spies in Miami, but he claimed not to have needed them. "We knew about 90 per cent of what was going on before the Girón invasion," he recalled, "because of what was being said publicly. We did not need spies." Castro declared a state of emergency and mobilized all of his armed forces. Within hours of the B-26 bombing campaign, three hundred thousand troops were deployed to beaches all over the island. The moment the exact location of the invasion became known, Castro drove down from Havana to take personal command of the defence. Rumours of large-scale anti-Castro uprisings in Cuban cities circulated in the press and on radio, but they turned out to be mainly U.S. propaganda—a grave disappointment for Cubans like the imprisoned poet Armando Valladares who had cheered the arrival of the bombers as a liberating force. Knowing that the invaders' strategy would include the incitement of insurgencies against the regime—this had, after all, been Castro's own strategy in 1952 and again in 1958— Cuban authorities moved immediately to clamp down on subversion. In the city of Havana alone, thirty-five thousand people suspected of counterrevolutionary tendencies were rounded up and detained on the first day of the invasion.

The combat at Playa Girón was intense. Yet, despite initial setbacks for the Cubans, the outcome was never in doubt. Within forty-eight hours, the invasion force was routed. One hundred invading soldiers lay dead, along with 160 Cubans. Another 1,180 invaders were taken prisoner. Castro issued a communiqué at 5:30 p.m. on April 19, declaring total victory and praising the courage of the Cuban defenders. In Washington, every effort was made to downplay the disaster. But within twenty-four hours, the true scale of the operation and the role of the CIA began to come to light. Recriminations rumbled through the corridors of power. Allen Dulles was singled out as having persuaded Kennedy to undertake the invasion against the advice of his State Department and his own better judgment. Dulles's refusal to disclose his own role in the planning of the invasion before the Senate Foreign Relations Committee fuelled speculation that the new president had been strong-armed into accepting his predecessor's flawed plan. The U.S. intelligence establishment was criticized for underestimating both Castro's popular support and the strength of his police apparatus. Exiles in Miami accused the CIA of failing to coordinate the landing with the efforts of the Cuban underground, and of neglecting to "soften up" the enemy with sabotage. The adoption of a single-thrust strategy rather than a campaign of smaller landings was also criticized.

President Kennedy admitted that the news from Cuba was not good. Even so, he put Castro on notice. "Let the record show that our restraint is not inexhaustible," the president said in a televised speech on April 20. "It is clear that this nation, in concert with all the free nations of this hemisphere, must take an ever closer and more realistic look at the menace of external Communist intervention and domination in Cuba." Such bravado did Kennedy little good. The administration's insistence that it was not behind the Bay of Pigs was viewed with skepticism by most observers. By early May, Kennedy advisers up to and including Secretary of State Dean Rusk were being grilled behind closed doors by the Senate Foreign Relations Committee. Things became so heated that ex-president Eisenhower came out of retirement to urge the Congress not to conduct a "witch hunt" over the U.S. involvement in the Bay of Pigs.

For his part, Fidel Castro spent the first few days after the battle incommunicado, fuelling speculation that he might have been hurt. When he finally reappeared he took masterful advantage of the American fiasco, spending hours at Havana's Sports Palace talking with captured members of the exile brigade while the world's media looked on. Once again, the vengeful rallying cry "Al Paredón—to the wall" was heard in Cuba, but this time Castro was taking the high road. "We believe the punishment should not be the death penalty at this moment," he said, "because the people's great victory should not be belittled by excess." In the court of world opinion, Cuba was now what Castro had always said it was, a victim of American aggression.

Back in Canada, Diefenbaker and his cabinet knew that public opinion was almost uniformly unsympathetic to Kennedy in the wake of the Bay of Pigs. For one thing, the Cuban government had taken pains to ensure the safety of the 260 Canadians then in Cuba. ("There is no danger to Canadians," said the Cuban ambassador in Ottawa, Américo Cruz. "We like them very much.") For another, like most of their European allies, many Canadians regarded the American rationale for the invasion with a jaded eye. The United States had announced its right to act unilaterally against communist influence in the hemisphere, which was itself contentious, but the fact remained that Castro had not yet declared himself a Marxist-Leninist. Many Canadians therefore concluded that the Bay of Pigs was just another episode in the schoolyard scrap between Washington and Havana, with the United States in the role of bully. The most alarming aspect of the Bay of Pigs for Canada, in fact, turned out to be the so-called Kennedy Doctrine announced during the president's televised speech. "If the nations of this hemisphere should fail to meet their commitments against outside Communist penetration," Kennedy had said, "then I want it clearly understood that this Government will not hesitate in meeting its primary obligations which are to the security of our own nation." The next day the front-page headline in the *Globe and Mail* shouted, "Kennedy Doctrine Applies to Canada." A heated national debate ensued. Neither Diefenbaker nor his leading ministers would comment publicly on the president's speech, but External Affairs confirmed on April 24 that the prime minister was pressing for "assurances from Washington that the Kennedy Doctrine does not apply to Canada."

Fidel Castro has never let his people forget the Bay of Pigs. For Cubans and also for others in the region, the battle is celebrated as "imperialism's first military defeat in Latin America." As for President Kennedy, he emerged from the fiasco frustrated, embarrassed and more determined than ever to get rid of Castro. He gave his brother, Robert Kennedy, the attorney general of the United States, full responsibility for the Cuba file. Together, the Kennedys created and oversaw Operation Mongoose, a covert program of paramilitary operations against the island that included hotel bombings, the sabotage of industrial and agricultural sites, and the contamination of Cuba's sugar crop. With an annual budget of $50 million, Mongoose employed four hundred Americans, two thousand Cubans and a private navy operating out of Florida. Operations were run directly out of the White House, with General Edward Lansdale in charge of logistics. And while it made extensive use of Cuban émigrés, recently declassified documents show that Mongoose was premised on the assumption that, sooner or later, the United States would have to invade Cuba. In June 1963, Kennedy replaced Mongoose with a Covert Action Plan that handed responsibility for Castro back to the CIA. After Kennedy's assassination in November 1963, President Lyndon Johnson would continue to back the paramilitary campaign and the covert action against the Cuban economy. Both were shelved temporarily in 1965, as Johnson became preoccupied with Vietnam, only to be revived and escalated by Richard Nixon after 1969.

Apart from Castro's seemingly overwrought claims about CIA involvement in counterrevolutionary activities in Cuba, Mongoose remained largely unknown to Americans until the congressional investigations of the mid-1970s. By the time White House "dirty tricks" were fully exposed, they came to be identified in the public imagination with Richard Nixon—that is, with Watergate, the bombing of Cambodia and the U.S.-backed coup in Chile. The Kennedy mystique, by the 1970s in full bloom, was not undermined in the least by the revelations that he had personally ordered the sabotage of vital Cuban interests and the assassination of Fidel Castro. On the contrary, and much to Nixon's consternation, the Camelot myth seemed to be enhanced by the ennui that had descended on U.S. politics by the bicentennial of 1976. Kennedy, many Americans had come to believe, was the last great president before Vietnam and Watergate destroyed the American presidency.

There was no ambiguity about Diefenbaker's contempt after 1961 for the Kennedys generally, for John F. Kennedy in particular and for what he saw as the new administration's bullying of both Canada and Cuba. The product of a privileged upbringing and Ivy League education, a youthful, handsome and telegenic figure, President Kennedy was anathema to Diefenbaker on practically every level. "President Kennedy had no knowledge of Canada whatsoever," Diefenbaker later complained. "More important, he was activated by the belief that Canada owed so great a debt to the United States that nothing but continuing subservience could repay it." For his part, Kennedy spoke of Diefenbaker—in his most exasperated moments at least—as a "fucker" and a "shit."

Diefenbaker had his first lengthy meeting with Kennedy in Ottawa in May 1961. (They had met briefly in Washington after Kennedy's inauguration but discussed little of substance and had not yet developed their mutual animosity.) The president was "still agitated by the humiliation of the Bay of Pigs fiasco," Diefenbaker later recalled, and thus keen to urge the other Western nations to follow the United States in disengaging from Cuba politically and economically. Diefenbaker dismissed this suggestion, reminding Kennedy that Canadians had enjoyed a long history of amicable relations with Cuba. He also remembered that this conversation about Cuba was paired with Kennedy's repeated insistence that Canada join the Organization of American States. "Having decided that he wanted Canada (he pronounced it 'Canader') as a member of the OAS, he wanted it done right now," Diefenbaker wrote. "I was not about to have Canada bullied into any course of action. This was the first of a number of occasions on which I had to explain to President Kennedy that Canada was not Massachusetts, or even Boston." When it was discovered that the U.S. delegation accidentally left behind a one-page memorandum Walt Rostow of the State Department had drafted for Kennedy's eyes only, Diefenbaker cited it in his public criticism of the president. Kennedy was furious. According to protocol, Diefenbaker should have returned the memo without comment, and he knew it.

Kennedy may have believed that John Diefenbaker's Cuba policy was rooted in anti-Americanism, but the Cuban ambassador in Ottawa, Américo Cruz, most certainly did not. Cruz was so struck by Canada's loyalty to NATO—a point that External Affairs officials made doggedly in his presence—that he recommended to Fidel Castro at one point that Cuba "break the union which it has forged with the socialist countries." Back in Cuba, meanwhile, much to his own surprise, Diefenbaker had come to be regarded as a hero of the Revolution. A Canadian journalist reported from Camagüey that there were four portraits hanging in the lobby of his hotel—Castro, Marx, Lenin and Diefenbaker. "Your Mr. Diefenbaker is a great man," the hotel clerk told him. "Mr. Diefenbaker is, I think, a lot like Fidel."

Castro did not take Ambassador Cruz's advice and loosen Cuba's ties to the Soviet Union. Instead, on December 2, 1961, he ended years of speculation and declared himself a dyed-in-the-wool communist. Backdating his conversion to Marxism to the days when he was fighting Batista from the Sierra Maestra, he told the Cuban people, "I am a Marxist-Leninist and will be one until the day I die." Castro announced that he would be accelerating Cuba's transformation into a one-party state. A new organization modelled on the Soviet Communist Party would be established to lead Cuba toward the dictatorship of the proletariat, and membership in it would be limited to "true revolutionaries." Henceforth, said Castro, Cuba would consider itself a member of the "Socialist Camp."

———

To an extent that became fully apparent only once the Cold War had ended, the nuclear stand-off that seemed like a tinderbox to ordinary citizens the world over was, in truth, a remarkably stable international system. Unlike the current "War on Terror," which is premised on the unpredictability and fanatical otherworldliness of an unseen, stateless enemy, the maintenance of Cold War stability was understood by each side to be essential to its survival. MAD (mutual assured destruction) worked. Only once did the superpowers come close to losing sight of this principle of self-preservation—during the Cuban Missile Crisis of 1962.

Six months after Fidel Castro declared himself a Marxist, his brother Raúl went to the USSR to negotiate a new military-aid package. The Soviets took full advantage of Cuba's move into the socialist bloc, laying plans for a strategic-missile capability in Cuba to counter the medium-range NATO arsenal arrayed against them in Europe. Within weeks of Raúl's visit, Soviet engineers began construction of forty-two medium-range ballistic-missile sites in Cuba. American U-2 overflights discovered and photographed one of the installations on October 14, 1962, and President Kennedy was briefed on its existence two days later. Although some historians have questioned whether the presence of the missiles actually upset the Cold War balance of power, there was never any doubt about Kennedy's position. He was uncompromising. He rejected some of his military advisers' more hawkish proposals, including an invasion of Cuba, but he also rejected any diplomatic solution that smacked of appeasement.

Khrushchev had hoped to present Kennedy with a *fait accompli* by installing the missiles clandestinely. Instead, Kennedy presented Khrushchev with a public ultimatum: dismantle and remove the missiles or the United States would take matters into its own hands. On the evening of October 22, 1962, the president went on American network television to put his case before the American people. A Soviet nuclear capability in Cuba posed a clear and present danger to the United States, he said, since it would significantly reduce American reaction time in the event of an all-out nuclear attack. What he did not say was that a nuclear-armed Cuba would almost certainly make the island impervious to an American invasion—something Castro well understood, hence his enthusiastic support for the missile installations. Having lost face at the Bay of Pigs and again in 1961 when the Berlin Wall was erected, Kennedy believed that the missile bases in Cuba represented a challenge to himself personally. Whether Khrushchev fully understood the implications of his

"Cuban adventure" in the summer of 1962 is unclear, but he certainly came to understand it on October 22 when Kennedy imposed a naval blockade on the island. For several days, the two leaders played a high-stakes game of brinksmanship, while the world waited anxiously to see if a third world war could be averted.

Khrushchev blinked. On October 29, the Soviets backed down and the United States ended the quarantine. The Soviet premier agreed to remove the weapons in exchange for a pledge from Kennedy that the United States would not invade Cuba. The president threw in a private assurance that he would dismantle and remove medium-range missiles from Turkey—Khrushchev's backyard—but this was not known publicly and in any case did not represent the kind of quid pro quo that would have allowed the Soviet leader to save face. Kennedy had taken an enormous gamble and won. Even as people all over the world climbed out of their cellars and breathed a collective sigh of relief, the "lessons" of the crisis had begun to change the tenor of the Cold War. Never again, both superpowers tacitly agreed, should a local crisis in an unimportant corner of the world threaten the possibility of all-out nuclear war. Communications must be improved and there must be more openness in the building and deployment of new weapons systems.

If the main lesson for American defence planners was that in a crisis the Soviet Union could be cowed, it should have come as no surprise that in Moscow their counterparts had drawn the same conclusion. The Soviet view of the crisis was that Kennedy had prevailed because both sides knew he had unquestioned superiority in nuclear forces. Thus, the USSR embarked on a breakneck arms-production program designed to achieve rough strategic parity with the United States. Within a decade, it would catch up. The immediate fallout in the United States was that Kennedy's resolve in standing up to the Soviets boosted his approval rating by 12 per cent. Future presidents would take note. It was not enough to simply duck the charge that one was soft on communism. What really counted, at least for the American public, was toughness.

As for Fidel Castro, he had not been consulted about the Soviet withdrawal and was predictably furious about Khrushchev's concessions to Kennedy. In a speech to the Cuban people on October 28, 1962, he observed that the president's promise not to invade Cuba would be meaningless unless the United States gave up the naval base at Guantánamo and ended its support of émigré terrorism. Cuba, said Castro, demanded the "cessation of all subversive activities, launching and disembarking of arms and explosives by air and sea, organization of mercenary invaders, infiltration of spies and saboteurs—all actions which are carried out from the territory of the United States and from some accomplice countries." He was hardly in any position to dictate terms, however; recently declassified State Department documents show that the CIA had continued its harassment of Cuba without interruption during the missile crisis. Even so, though Castro was seen as "the big loser" in the immediate aftermath of the crisis, in the long run the American pledge not to invade Cuba benefited him enormously. For the remainder of the Cold War, the U.S.-Soviet quid pro quo on Cuba held. Right up to the present day, Castro has used the spectre of an American invasion of Cuba as a galvanizing force for his Revolution, and as a primary tool in the maintenance of his own authority. As far as the superpowers were themselves concerned, however, after the missile crisis of 1962 Cuba was off limits to both sides.

———

Prime Minister John Diefenbaker came to believe that the Cuban Missile Crisis sank his government, not only because he ended up on the wrong side of President Kennedy but because his political enemies turned Canadians against him. He also believed that the charges levelled against him in the aftermath of the crisis—that he had acted indecisively and against Canadians' wishes—were unfounded. He was correct on both counts.

At 5 p.m. on October 22, just hours before Kennedy took to the U.S. airwaves, Diefenbaker and his top ministers were for the first time presented with the details of the crisis. Livingston Merchant, a former

U.S. ambassador to Canada, had come out of retirement to carry the information in person from Washington to Ottawa. He returned to the United States believing that Kennedy had the full support of the Canadian government and in particular that Diefenbaker would do nothing to undermine NATO support for the blockade. However, with the terrifying prospect of nuclear war now before Canadians, the prime minister rose in the House of Commons after the president's televised speech and suggested that the best course of action would be a UN inspection of the situation in Cuba. He would later be pilloried for this suggestion, his critics charging that it appeared to give the Soviets, and not President Kennedy, the benefit of the doubt.

The status of the U.S. military had been upgraded in the meantime to "Defcon 3" in anticipation of a possible Soviet attack. North American Air Defence (NORAD) headquarters alerted the Canadian armed forces to this heightened state of alert, expecting them to follow suit. In a cabinet meeting on October 23, however, Howard Green made an impassioned appeal to his colleagues to decline the American request to put the Canadian forces on alert. "If we go along with the Americans now," Green reportedly said, "we'll be their vassals forever." Diefenbaker agreed, much to the chagrin of his defence minister, Douglas Harkness, and refused to order the alert. President Kennedy was "dumbfounded," as his brother Robert later put it. He called Diefenbaker in person the same day to express his displeasure in no uncertain terms. The prime minister, every bit as furious, told the president that as an equal partner in NATO, Canada should have been consulted (as the British had been) rather than merely informed of a threat to the alliance. Diefenbaker later allowed Harkness to place the Canadian forces on alert informally, but declined a request from the U.S. Defense Department to move nuclear-armed fighter aircraft from American to Canadian bases. For this refusal, his critics on both sides of the 49th parallel would later call him obstructionist.

In a speech to the House of Commons on the afternoon of October 25, the third day of the crisis, Diefenbaker left no doubt about his conviction that the Soviet missile installations in Cuba were a threat to Canada and to the West. "The Soviet Union has reached out across the Atlantic to challenge the right of free men to live in peace in this hemisphere," he said. "Canadians are in general agreement that these offensive weapons, located so contiguously to our border, are a direct and immediate menace to Canada. Furthermore, they are a serious menace to the deterrent strategic strength of the whole Western alliance on which our security is founded." It was too little, too late for Diefenbaker's critics, both in Canada and in the United States. They believed he should have fallen in behind Kennedy, promptly and unquestioningly, and they interpreted his intransigence as a failure to recognize the Soviet threat coupled with opportunistic anti-Americanism.

One week after the Cuban Missile Crisis had ended, the Canadian Peace Research Institute polled Canadians on whether they supported Kennedy's blockade strategy. Roughly 80 per cent said yes. This statistic has been cited regularly since 1962 as evidence that Diefenbaker's normally infallible instincts on Canadians' sensibilities had gone awry during the crisis. Such a claim is counter-historical. Canadians may well have been emboldened to express confidence in the blockade in hindsight. But, while the crisis was in progress, with the world on the brink of nuclear war, they were every bit as unsettled as their leader. "It seems to me this is a violation of international law to stop and search ships when a nation is not at war," New Democratic Party (NDP) leader Tommy Douglas had said at the height of the crisis. "It could lead to an incident that might precipitate a nuclear war." For his part, Liberal leader Lester Pearson had commended Diefenbaker. "It is good to know," he said, "that the Canadian Government in this situation is working, as it is working, to bring about a strengthening of peace and security, to remove the awful threat of war. It is good to know that the Canadian Government is right up behind its friend and neighbour, the United States, in this issue." Editorials in Canada had echoed these sentiments. The *Toronto Star* had expressed "the gravest misgivings" about Kennedy's quarantine.

"Cuba has not invaded anyone nor has it committed aggression against anyone," which made the blockade illegal, said the paper. The *Globe and Mail* praised Diefenbaker, calling his role in the crisis "statesmanlike" and defending his insistence on consultation within the Western alliance. Between October 22 and 25, various other Canadian dailies were divided on their view of Kennedy's brinksmanship strategy, some praising him for drawing a line in the sand, others calling him reckless. The common theme in all of these editorials, however, was profound anxiety about the fact that Cold War tensions had been allowed to reach such an unprecedented pitch. Diefenbaker was hardly mentioned.

The claim that Prime Minister Diefenbaker's initial response to the Cuban Missile Crisis was symptomatic of chronic indecisiveness and paranoia (or even of declining mental health) does not hold up. The worst that can be said of the prime minister is that he fumbled for two and a half days before reaching a position that would simultaneously represent Canada's interests, the interests of the NATO alliance and, above all, the interests of world peace. That he had to steer this course under the threat of nuclear war and the inexorable pressure of the Kennedy administration made his struggle more, rather than less, difficult. Only in retrospect, after Kennedy's brinksmanship strategy had so decisively humbled the Soviets, did it become possible to paint Diefenbaker's equivocation as self-serving and disloyal. It would have been a different story had Khrushchev not backed down. In such circumstances, Diefenbaker's call for a face-saving UN-brokered solution to the crisis—an eminently "Pearsonian" position for a Canadian prime minister to take—might have been the world's only hope for averting nuclear war.

———

In February 1976, John Diefenbaker would condemn Prime Minister Pierre Trudeau in the House of Commons for cuddling up to Castro during his state visit the previous month. Cuban troops were pouring into Angola, Diefenbaker railed, and yet the prime minister was still "canoodling with Castro." Trudeau, by this time a seasoned political brawler, delighted in turning the tables on Diefenbaker. He reminded the old Tory that it was his own government and not the Liberals who had pioneered Canada's policy on revolutionary Cuba. If Diefenbaker had been so concerned about Castro's danger to world peace, Trudeau taunted him, he might have backed Kennedy during the "dark days" of the Cuban Missile Crisis. This was a mischievous claim, given that Trudeau himself had been highly critical of Kennedy during the crisis. Diefenbaker called him on it. "Mr. Speaker," he told the House, "in 1962 the Prime Minister of this day was supporting my government in what was done. But he changed strongly when he saw the light and switched from socialism to the Liberal party."

Again in May 1978, when Pierre Trudeau finally agreed to punish Castro for meddling in Africa, Diefenbaker was only too happy to invoke his own record as prime minister. In the early 1960s, he pointed out, when his government had had to confront some of the gravest challenges of the Cold War, Trudeau was enjoying an extended adolescence, dabbling in federal politics, jet-setting around the globe and enjoying the trivial pursuits of the idle rich. Mocking Trudeau's attempt to paddle across the Straits of Florida, Diefenbaker told the House that Trudeau's "love affair" with Castro had begun "by canoe." Just to twist the knife, he added that the CIA had done the right thing in refusing Trudeau entry into the United States at that time.

Diefenbaker's jousts were chock full of half-truths but his characterization of Pierre Trudeau as a dilettante in the early 1960s was not baseless. Trudeau's partisan sympathies in those days lay with the NDP, the political home of his old McGill University friends Frank Scott and Eugene Forsey, but he was a fickle fellow-traveller. By the time of the tumultuous 1963 federal election in Canada, Trudeau was again politically homeless. The New Democrats he renounced for their "two nations" concept of Canada. Lester Pearson and the Liberals he branded "idiots" for their opportunistic *volte-face* on the acquisition of nuclear weapons for Canada. As for

Trudeau's attempt in May 1960 to paddle to Havana, Diefenbaker was amiss in suggesting that it had political overtones. It had been a lark and nothing more. When Trudeau was pulled from his canoe, sunburned and seasick, he made no reference to Fidel Castro, nor did he even bother to make his way to Cuba by more conventional means. His failed channel crossing was of so little consequence that the CBC casually scrapped its film footage of the voyage. Diefenbaker was also wrong about the CIA. It was the FBI that had refused Trudeau entry into the United States, and only because he had visited the Soviet Union in 1952.

As much as Pierre Trudeau liked to spar with John Diefenbaker in the House of Commons, the truth is that he held him in the highest esteem for refusing to follow the Americans' hardline policy on Cuba while he was prime minister. During his 1976 state visit to Cuba, Trudeau told Fidel Castro that the "Canadian government is proud to have maintained relations with Cuba during the embargo," and he praised Diefenbaker explicitly for having the courage to stick to his principles.

As Trudeau well knew, October 1960 marked the decisive fork in the road for Cuban-Canadian relations—far more so than anything that has followed. Although Diefenbaker paid a high political price for getting on the wrong side of Kennedy, his instincts about where Canadians stood on Fidel Castro were impeccable. The proof came in 1964. On July 26 of that year—a date chosen specifically to annoy Castro—the American-led OAS imposed economic sanctions on Cuba because it had been training revolutionaries in Venezuela. As the only nation in the western hemisphere outside the OAS, Canada was not subject to the terms of the Rio Declaration, as the new round of sanctions became known. (Only Mexico broke ranks within the OAS and refused to sever relations with Castro.) U.S. Undersecretary of State W. Averell Harriman did his best to pressure the Canadian government to support this new campaign to isolate Castro. But, in keeping with its established position, Ottawa politely refused. Liberal External Affairs Minister Paul Martin stated confidently that most nations belonging to NATO and the Organisation for Economic Co-operation and Development (OECD) concurred with Canada that the maintenance of diplomatic relations with others ought not to be contingent on agreeing with their political principles. Canada would therefore "continue diplomatic and commercial relations with Cuba," he said.

Pierre Trudeau was delighted with this decision. In 1964, the year of the Rio Declaration, he ventured to Cuba for the second time in his life to see the Revolution first hand. He spent three weeks there, traversing the entire island and immersing himself as much as possible in the daily rhythms of ordinary Cubans. He would later express his admiration for the fact that such a poor country, now hobbled by economic sanctions, was working against the odds to improve the lives of even its poorest citizens. Whether Paul Martin's decision not to fall in behind the OAS had helped to inspire Trudeau's taste for politics is not a matter of the public record. But it might well have. For the following year he packed up his Mercedes convertible, drove up to Ottawa and joined the Pearson Liberals, the very "idiots" he had written off just two years earlier.

3

The "Canadian Castro"

Pierre Trudeau in Power

Pierre Trudeau decided to join the Liberal Party just before the 1965 federal election. From this point on, his rise to power was meteoric. He was dropped into the safe Montreal riding of Mount Royal, and elected to Parliament. By April 1967, he was minister of justice. By December, he was shepherding through the House of Commons an omnibus bill liberalizing divorce, homosexuality and abortion laws, telling Canadians, "The state has no business in the bedrooms of the nation." In April 1968, he succeeded Lester Pearson as party leader and prime minister of Canada.

Trudeau surprised Canadians by calling an election immediately. He chose June 25, 1968, as the day of the election knowing that the

Saint-Jean-Baptiste celebration in Quebec fell on the 24th. Just in case Canadians missed the symbolism, Trudeau insisted on watching Montreal's Saint-Jean-Baptiste parade from the official reviewing stand on Sherbrooke Street, even though Mayor Jean Drapeau and others feared that his presence might provoke a riot among the separatists. What followed became part of the Trudeau legend. An extraordinary bit of film footage shows Pierre Trudeau sitting on a balcony between the archbishop of Montreal and Quebec Premier Daniel Johnson. Suddenly, a group of separatist militants begins to throw rocks and bottles at the prime minister. Panic ensues. The dignitaries in the reviewing stand duck for cover and are quickly sheltered by plainclothes Mounties. But not Trudeau. With defiance etched into his normally inscrutable face, he waves off his bodyguards and maintains his seated position in full exposure to the projectiles of the agitators. The scene was as unscripted as it was electrifying, and it revealed plainly that Pierre Trudeau did not cower when threatened with violence.

The day after the Saint-Jean-Baptiste row, Canadians handed Trudeau a majority government. He wasted no time moving to implement his agenda for a new Canadian federalism. In October 1968, the Official Languages Act was introduced, guaranteeing that Canadians could enjoy the services of the federal government in French or English anywhere in the country. Meetings with the premiers set in motion the repatriation of the British North America Act. And major reviews of foreign policy and Aboriginal issues were launched.

The big story remained Trudeau himself, however, the swinging bachelor who dated Barbra Streisand, sunbathed in the nude and held talks with John Lennon and Yoko Ono.

———

Pierre Trudeau had a sign on his door while he was a student at Harvard: "Pierre Trudeau, citizen of the world." And this is precisely how he saw himself.

When it came to international relations, Trudeau was a man of high ideals. His world travels, his international education, his mastery of languages, his genuine interest in the lives and living conditions of people all over the globe—these made of Trudeau a leader more worldly than any Canadian prime minister before him or since. He wrote in his *Memoirs* that, apart from his concern about nuclear weapons, foreign policy "really didn't interest me greatly" before entering politics. Yet he assumed the office of prime minister with a strong conception of what Canada's role in the world should be. "I felt it was a duty of a middle power like Canada," he said, "which could not sway the world with the force of its armies, to at least try to sway the world with the force of its ideals. I wanted to run Canada by applying the principles of justice and equality, and I wanted our foreign policy to reflect similar values."

Trudeau did not hesitate to put his own imprimatur on Canadian foreign policy—a brash move for the successor to Lester Pearson, the man who had put Canada on the postwar map and won a Nobel Peace Prize in the process. After a two-year foreign policy review, Trudeau jettisoned the "helpful fixer" role that had once made Canada the world's favourite peacekeeper and truce supervisor. He also overhauled the entire foreign service bureaucracy so as to increase what he called rational decision making and enhance his own power. For the first time since the founding of the Department of External Affairs in the early twentieth century, it did not matter who the minister was. Ivan Head, a University of Alberta law professor, became Trudeau's senior policy adviser, primary speech writer and, as Margaret noted perceptively, "Canada's Henry Kissinger." When Trudeau went to Cuba in 1976, he was accompanied by Head, and not by his secretary of state for external affairs, Allan MacEachen, a breach of diplomatic protocol that still brings a wry smile to the face of his friend and former ambassador to Cuba, James Hyndman.

Throughout his political career, Pierre Trudeau was smeared with the charge that he was a closet Red. At every stage in this offensive, one

theme was repeated endlessly. *Pierre Trudeau was the Canadian Castro.*
The trajectory of this smear campaign was typical of all conspiracy
theories. It started on the extremist fringe and moved into mainstream
political debate as Trudeau's enemies sought ammunition against him. In
March 1968, when Trudeau was campaigning against Paul Martin for the
Liberal Party leadership, a direct-mail campaign run by an organization
calling itself the Canadian Intelligence Service claimed that Trudeau, a
"Communist," was using the Liberal Party as an "instrument" to impose
his radical views on Canada. It referenced the magazine *American Opinion*,
a publication of the right-wing John Birch Society. This direct-mail "bul-
letin" was sent to every Liberal convention delegate, apparently using a
mailing list poached from the Martin campaign (the evidence for which
was that misspellings and typos were reproduced exactly as they appeared
in the original). It later came to light that the Canadian Intelligence
Service was run by Ron Gostick of Flesherton, Ontario, who claimed,
among other things, that fluoridation, racial integration and the United
Nations were subversive, and that International Brotherhood Week was
"the brainchild of organized Jewry."

Even so, the innuendo against Trudeau persisted. The Montreal-based
Pilgrims of St. Michael claimed that the "pro-Soviet, pro-Castro and pro-
Mao" Trudeau was "plotting the moral collapse of the nation." A twenty-
five-page pamphlet distributed by the Toronto-based Edmund Burke
Society warned that Trudeau was "a potential Canadian Castro."During
the June 1968 election campaign, the press badgered Trudeau on some
of Gostick's more outrageous statements, including the accusation that
his attempt to paddle to Havana in 1960 had political motivations. "I've
canoed from Hudson Bay to Montreal, I've canoed down the Coppermine
River and down the Mackenzie, I've barged up the Nile," the prime minister explained patiently, "and so I tried to canoe across to Cuba." He
urged the press to be more discerning. "I suggest it is our duty to dissociate ourselves from this type of garbage," he said. It was no use. The
smear campaign was so successful leading up to election day that the *New*

York Times covered it. An exasperated Peter C. Newman, one of Canada's foremost political journalists, devoted an entire column to dispelling its claims. "Never before in a Canadian election," wrote Newman, "has a prime minister been the subject of so much hatred and innuendo as has been flung at Pierre Elliott Trudeau in the current campaign."

American extremists added their own voices. "We've got a crypto-Communist premier in Canada just above us," said Alabama governor George Wallace in 1971 while he was testing the waters for a second run at the U.S. presidency. "He's got a worse background than Cuban Premier Castro himself." That same year, the John Birch Society direct-mailed to doctors and dentists in the Toronto area a glossy publication for their waiting rooms. "Since June of 1968," it read, "Canada has had as a Prime Minister a Communist named Pierre Elliott Trudeau, with a known record more blatant than that of Castro." The following year the Birchers, as they were known, published a booklet entitled *Canada: How the Communists Took Control,* in which "Red Mike" Pearson and the communist Pierre Trudeau were the main villains. By the mid-1970s, this right-wing campaign against Trudeau had begun its migration toward the political mainstream, where it would inform the "neo-conservative" critique that was building against him. A 1976 editorial in the U.S. business magazine *Barron's,* for example, accused the prime minister of "virulent collectivism" and was reprinted in its entirety in the *Globe and Mail* without comment. What many mainstream conservatives later co-opted from the extremists was the idea that Trudeau had sought by design (and thus by stealth) to impose his socialist ideals on an unsuspecting Canada via the once-great party of C. D. Howe. This is what put the bite in comparisons of Trudeau and Castro, since the Cuban leader *had* concealed his radical intentions while claiming to be a democrat.

Pierre Trudeau loathed totalitarianism and the repression it meant for its subject peoples. And when it came to the communist world, Trudeau understood that a Canadian prime minister must always walk the razor's edge. In this, his views were virtually identical to those of Diefenbaker and

Pearson. No matter who was in power, Canadian foreign policy was constrained by what Trudeau called "orthodox alliance priorities," meaning
that the government of the day could never compromise Canada's NATO
commitments. It must also respect "the strong feelings of Canadians of
Eastern European origin," Trudeau wrote, "who had watched with justifiable horror the occupation of their homelands and the reduction of
their remaining relatives and neighbours to conditions of near slavery."

Yet Trudeau believed as well that in a world that was ideologically
polarized, armed to the teeth and flirting with nuclear disaster, dialogue
was preferable to confrontation. Finding a common language of peace
and security thus meant engaging one's adversaries at a level that recognized their humanity. Anything less, Trudeau believed, was both dishon-
est and dangerous. Questioned in 1952 about why he had attended an
economics conference in Moscow, he replied, "I felt that people must use
every possible means to get to know each other. For, on either side, it is
precisely the fear of the stranger which is at the root of this pathological
hatred that is bringing us relentlessly closer to the third and final world
war." Getting to know each other meant discovering those areas in which
even the most determined of enemies could find common ground—trade,
for example, or cultural exchange, or arms reduction. When, as prime
minister, Trudeau conversed with communist leaders, he was taking their
measure. Thus, he preferred Soviet Premier Alexei Kosygin to General
Secretary Leonid Brezhnev because, of the two, he was less doctrinaire
and more open to reform. Kosygin was, as Trudeau put it in his *Memoirs*,
"a fatherly man who was a forerunner of Mikhail Gorbachev." One could
talk to Kosygin.

When Mikhail Gorbachev appeared on the international scene in the
1980s promoting glasnost and perestroika —openness and reform—North
Americans caught their first glimpse of what Trudeau had been seeking
all along: the humanity of the enemy. Until Gorbachev, North Americans
had thought of the Soviets in the most simplistic of terms, as Reds, as
hard-nosed ideologues and ruthless geopolitical adversaries. They may

well have been all of these things, but they were also people for whom the cultivation of peace and prosperity was preferable to nuclear war. Pierre Trudeau spent the Cold War trying to promote dialogue on the basis of these common aspirations. This did not preclude his treating people with whom he disagreed with respect and even warmth. Apart from his friendship with Fidel Castro, the most notable case in point was his close personal relationship with Alexander Yakovlev, the Soviet ambassador to Canada between 1973 and 1983 (and Sacha Trudeau's namesake). Yakovlev had earned a doctorate at New York's Columbia University, and although he held to the Soviet line ideologically, he was an original thinker whose opinions on international affairs Trudeau came to value highly.

Pierre Trudeau's resolve to improve relations between the West and the communist world raised eyebrows—and sometimes voices—in Washington, but at home it accorded perfectly with many Canadians' changing views of themselves and their world. Well before he became prime minister, Canadians knew that Pierre Trudeau stood for China's admission to the UN, for détente with the USSR, for a review (and later a reduction) of Canada's NATO commitments in Europe, for increased aid to the developing world and especially for a de-escalation of the nuclear-arms race. He had been saying these things throughout the 1960s, and in 1968 he campaigned on them. Canadians voted for Trudeau's foreign-policy agenda four times out of five between 1968 and 1984, and to a remarkable degree the prime minister delivered on it. Pierre Trudeau became an international star in an age of mediocrities, as Richard Gwyn once put it. Many Canadians were immensely proud of his contributions to world peace and, more generally, of his place on the world stage.

It may seem a facile comparison, but consider this. Most Canadians have never heard of Alexander Yakovlev, but they certainly remember Vladislav Tretiak. In the fall of 1972, Canada's best professional hockey players squared off against the Soviets in an eight-game summit series that has since become the stuff of sport legend. Tretiak was the twenty-year-old goalie for the Soviets, one of many Russian players to astound Canadian hockey fans with his athletic prowess. Paul Henderson was the hero of the '72 series, of course, but Tretiak was the star. He became the only Soviet player from the pre-glasnost period to be inducted into the Hockey Hall of Fame, and he went on to a coaching career in the NHL. After the eighth game of the series, Pierre Trudeau sent a friendly telegram to Soviet Premier Kosygin. When asked about it by a CBC reporter, the prime minister offered a reply that illustrated why the game had been, for him, such an important international milestone. The best part of the game was not the Canadian victory, said the prime minister, but the "possibility of the two countries getting to know each other better in this way. I know personally I've been exchanging some banter with Premier Kosygin about the outcome of the game—teasing each other a little bit—and he was proud to send me a telegram saying that even when the Russians were behind, they were still yelling 'Friendship!' I think we'd still be yelling 'Friendship!' if we'd lost the game."

It was vintage Trudeau, and it encapsulated the politics of dialogue for which he had so long been a voice in the wilderness.

———

Prior to the Cuban Revolution, the number of Cubans living in the United States did not exceed 20,000. There were only 10,000 Cubans in Miami in 1958, and roughly three-quarters of these had emigrated since 1952 in protest against Batista. After Castro took power in 1959, this trickle of immigrants turned into a flood. In the first year of the Revolution, 35,000 people left Cuba. The regime called such émigrés worthless *gusanos* (worms) but, in truth, almost all were highly educated professionals whose exodus deprived Cuba of invaluable research, managerial and entrepreneurial talent when it was most needed. By 1970, there were over 560,000 Cubans living in the United States, roughly half of them in Florida. By 1977, there were 665,000 Cubans living in Miami alone. Dade County thus emerged as the cultural and political centre of the exile community, the preferred destination for subsequent waves of Cuban émigrés and the epicentre of hardline anti-Castro politics in the United States.

This first wave of anti-Castro exiles in the United States was, in fact, composed of two distinct groups whose relationship was somewhat uneasy. One had left Cuba before Castro took power and never viewed him with anything but contempt. The other had cheered the rebel victory and supported the principles of the Revolution early on but left the island when Castro betrayed his promise of democracy and began employing repressive measures to consolidate his own power. Because both groups fully expected that the United States would invade Cuba and defeat the Revolution, they saw their sojourn in Florida as temporary. They began organizing against the Castro regime almost immediately.

The role of anti-Castro émigrés in shaping Washington's response to Castro, then and now, cannot be overstated. In the early years of the Revolution, the Cuban exiles mobilized American public opinion against the regime, providing money, materials and moral support for counterrevolutionary activities of every description. In 1961, they formed a provisional government headed by José Miró Cardona, Castro's deposed premier. They provided a critical mass of willing combatants in America's covert war against Castro, most notably during the Bay of Pigs. Some of them intimidated Miami Cubans who expressed opposition to their anti-Castro politics or sought dialogue with the Castro regime, enhancing the general perception that the émigré population was a one-issue voting bloc. And the extremists among them conducted a long-running campaign of terror against the Revolution that alarmed even some of their contacts in the U.S. intelligence establishment.

To observers outside Miami, the cloak-and-dagger world of the anti-Castro exiles has been a source of endless fascination. Hollywood deserves much of the credit for this. Oliver Stone, who directed *JFK* and wrote the screenplay for *Scarface*, has done more than his fair share to cast Cuban émigrés in the light of "black-ops" conspiracy theories and underworld intrigue. Serious studies of Cuban-Americans show them to be one of the most successful immigrant groups in American history, one of the most assimilated and also one of the most culturally and socially dynamic. Even so, anti-Castro extremists have been the ones making headlines the world over since 1959, contributing to the perception that Cuban-Americans are united by their burning hatred of Fidel Castro. Miami's reputation as "Little Havana" has produced a mystique almost as exotic as the city on which it was modelled, for the obvious reason that there is no Cuban émigré community like it anywhere else in the world.

Canadians have always been fascinated by the Miami exiles. In the mid-1960s, for example, a period notable for Castro's relatively low profile in the Western media, Canadian press coverage of the exiles exceeded coverage of Cuba itself. The odd time Cuban exiles have been discovered hatching anti-Castro plots on Canadian soil, media coverage has been extensive. It was front-page news in Canada in October 1960, for instance, when a group of fifty exiles from all over the western hemisphere met at the Montreal home of Major-General José Eleuterio Pedraza Cabrera, the one-time commander-in-chief of Batista's army and now the head of a group calling itself the Anti-Communist Liberation Movement. The story remained on the front pages when Cabrera was later apprehended by U.S. border officials for trying to sneak into the United States, and when three of his co-conspirators were deported from Canada.

But the fact remains that Cuban émigrés have never had the sort of direct impact on Canadian politics that they have in the United States. The main reason for their negligible influence is that their numbers have always been negligible. The Canadian census of 1961 showed that there were only 150 people of Cuban origin residing in the country; by 1980, the number had risen to only 295. Every once in a while a high-profile Cuban has made a splash by defecting to Canada, such as in 1960, when the "dashing" Cuban ambassador to Canada, Luis A. Baralt Mederos, publicly resigned his position and sought political asylum in Canada, claiming, "I can no longer defend major items of Cuban policy." But such incidents, though dramatic, have seldom spawned Miami-styled anti-Castro activism. The exiles' main influence in Canada has come instead in the form of external pressure. As one of only two nations in the western hemisphere never to break with Castro (Mexico being the other), Canada has been denounced continuously by exile lobbyists and demonstrators in the United States, and only slightly less frequently by their allies in the U.S. Congress. In the Trudeau years, when exile violence peaked, Canadians were targeted by anti-Castro terrorists and their businesses were occasionally bombed.

If Canadians' encounters with Cuban-Americans have been troubled, it is only because it is the troublemakers who venture north to Canada. Canadians rightly denounce terrorist acts by Cuban-American exiles, and they take justifiable exception to the United States any time it attempts to trample Canadian sovereignty in the name of militant anti-Castro politics. Certainly, moderate elements within the Cuban-American community deserve Canadians' utmost respect. After all, the promotion of dialogue with the Castro regime has become a distinguishing feature of Canada's foreign policy, and one that makes many Canadians proud. But the truth is that this stance has seldom demanded much of either Ottawa or ordinary Canadians. In Cuban Miami, by contrast, *El Diálogo* has always demanded the utmost in courage and sacrifice, and it has exacted an enormous cost in lives and property. (In 1974–77 alone, a period that included Pierre Trudeau's visit to Havana, over one hundred Cuban-Americans were attacked for being soft on Castro, many fatally.) Even the hard-liners in the Cuban-American community, the great majority of whom eschew terror, are driven by a passion for the very values that Canadian liberals hold dear—democracy, free elections, the rule of law and respect for basic human rights.

———

In 1968, Richard Nixon was elected president of the United States, in large measure because the beleaguered Lyndon Johnson had been forced by the war in Vietnam not to seek a second term. Henry Kissinger, a Harvard-trained German émigré, became Nixon's national security adviser and, after 1973, his secretary of state. As one of the only members of the Nixon administration to survive the Watergate scandal, Kissinger stayed on as secretary of state in the Ford administration. Unelected, secretive and without compunction when it came to the use of force to achieve American security objectives, Kissinger became the primary architect of U.S. foreign policy in one of the most tumultuous periods in American history.

Although achieving "peace with honor" in Vietnam was the single most pressing issue for Nixon and Kissinger, the overriding goal of their foreign policy was détente. Kennedy had humbled Khrushchev during the Cuban Missile Crisis because he had enjoyed vast strategic superiority. Less than a decade later, the Soviets' breakneck arms program had achieved rough nuclear parity with the United States, fundamentally changing the Cold War equation. Both Nixon and Kissinger viewed communism with contempt and believed the USSR to be an international menace. But they also acknowledged that the Soviet Union was now a bona fide superpower, and that any U.S. policy that failed to treat it as such would be folly. Thus, they adopted détente as a strategy to "tame the bear," as one White House insider put it. This meant drawing the Soviets into a matrix of linkages with the West—trade, technology, cultural exchanges, arms control—that would give them good reason to maintain the geopolitical status quo.

The defining moment for détente came in May 1971, when Nixon announced to the American people that he had concluded a Strategic Arms Limitation Treaty with the Soviets. One year later, President Nixon met General Secretary Leonid Brezhnev in Moscow. Their historic summit meeting laid out twelve principles by which superpower relations would be conducted, starting with an ideological truce that would have been unimaginable just years earlier. "Differences in ideology and in the social systems of the USA and the USSR," the two leaders told a Cold War–weary world, "are not obstacles to the bilateral development of normal relations based on the principles of sovereignty, equality, non-interference in internal affairs and mutual advantage." So unexpected and dramatic was this Soviet-American rapprochement that people began speaking of the end of the Cold War.

A steady stream of what Henry Kissinger called "incentives for restraint" were also negotiated with the Soviets in the early 1970s. In February 1972, the U.S. Department of Commerce approved licences for the export of $367-million worth of truck-manufacturing equip-ment to the USSR. The following July, a grain deal worth $750 mil-lion to the United States was inked—the largest commercial agreement in U.S.-Russian history. In October 1972, a maritime shipping agree-ment was signed, terms for the repayment of the Soviets' Second World War debts were finalized, and the United States extended to the USSR most-favoured-nation (MFN) status. Between 1972 and 1975, the value of Soviet-American trade tripled to $1.83 billion. Pepsi signed a deal to manufacture soft drinks behind the Iron Curtain in exchange for the USSR being allowed to sell its vodka in the United States. The Chase Manhattan Bank set up a branch office in Moscow.

In July 1971, President Nixon astonished the world again by revealing that Henry Kissinger had just returned home from China. Kissinger had met with top officials in Beijing and laid the groundwork for a state visit by the president the following year. The immediate goal of Kissinger's trip was to secure Chinese support for an end to the Vietnam War on terms favourable to the United States—something Nixon had also been working toward in his conversations with the Soviets. As Kissinger well knew, offering the carrot of improved relations with the United States to the two communist giants was also a means of playing them off against each other. (By definition, Kissinger believed, any Sino-Soviet split was good for the United States. He was thrilled when they began amassing troops at their common border in the late 1960s.)

Nixon's and Kissinger's efforts to engage both the Soviets and

the Chinese in dialogue in the early 1970s had one further implica-
tion. The administration was signalling that the United States could no
longer afford—in any sense of the term—to pursue a policy of global
anti-communism, if this meant confronting insurgency in every corner
of the world. This was one of many lessons they learned in Vietnam.
Henceforth, the United States would pick its fights. It would disengage
from the zero-sum game of containment unless its national interests
were directly threatened. This new, downsized Cold War strategy was
dubbed the Nixon Doctrine.

———

By the mid-1970s, the people of Moscow could drink Pepsi, eat pork from
pigs fed on American corn and do their banking at the Chase Manhattan.
The people of Cuba could do none of these things. Why this double
standard persisted in American foreign policy boiled down to one incon-
trovertible fact. Richard Nixon hated Fidel Castro.

"There will be no change toward that bastard while I'm president,"
Nixon said of Castro as he entered a National Security Council meeting
in the fall of 1969. As noted earlier, Nixon had met the Cuban leader
during his North American tour of 1959 and concluded that he was a
communist. That fact alone was enough to put Castro on the wrong side
of Nixon. But during the Kennedy and Johnson years, when Nixon was in
the political wilderness, his loathing of Castro had also grown increasingly
personal. The Cuban Revolution had handed John F. Kennedy a critique
of Republican foreign policy powerful enough to give him the White
House in 1960, which irked Nixon. (In his 1997 book on the Kennedys,
The Dark Side of Camelot, Seymour Hersh revealed that Kennedy had
used classified intelligence on Cuba against Nixon during the campaign.)
Then in 1962, Kennedy's popularity after the Cuban Missile Crisis delivered the California governorship to Democratic incumbent Pat Brown,
robbing Nixon once again. ("You won't have Dick Nixon to kick around
any more," he told the press bitterly after losing the 1962 gubernatorial

election.) Equally important was the fact that Nixon also had—as he put it himself—"too many good friends" in the Miami exile community to treat Castro as anything other than a pariah.

During the 1968 presidential race, Nixon campaigned on a hard line against Castro. Something was definitely wrong, he said in his first speech of the New Hampshire primary campaign, when Cuba was the strongest military power in the western hemisphere after the United States— "stronger than Brazil, stronger than Canada." For the remainder of the campaign, Nixon left to the imagination what measures he might take against Cuba beyond pressuring America's allies to support the embargo. But, as soon as he took office, he ordered the CIA to step up its covert harassment of the island. "The first thing the administration wanted us to do was double our operations against Cuba," CIA analyst Roy Burleigh later recalled. "We couldn't believe it. We thought the American people had matured more than that."

Fidel Castro could believe it, of course, and so could the Cuban people. An air of anxiety descended on the island when Nixon entered the White House. It was inevitable that the new president would continue to make life miserable for them, Cubans believed. The only question was whether he would renege on Kennedy's pledge not to mount a U.S. invasion. Castro rallied his people once again to the defence of the Revolution. In a January 1969 speech that coincided both with Nixon's inauguration and with the tenth anniversary of the rebel victory, he told six hundred thousand cheering Cubans that Nixon was "fifteen years behind the times." Castro ridiculed the new president for supporting the Bay of Pigs invasion eight years earlier, and exclaimed that he would now have the "bitter experience of seeing the blockade destroyed!"

The main effect of Nixon's policy of harassing Cuba was not to destabilize the Cuban regime but to impress upon both Fidel Castro and his enemies in Miami that Washington had no interest in rapprochement with Havana. Détente was the watchword for U.S. relations with the USSR and China, Nixon was signalling, but not with Cuba. Cuba remained in a class by itself. It fell to Soviet Premier Kosygin to explain this not-so-subtle distinction to an understandably distrustful Fidel Castro. In October 1971—the period between the SALT announcement and the Nixon-Brezhnev summit—Kosygin flew to Havana to reassure the Cuban leader. Although Moscow's foreign policy was now oriented toward "dialogue and détente" with the United States, he said, its relations with Havana and its commitment to protecting Cuba's national interests were stronger than ever. Castro was reported to have taken some comfort in Kosygin's words. In March 1972, he began indicating through unofficial channels that he was no longer "inflexibly opposed to resuming a more friendly relationship with the United States." A month later, rumours began to swirl in the press that Henry Kissinger was about to surprise the world with news that he and Nixon had secretly normalized relations with Cuba.

———

Cuba was not Premier Kosygin's first stop in October 1971. Before heading to Havana, he spent eight days in Canada enjoying what could only be called—in the parlance of the day—a love-in. His Canadian travels included several days in Toronto, a four-hour boat tour around the shores of Vancouver harbour, and a packed itinerary of speeches and receptions. Interviewed extensively by the press, he expressed his liking for Canadians in the warmest of terms. When he left Toronto for Cuba, he was accompanied by the prime minister and his wife, who had struck up a friendship with his daughter, Ludmila Gvishiani. As they were exchanging their farewells, Kosygin joked with Pierre that he might steal Margaret away for the Cuban leg of his jaunt.

Pierre Trudeau's amicable rapport with Soviet Premier Kosygin stood in marked contrast to his cool relationship with President Nixon. Trudeau recalled Nixon as a "complex man" in his *Memoirs*, charming in public but "stiff and perspiring" in private, a man "obviously not at ease in his skin." It was probably inevitable that two such different men with such different views of the world would not hit it off. Henry Kissinger acknowledged as much when he and Nixon met Trudeau for the first time in 1969. "It cannot be said that Nixon and Trudeau were ideally suited for each other," Kissinger reflected. "A scion of an old Quebec family, elegant, brilliant, enigmatic, intellectual, Trudeau was bound to evoke all of Nixon's resentments against 'swells' who in his view had always looked down on him. He disdained Trudeau's clear enjoyment of life; he tended to consider him soft on defense and in his general attitude toward the East."

Many issues put the president and the prime minister at odds but none more so than the Vietnam War, which cast its grim shadow over the whole of Nixon's presidency. "Clearly," Trudeau later recalled of Vietnam, "there was no way the United States should have been there in the first place." In the 1970s, the prime minister was criticized in Canada for not doing enough to oppose the U.S. action in Vietnam. Yet in retrospect it is striking just how anti-war he allowed his government to be. The Trudeau Liberals openly criticized the U.S. invasion of Cambodia in 1970 and the massive "Christmas" bombing of Hanoi in 1972. They freely admitted American draft dodgers to Canada. And in 1973 they pulled Canada out of the International Control Commission (the body established in 1954 to monitor ceasefires in Indochina)—a policy that so infuriated President Nixon that he called Trudeau an "asshole" on one of his famous White House tapes. (To this epithet Trudeau later responded, "I had been called worse things by better people.") The prime minister believed that Canada's more enlightened foreign policy was blazing the trail toward international peace and security, and that the United States was on the trailing edge. "I laid the foundations for what would later be called 'détente' in East-West relations," Trudeau recalled immodestly of his 1971 meeting with Leonid Brezhnev. There was truth in this boast, but there was certainly never any evidence that Richard Nixon saw things this way.

Predictably, Cuba was another divisive issue on the Canadian-American agenda. Nixon took a dim view of Canada's continuing diplomatic and trade relations with Cuba. He had campaigned in 1968 on the promise to bring new diplomatic pressure to bear on "our Canadian friends" who continued to trade with Castro. When his secretary of state, William P. Rogers, suggested in late 1969 that the Kennedy-era Alliance for Progress be renamed the "Hemispheric Alliance for Progress," Nixon retorted, "Oh yeah, then we could let that fucking Trudeau grow a beard and go play with Castro." Yet, as Henry Kissinger understood but the president did not, it was a virtual certainty that as prime minister Pierre Trudeau would take a strong interest in Cuba. Easing East-West tensions and bridging North-South disparities were the overriding themes of his foreign policy, and Cuba was one place in the world where the two intersected. Thus, while Trudeau, most Canadians and virtually all of America's NATO allies could see no reason to exclude Cuba from détente in the early 1970s, Nixon remained a captive of his own anti-Castro convictions and those of his Cuban-American friends. "Cuba is still in the icebox as far as Washington is concerned," pronounced the *Toronto Star* in November 1971. "This is rather silly. The Nixon government no longer fears to deal with the giants of communism, Russia and China; why should it fear closer contacts with a country as small as Cuba?"

An increasing number of Americans, it turned out, saw things the same way. During Trudeau's first official visit to Washington in 1969, he got an unexpected round of applause at a National Press Club luncheon when he suggested that the time had come for the United States to recognize the government of Fidel Castro. "It is important to recognize that the force of nationalism, the feeling of independence, are pretty hard to stifle," Trudeau said. The Canadian view was that international grievances should be dealt with through communication and dialogue, he continued. "We think in the case of Cuba this is the same." Asked about Canadian trade with the island, Trudeau suggested that commercial linkages with Cuba were important not so much for their economic benefits but for their broader value in promoting dialogue. "Short of being at the state of war with another nation," he said, "we do not believe that curtailment of trade is in any sense conducive to a lessening of tensions between countries. On the contrary. We trade with Communist China. We trade with Cuba." Back in Canada, Trudeau's comments played extremely well. The prime minister, it was widely agreed, had capped a fruitful meeting with Nixon with a real "stinger" on the Cuba question.

———

The Cuban Revolution coincided with Quebec's Quiet Revolution, the sweeping modernization of the province that began with the election of Jean Lesage's provincial Liberals in 1960. René Lévesque, the CBC reporter who would join Lesage's cabinet and later lead the Parti Québécois, admired Fidel Castro. So did the young Quebeckers who founded the FLQ in 1963—"a couple of dozen young terrorists," Lévesque called them, "whose ideology was a hopeless hodgepodge of anarcho-nationalism and kindergarten Marxism." For eight years, the FLQ's campaign of mayhem and murder would draw its main inspiration from the revolutionary principles of Che Guevara. And yet, ironically, it was Fidel Castro to whom Pierre Trudeau would end up owing a debt of gratitude for helping to defuse the October Crisis. Never before had the fates of Canada and Cuba been so closely intertwined.

The goal of the FLQ was the creation of an independent socialist state in Quebec. Like many similar movements elsewhere in the world, it was inspired by Che Guevara's *La Guerra de Guerrillas*, the book that John F. Kennedy had used as a backgrounder for U.S. Cuba policy. The terror campaign that would end in 1970 with the murder of Pierre Laporte began in the spring of 1963. Self-styled "FLQ suicide commandos" detonated bombs in the mailboxes of three Montreal armouries and seventeen homes in the English-speaking suburb of Westmount, sending shock waves through Canada and Quebec alike. The following year, during an FLQ holdup at a Montreal gun shop, two employees were killed (one of them by the police, who mistook him for a terrorist). Later targets of FLQ bombs included federal government buildings in Montreal, the mayor's residence, McGill University, the Montreal Stock Exchange and, one week before the 1965 election that gave Pierre Trudeau his first seat in Parliament, a Liberal rally in Montreal. In 1967, a seventeen-year-old boy enrolled at Pierre Trudeau's alma mater, Collège Jean-de-Brébeuf, blew himself up while planting a bomb at a Montreal textile mill.

At one point in 1965, a group of Quebec "revolutionaries" including Pierre Vallières, author of the inflammatory book *White Niggers of America*, made contact with the Cuban consul in Montreal, Julia González. She, too, was a Guevarist and openly sympathized with radical separatists in Quebec. Acting on the advice of the RCMP, the Pearson government quietly requested of Fidel Castro that the consul be recalled. He obliged, reasoning that backing Québécois activists was hardly worth provoking the ire of the Canadian government, whose good graces he needed more than ever. In the wake of the news that Che Guevara had been killed in Bolivia in 1967, however, came reports in the Canadian press that Castro himself was sanctioning Cuban aid for "Québec separatists and unhappy Indians in Canada." Canadian MP Robert Thomson accused Radio Havana of broadcasting instruction on guerrilla warfare to the Cree in Quebec. Self-styled revolutionary and convicted armed robber Gaston Plante told a Quebec judge that he had undergone intensive guerrilla training in Cuba. The RCMP in Quebec accused the Cubans of training many more FLQ members, and rumours swirled around Cuba's Expo pavilion that militant separatists had the ear of the Cuban regime. Fidel Castro again acted decisively. When José Fernández de Cossío began his tenure as Cuba's ambassador to Canada in 1968, he conveyed to Prime Minister Trudeau Castro's personal assurance that reports of Cuban support for separatism in Quebec were baseless and that Cuba had no intention of "undermining the national integrity of Canada."

In 1969, the FLQ divided into two cells, one calling itself the Liberation Cell, headed by Jacques Lanctôt, and the other Paul Rose's Chenier Cell. The following year, on October 5, 1970, members of both cells kidnapped British Trade Commissioner James Cross. He ended up in the custody of the Liberation Cell, which demanded as his ransom

$500,000 in gold bullion, the release of twenty-three "political prisoners," the publication and broadcast of the FLQ "Political Manifesto" and a plane to carry the kidnappers and their freed comrades to Cuba or Algeria. The Canadian press reported that the FLQ "Manifesto" praised Fidel Castro, but in fact the document made no mention of the Cuban leader, or of Che Guevara. It did, however, seek to inspire the Quebec working class to mobilize in the class struggle. "Make your revolution yourselves in your neighbourhoods," the manifesto exhorted, in language borrowed directly from the Cuban revolutionaries.

On October 10, 1970, just when it appeared that negotiations with the Liberation Cell would secure Cross's release, the Chenier Cell kidnapped Pierre Laporte, Quebec's minister of labour and immigration. Five days later, Premier Robert Bourassa requested of Prime Minister Trudeau that the Canadian Armed Forces be mobilized to assist the local police. Trudeau agreed and on October 16 proclaimed a state of "apprehended insurrection" under the terms of the War Measures Act. The FLQ became an unlawful organization, civil liberties were suspended, and arrests and detentions without formal charge were authorized. "If a democratic society is to continue to exist," Trudeau told Canadians in a sombre and carefully worded speech, "it must be able to root out the cancer of an armed, revolutionary movement that is bent on destroying the very basis of our freedom." The prime minister stressed that the governments of both Montreal and Quebec had asked him to act but, of course, he well knew the political and personal implications of his decision to impose martial law. "These are strong powers and I find them as distasteful as I am sure do you," he told Canadians. "They are necessary, however, to permit the police to deal with persons who advocate or promote the violent overthrow of our democratic system. In short, I assure you that the Government recognizes its grave responsibilities in interfering in certain cases with civil liberties, and that it remains answerable to the people of Canada for its actions. The Government will revoke this proclamation as soon as possible."

As happened so often in Pierre Trudeau's political career, his carefully scripted pronouncements were all but eclipsed by his spontaneous jabs at his critics. Confronted by a CBC reporter who asked him how far he would go in the imposition of emergency measures, he responded, "Just watch me." It was a brash threat coming from a man who had made the study of citizens' rights his life's work. What tipped the balance in favour of a hardline policy, Trudeau later recalled in his *Memoirs*, was his perception that within Quebec even moderate nationalists—including future premiers René Lévesque and Jacques Parizeau—were prepared to negotiate with the terrorists. For Trudeau, the short-term battle against terrorism had thus dovetailed with the long-term war against separatism. In this war, he would give no quarter. In the end, roughly four hundred and fifty Quebeckers were detained without hearings in the emergency dragnet, only one-third of whom were suspected of links to the FLQ. Civil libertarians across Canada were outraged. Even some of the prime minister's most loyal allies were, as one of them put it, "jarred by the rigidity of Trudeau's reasoning on the indivisibility of basic national rights and federal powers." As for ordinary Canadians, opinion polls showed that the great majority supported his forceful stand against the terrorists.

On October 17, Pierre Laporte's body was found in the trunk of a car, turning the unpredictable threats of the kindergarten Marxists into a case of cold-blooded assassination. Seeking to prevent Cross's murder, the federal government engaged the Liberation Cell in a secret negotiation. Allowing the kidnappers safe transit out of Canada was a concession even Pierre Trudeau was prepared to make, though not publicly and certainly not on a basis that would include Laporte's murderers. The government thus sought the assistance of a foreign country willing to accept the increasingly desperate terrorists. Algeria and Cuba were approached. Fidel Castro put himself at Canada's disposal and agreed to provide sanctuary for the members of the Liberation Cell and their families. In December 1970, eight weeks after he had been abducted, Cross accompanied five of his kidnappers first to Cuba's Expo pavilion and then to Dorval. (A sixth remained in Montreal and was brought to justice in 1980.) From there, the terrorists and their families were flown to Havana. Cross was released. The October Crisis ended a month later when the members of the Chenier Cell were found and arrested.

Just days after the FLQ exiles arrived in Havana, Prime Minister Trudeau sent Fidel Castro a short thank-you letter. "Dear Mr. Prime Minister," he wrote. "On behalf of the Government of Canada I wish to express to you our sincere thanks for the co-operation extended by your Government in the arrangements leading to the safe release of Mr. James Cross. The co-operation of your officials in Havana and in Canada proved to be a vital element in the early stages of working out the details of the safe conduct offer, as well as in the subsequent lengthy period waiting and on the day when these plans finally bore fruit." Trudeau made a special point of thanking Cuban Ambassador de Cossío and his staff, whose role in transporting the kidnappers and their families had been indispensable. "I also understand," added Trudeau suggestively, "that in keeping with the good relations between our two countries, the individuals who have been given safe-conduct will not while in Cuba undertake any activity directed against Canada."

Toward the end of 1971, the CBC sent journalist Tom Leach to Havana to see how the exiled terrorists were making out. He found four of the original five—Jacques Cossette-Trudel, Marc Carbonneau, Jacques Lanctôt and Pierre Seguin—living in the once-ritzy Deauville Hotel, a fourteen-storey building overlooking Malecón Drive. (Lanctôt's wife Marie made page two of the *New York Times* in December 1970, when it was discovered that she had no sooner arrived at the at the hotel than she had given birth.) The exiles' amenities included a private beach, swimming pool and free meals and liquor—all courtesy of the Cuban government. Even so, the men were lonely, bored, ideologically divided and so resentful of each other after only one year in Cuba that they no longer spoke. They were also annoyed that, out of a sense of obligation to Canada, the Cubans refused to train them in guerrilla warfare. "For visiting Canadians,"

Leach observed, "they're putting on a brave front. But as one of them was heard to admit privately, the sense of isolation is beginning to eat into their souls." Five years later, the disgruntled Canadian exiles left Havana for France. All would later return to Canada and serve jail terms.

Ambassador de Cossío, always an indefatigable booster of Cuban-Canadian relations, later observed that the two countries' collaboration during the FLQ crisis was a pivotal moment for the bilateral relationship. Had it not been for Pierre Trudeau's sizeable debt to Fidel Castro, it is likely that the state visit of 1976 would never have taken place. Ironically, the fact that the Cubans were willing to provide a refuge for exiled Canadian terrorists was taken by the RCMP as evidence of Castro's support for the FLQ. For their part, the Soviets were so annoyed by Trudeau's cancellation of his state visit to Moscow during the October Crisis that they scolded Castro for meddling in it.

———

By the early 1970s, there were two areas in which Canadian differences with the United States over Cuba had grown serious—one of them deadly serious.

The first concerned trade. As part of its ongoing efforts to cripple the Cuban economy, the United States had embarked on a campaign in the early 1960s to constrain its allies' trade with Cuba. This meant broadening support for the U.S. embargo and stigmatizing those nations that continued to trade with the island. It also meant invoking the Trading with the Enemy Act. The act, which dated from the First World War, allowed U.S. authorities to prosecute American directors of multinational corporations if they traded with blacklisted countries. Starting in 1963, the United States put Canada on notice. The Trading with the Enemy Act, it warned, would apply to Canadian branch plants of U.S. corporations doing business with Fidel Castro. Penalties would be steep, ranging up to $10,000 and/or ten-year prison terms. For more than a decade thereafter, this extraterritorial application of U.S. law raised hackles among

Canadian business people, intellectuals and politicians, up to and including Pierre Trudeau. The issue became part of a much broader national debate about U.S. control of the Canadian economy, thus assuming a symbolic importance that far exceeded any actual trade-related repercussions it might have had. At least one thoughtful American had predicted that this would happen. "The stiletto with which we endeavor to prick our enemies can, if we are not careful, wound us grievously," wrote the U.S. ambassador to Canada to his superiors in 1965.

The second Cuba-related issue to cloud Canada's relationship with the United States was terrorism. Washington's enthusiasm for covert operations against Castro tended to wax and wane, but for the militant Cuban-American exiles the United States had trained and armed under presidents Eisenhower and Kennedy, destroying the Castro regime became an obsession. The worst terrorist acts against Cuba in the four decades after the Bay of Pigs were masterminded by men who had served in Brigade 2506, Orlando Bosch and Luis Posada most notably, and carried out by paramilitary organizations founded by them. These included the Movimiento Nacionalista Cubano (MNC), Poder Cubano, Gobierno Secreto Cubano (GSC), Alpha 66, OMEGA 7 and, after 1974, an umbrella organization called the Comandos de Organizaciones Revolucionarias Unidas (CORU). Their lifelong passion for the cause of freeing Cuba from communist control, even by violent means, was summarized by Posada in 2005, then seventy-seven years old and in U.S. custody. "I've always believed in rebellion, in the armed struggle," he said. "I believe more and more every day that we will triumph against Castro. Victory will be ours." The Cuban government, which regularly publishes the résumés of ex-patriots it regards as terrorists, claims that Orlando Bosch was responsible for forty terrorist bombings against Cuban targets in 1968 alone.

The extent of direct U.S. complicity in Cuban-American terrorism in the 1960s and 1970s has always been a matter of dispute. Noam Chomsky has bluntly called the covert war against Cuba an example of "U.S.-directed international terrorism," but he also acknowledges that federal authorities took the surveillance of Cuban exile groups seriously. This is not surprising, since many of the most dramatic terrorist attacks against Cuban interests took place on American soil. These included the 1964 bazooka attack on the UN (while Che Guevara was addressing the General Assembly), the 1968 armed takeover of New York's Spanish-language radio station WBNX, the 1974 bombing of the OAS office in Washington, and the 1977 bombing of the Lincoln Center in New York after a performance of the Ballet Nacional de Cuba. In 1962, according to the *Washington Post*, a Canadian agricultural technician was paid by U.S. military intelligence to infect Cuban poultry with the virus that causes Newcastle disease. In 1977, *Newsday* reported that the African swine fever outbreak that swept Cuba in 1971 had been clandestinely introduced by a Miami exile group backed by the CIA. The same year, Bill Moyers, a highly respected journalist and former press secretary for Lyndon Johnson, reported in a CBS television documentary that exile guerrillas trained by the CIA and based in the United States were continuing the covert war against Castro that had begun at the Bay of Pigs. In Miami and Washington, "moderates" in the Cuban-American lobby openly defended paramilitary attacks against Cuba and raised money for what they called *la guerra*.

Cuban-American violence extended to Canada and to Canadian interests abroad, heightening Canadians' already considerable wariness about Washington's connections to anti-Castro militants. Throughout the 1960s and the 1970s, Canadian diplomats in New York, Washington, Ottawa and especially Havana were threatened with reprisals for Canada's policy of "aid and trade" with Castro, as one Miami-based organization put it. Even before Air Canada began running charter flights to Cuba in 1970, it was a favourite target of terrorists. In October 1968, for example, exile Hector Cornillot went on a bombing rampage in the United States that included blowing up Air Canada's Miami office, a crime for which he was convicted in 1973. Far more frequently—and with far more damaging results—were Cuban targets in Canada bombed by anti-Castro groups. In August 1964, a cell of the New York–based MNC kicked off a rash of attacks on Cuban properties in Montreal with the bombing of the Cuban freighter *María Teresa* in the city harbour. In 1966, the same organization detonated a time bomb made from a bazooka shell outside the Cuban Embassy in Ottawa. No one was hurt in the explosion, but the windows of the Embassy and of several nearby houses in Ottawa's Sandy Hill neighbourhood were blown out. The head of the MNC, Felipe Rivero Díaz, a veteran of the Bay of Pigs, told the Miami press that Canada had again been targeted "because of the insulting and provocative attitude maintained by the Canadian Government with respect to the tragedy of the Cuban people enslaved by international communism."

Canadians were shocked by the Embassy bombing. Prime Minister Lester Pearson promised a full inquiry into the incident. But only six months later, the "Canadian branch" of the MNC struck again, this time detonating a cigar-box bomb outside Fraser Bros., a Montreal auction house. Forty-year-old Quebec cabinetmaker Dieudonné Boudreau was injured in the incident, as he tried to defuse the bomb. Again Felipe Rivero Díaz admitted responsibility for the crime, claiming that Fraser Bros. had been targeted because it was selling off furniture stolen from Cuban refugees by the Castro regime. Related terrorist acts against Canada included the bombing in May 1967 of the Cuba Pavilion at Expo '67, for which Díaz was detained and evicted from the United States but never charged; the bombing of the Cuban Consulate in Montreal in October 1967 (a building that also housed the Cuban trade commission); MNC threats against the Canadian Embassy in Havana and Canadian banks with branches in Cuba; the July 1968 bombing of a Canadian tourist office in the United States attributed to Poder Cubano; the attempted bombing of the Cuban Consulate in Montreal in May 1969; and attacks on Cuban ships docked at Montreal.

In June 1969, a U.S. federal grand jury indicted three MNC members for conspiring to bomb Cuban properties in Montreal, temporarily halting the terror campaign. A rash of bombings commenced eighteen months later, however. It included the December 1970 bombing of the

Cuban Consulate in Toronto (the day after FLQ terrorists were flown to Havana); the July 1971 and April 1972 attacks on the Cuban Consulate in Montreal, attributed by Cuban authorities to the Gobierno Secreto Cubano; the attempted bombing of the Cuban ambassador's residence and the Cuban Embassy in Ottawa in March 1972; the attempted bombing of the U.S. office of the Canadian firm Michael's Forwarding in December 1972; the January 1974 bombing of the Cuban Embassy in Ottawa; and the September 1976 bombing of the Cuban Consulate in Montreal. Canadians were appalled by evidence of organized terrorism against Cuban targets, and by reports that sympathetic elements in the U.S. intelligence establishment were complicit. They were also plainly spooked by the fact that their country had become a prime target for foreign terrorists, a perfectly understandable response that had ramifications for Cuban-Canadian diplomacy. Concern over security was the main reason Canadian officials insisted—quietly but firmly—that Fidel Castro not attend Expo '67 in person.

An interesting twist on the Cuban-American terror story in Canada was revealed by journalist John Sawatsky in 1980. The April 1972 bombing of the Cuban Consulate in Montreal, which killed Cuban security guard Sergio Pérez, is alleged to have taken place with the prior knowledge of the RCMP Security Service. The Cuba Desk of the Security Service in Montreal had for years worked closely with the CIA on cases of violence against Cuban targets in Canada. It was well known within both agencies that the Consulate was the North American headquarters for Cuban espionage. When the explosion took place, at 12:45 a.m., the Mountie in charge of the Cuba Desk was ostensibly at home in Sainte-Thérèse. But he arrived at the Consulate so quickly that some of his colleagues later calculated that he must have left home before the bomb was detonated. In the chaotic aftermath of the explosion, which saw armed Consulate personnel frantically try to stall the Montreal police and burn sensitive files, the RCMP officer helped himself to whatever documents he could salvage, including a code book used by Cuban cipher clerks. According to Sawatsky, the entire cache of hundreds of documents, including the code book, were being perused at CIA headquarters in Langley, Virginia, just hours later.

The most devastating attack by Cuban-American terrorists against their home country came not in the 1960s but in the autumn of 1976, just ten months after Pierre Trudeau's state visit to Havana. On October 6, CIA-trained Cuban exiles planted a time bomb in an Air Cubana jetliner, killing all seventy-three people aboard just after takeoff from Bridgetown, Barbados. The timing of this crime was not coincidental. The prime minister's trip was but one of many indicators in the mid-1970s that the Western world was ready to begin a new dialogue with Fidel Castro, one that would include the United States and thus presage an end to economic sanctions. Militant anti-Castro exiles based in the United States read the signs, and stepped up their attacks on Cuba accordingly. The era of *El Diálogo* thus also became the era of the worst anti-Castro terrorism in history, with doubly tragic results for the Cuban people. The dialogue failed, and Cuban-American terrorism against the Castro regime persisted for another thirty years.

———

While Pierre Trudeau's political toughness was an asset when he was doing battle with terrorists, it was the worst of liabilities when turned against the Canadian people. The Liberals were returned to power in October 1972, but they were reduced to a minority government. The election campaign, Trudeau said in retrospect, had been "too cerebral." Perhaps, but by 1972 Canadians had also witnessed Trudeau at his least cerebral—when he mouthed the words "fuck off" to an opponent in the House of Commons, for example, or when he told some laid-off postal workers to "mangez la merde." And, although he had emerged from the FLQ crisis a hero to many Canadians, Trudeau had also shown contempt for the "bleeding hearts" who were worried about soldiers in the streets. In 1972, the electorate sent the prime minister a message and he knew it. For the next two years, Canadians would see a kinder, gentler Pierre Trudeau.

Trudeau stated in his *Memoirs* that he was quite happy during the minority government of 1972–74 to collaborate with the NDP. Because he had had a reputation as a "leftist" before entering federal politics, he recalled, he had taken pains during his first mandate to "maintain a careful equilibrium between progressive measures and more moderate ones." Remarkable though it seems in retrospect, given the scorn that would later be heaped on Trudeau for his "bloated" deficits, between 1968 and 1972 he had a reputation, as Richard Gwyn put it, "for caring more about balanced budgets than the poor." Trudeau's first war on inflation, between 1968 and 1970, was fought by conventional means. He froze spending, made deep cuts to the civil service, forced the Bank of Canada to adopt a tight-money policy and in 1969 balanced the budget for the first time in over a decade. The minority government of 1972–74 thus presented Trudeau with the opportunity, as he put it, to "institute policies that I had been dreaming about for a long time." Seniors' pensions were indexed for the first time, and family allowance and unemployment-insurance benefits were increased. Government spending took its largest jump in history.

As noted above, Trudeau's rise to power coincided with a national crusade to regain control of the Canadian economy. Trudeau felt the pressure of this "new nationalism" and, pragmatic politician that he had become, he knew that he had to make some concessions to it. In 1972 he launched his Third Option policy to diversify Canadian trade and, as he put it himself, to "reduce our economic dependence on the U.S." Other Liberal measures to protect Canada's economic sovereignty would include the Foreign Investment Review Agency (FIRA), the Canada Development Corporation, Petro-Canada and the National Energy Program. Trudeau took credit in his *Memoirs* for "turning the tide" on foreign ownership of the Canadian economy by the mid-1980s. But the truth is that he was never much of an economic nationalist. Ottawa insiders claim that Trudeau showed little interest in the Third Option as it was being hammered out, and when the initiative fizzled it neither surprised nor concerned him. Trudeau's endorsement of FIRA was equally luke-warm, for the simple reason that he believed foreign investment to be the engine of the Canadian economy. It is probably fair to say, as a dejected Peter C. Newman came to believe, that when it came to repatriating the Canadian economy, Trudeau was merely going through the motions.

For many student radicals and countercultural activists in these years, not all of them terrorists by any means, Fidel Castro's Revolution beckoned as a social and economic experiment with promising possibilities for Canada. Even among mainstream Canadian politicians, Castro's elixir of uncompromising nationalism and social reform struck an inspirational chord. Former Newfoundland premier Joey Smallwood, for example, started up a personal friendship with the Cuban leader when they met for the first time in May 1973. They would meet at the Gander airport whenever Castro's plane stopped to refuel—"very buddy-buddy," said Smallwood. David Lewis was another Canadian politician to visit Cuba and sing the praises of the Revolution. "What impresses one is the immense progress made in only a dozen years," wrote Lewis in 1975. "What is equally impressive is the fact that plans for the future continue to emphasize education, health, food and shelter."

Pierre Trudeau also spoke favourably of Cuban social ideals. But never did he view Castro's economic and trade policies as anything but disastrous. Prior to his official trip in 1976, in fact, the prime minister regularly cited Cuba as a worst-case scenario for Canada if the nationalists got their way. In September 1970, for example, the prime minister engaged in a frank discussion of Canada-U.S. relations with a group of Montreal high-school students. When they took him to task for doing too little to reduce American control of the Canadian economy, he bluntly defended foreign investment. "It is easy to get rid of foreign capital," Trudeau said. "Castro did it in about three weeks, but the standard of living in Cuba went way down and now he has to borrow money from the Soviet Union and China." An indignant student challenged the prime minister on his claim that ordinary Cubans were worse off under the

Revolution. "Read Castro's last speech," Trudeau shrugged, alluding to the Cuban leader's public apology for missing his ten-million-ton sugar quota in 1970. "He offered his resignation because of the economic problems. Certainly, there is less money and capital in Cuba now than there was before the U.S. investors were driven out."

This was not an isolated exchange. Trudeau regularly asked Canadians whether they wanted to sacrifice their prosperity, only to end up like Cuba. It was a politically risky question in the 1970s, since it put him on the wrong side of the nationalists. But it illuminated something central to Trudeau's thinking about the Canadian economy. Tinkering with the odd corporate takeover in FIRA was one thing, but cutting off the flow of American capital was quite another.

———

Sensing that his political fortunes had improved, or at least that the electorate owed him one for all of his new social spending, Trudeau called an election for July 1974. His instincts proved correct, and the Liberals were returned with a majority government.

The tanking Canadian economy was the major issue of the 1974 election campaign, and it turned out to be a gift to the Liberals. Tory leader Robert Stanfield campaigned on a platform of government-imposed wage-and-price controls as a cure for Canada's rampant inflation. Trudeau attacked him mercilessly for it, arguing that government should not be in the business of micromanaging the national economy. Once they had their majority, Trudeau and Finance Minister John Turner tried to persuade Canadian businesses and workers to reign in their expectations voluntarily. They met with little success, and the economy got no better. When the Finance Department began working on scenarios that included wage-and-price controls, Turner resigned, enhancing the atmosphere of an economy in crisis and a government immobilized by it. On Thanksgiving Day 1975, Trudeau went before Canadians on national television and announced the creation of the Anti-Inflation Board. It would directly impose controls on

wages and prices in Canada, starting with a freeze on the salaries of politicians and civil servants in Ottawa. Trudeau later claimed that this "harsh
medicine" worked, bringing the national inflation rate down to 7.5 per cent
in 1976. But he could never overcome the perception that he had cynically
adopted the very policy he had criticized in Stanfield. Canadians, he said,
lost their faith in him as a "straight-shooting guy."

Trudeau's apparent *volte-face* on wage-and-price controls prompted
many of his critics to question his commitment to a free-market economy
in Canada. Their worst fears seemed to be confirmed just weeks later
when the beleaguered prime minister mused aloud in a year-end interview about Canada's economic problems. "We haven't been able to make
it work—the free-market system," he said, so it might be necessary to
consider a "new society" in the future, in which government might have
to play a more active role.

Trudeau recalled in his *Memoirs* that his New Society comments, as
they became known, caused an uproar in Canada. "I found myself being
accused of everything from communism to fascism," he wrote. He was
right. All hell broke loose. Business people from every corner of Canada
went after the prime minister with a vengeance. Edgar G. Burton, president of the Metro Toronto Board of Trade, spoke for many when he
exclaimed that "Trudeau is trying to scramble an egg by beating the
chicken." The political fallout was equally intense. The federal Tories,
then in the middle of an unofficial leadership race to replace Stanfield,
knew a political gift horse when they saw one. Calgary Tory Peter Bawden
remarked that Trudeau's musings had merely "confirmed what a lot of
people here have suspected for a long time—that Trudeau is leading
Canada down a more socialistic path." Conservative leadership hopeful
Flora MacDonald said that Trudeau did not seem to understand the term
"free enterprise." Jack Horner, one of her rivals, suggested that there were
"similarities" between Pierre Trudeau and Adolf Hitler. Liberals rallied
to Trudeau's defence, but he knew that he had fumbled the ball. A week
after his New Society comments, he went back on television to clarify

his position. "I do think that the habits we've acquired, the behaviours that we've acquired in this two or three hundred years of an industrial society had led to sending the system out of joint," he said. "Obviously the system isn't working very well." His critics were not comforted.

The month-long spectacle of a Canadian prime minister backpedalling on one or two unguarded remarks turned out to be of little consequence over the longer run. Most Canadians conceded grumpily that Trudeau had been merely "thinking out loud," as Richard Gwyn noted in the *Toronto Star*. Gallup polls showed that the number of Canadians who believed Canada was "heading toward socialism" had risen by only 5 per cent since 1968. (More than one observer noted that if Trudeau's remarks had been anything other than idle chit-chat—if he had really intended to signal a radical shift in Liberal economic policy—Canadian stock markets would have taken a beating. In fact, in the days after the prime minister's New Society interview, the TSE actually rose. "Can you imagine the decline on Wall Street," asked finance columnist Jack McArthur, "if President Gerald Ford had said similar things about the U.S.?") For his part, Pierre Trudeau never understood what all the fuss was about. His New Society comment, he recalled in his *Memoirs*, had been an off-the-cuff remark and not a policy statement. And in any case, he subsequently gave Canadians every assurance that he had "no plans to subvert the free enterprise system." It was no big deal.

Perhaps not, but if he was going to share with Canadians his growing disillusionment with capitalism, the prime minister's timing could have been better. Just a month after he told them the free-market system did not work, he was in Havana cheering, "*¡Viva el Primer Ministro Fidel Castro!*"

4

El Diálogo
Thawing the Cold War

When Pierre Trudeau told the American press corps in 1969 that he thought the time had come for Washington to make its peace with Cuba, he got a surprisingly warm response. This was but one sign that the decade-old American consensus on Fidel Castro was crumbling, and playing to Trudeau's advantage. President Nixon remained hawkish on Castro but others in Washington (including the late President Kennedy's brother, Senator Ted Kennedy) were by 1970 openly critical of the U.S. embargo and keen to restore diplomatic relations. American students and other activists inspired by the ideals of the Revolution volunteered in the hundreds to cut cane in Cuba as part of the Venceremos Brigades, sailing illegally from Saint John, New Brunswick, and other

Canadian ports. Washington continued to press Canada to join the OAS, but this effort had become half-hearted. Anti-Castro business people in the United States occasionally trotted out the old argument that Canada would do anything for a buck. But this accusation, too, had lost much of its sting. In 1969, Canada's total sales in the Cuban market remained a paltry $40 million annually, while Cuban imports to Canada were stalled in the $7-million range.

Not only had the American critique of Canada's Cuba policy run out of steam but, as Pierre Trudeau well knew, Canada's cordial relationship with Cuba had acquired an increasingly important symbolic significance at home. Asserting Canadian independence from the United States had become politically popular in the aftermath of the Canadian centennial celebrations, and not just among the growing ranks of left-nationalists who detested Richard Nixon, the Vietnam War and the draft. The Trading with the Enemy Act remained a thorn in the side of Canadian business, for example, a constituency that might otherwise have been supportive of Washington's anti-Castro position. Canadian branch plants of U.S. multinationals had to fight Washington just to send spare parts to Cuba. They included the Montreal locomotive firm MLW-Worthington and the Scarborough, Ontario, subsidiary of Litton Industries. Occasionally, the federal government had to run interference for Canadian businesses in Washington, an exercise that visibly frustrated Trudeau's trade minister, Alastair Gillespie. "This return to a type of commercial colonialism we find intolerable," he said in 1974, and not for the first time.

Extending a helping hand to Cuba also accorded with Trudeau's own view of Canada's role abroad. In 1969, the Canadian University Services Overseas (CUSO) became the first foreign non-governmental organization (NGO) to set up shop in Cuba, a milestone that won many Canadians' approval. "Cuba has a serious shortage of teachers, and needs many who can teach English," remarked the *Globe and Mail*. "A bridge of this sort to Cuba could teach Canada, as much as Latin American states, a lot." Four years later, the CUSO exchange program was expanded using $1 million from the Canadian International Development Agency (CIDA), making it the first major aid program in Cuba to be funded by Canadian taxpayers. Under the expanded program, Canadian professors were recruited to teach post-graduate engineering at Fidel Castro's alma mater, the University of Havana, and Cuban teachers were trained at Canadian universities. In February 1974, a CIDA delegation headed by agency president Paul Gérin-Lajoie visited Cuba and signed a Technical Aid Agreement. Gérin-Lajoie gave an enthusiastic speech to a large group of Cuban officials, praising Cuba's achievements in education, literacy and public health. "The message which I bring to you," he said, taking a page from the Trudeau playbook, "reflects our desire to strengthen, through co-operation, a community of understanding; it will take on concrete form in the co-operation programs between Cuba and Canada as well as in our joint search for human dignity, social justice and world peace." In January 1975, a 180-member team of athletes from Canada enjoyed ten days of friendly competition in Cuba, a visit that was reciprocated several times later the same year in the lead-up to the 1976 Olympic Games in Montreal.

In the mid-1970s, at Trudeau's urging, the federal government also redoubled its promotion of Cuban-Canadian trade. In January 1974, a group of seven Canadian MPs visited Cuba as guests of Fidel Castro. One of their many stops was a tour of a cattle-breeding station stocked with Canadian cows and managed by the *Comandante*'s brother, Ramón Castro. Exchanges between Canadian and Cuban government officials followed. Beefing up bilateral trade turned out to be fairly good for Canada's bottom line. By 1973, Canadian sales to Cuba were in the $80-million range (not including the $50 million in wheat exports to the USSR that ended up in Cuba), a doubling since 1969. By 1974, they had reached $144 million, with $76-million worth of Cuban sugar, tobacco and rum entering Canada.

Canadian tourism was also way up, and helping to balance Castro's trade with Canada. In 1971, roughly seventeen hundred Canadian tourists visited Cuba. Three years later, the number had risen to six thousand, making Canada the largest non-socialist market for the decrepit Cuban tourist industry. Then, in the 1974–75 season, it doubled again to twelve thousand, with projections for 1975–76 reaching forty thousand. Tourism had been a pillar of the Cuban economy in the Batista era, but with Castro's criminalization of gambling and the imposition of the U.S. embargo, it had withered almost to insignificance. Not until the mid-1970s did the regime show any interest in making the island hospitable to Western tourists. And even then, as Canadian travel writers complained regularly, a visit to Cuba had the same gloomy atmospherics as a visit to the communist-bloc countries. The only means of getting to Cuba from Canada until 1975 were weekly Unitours charter flights to Havana, heavily discounted all-expenses-paid trips to "Castro-land" launched by Air Canada in 1970. In 1975 a second charter company, Suntours, began offering similar all-inclusive packages. In light of increasing business and tourist demand, Air Canada floated the idea of a direct air link to Havana early in 1974, later collaborating with Air Cubana on a feasibility study for direct flights from Toronto or Montreal to Havana. In 1975, the carrier announced five special charter flights by Air Canada and Quebecair in lieu of a regular air link. As it happened, regular flights to Havana would not begin until 2003.

Ironically, the property of choice for many Canadian tourists in Havana was the Deauville Hotel—the home away from home of the FLQ terrorists exiled after the October Crisis. Then as now, Canadian tourists claimed that the absence of Americans was one of the main reasons Cuba was their preferred vacation spot. "Right now," said Fred Miller, an Agincourt man visiting Havana in 1973, "this is almost the only country where a Canadian can never be confused with an American. They know who we are, all right, and they are happy." (Miller, an Austrian-born Canadian who had fought in the Second World War and identified himself as a staunch anti-communist, also expressed his admiration for the Cuban people. "The Batista regime that was overthrown by Castro was one of the most corrupt and evil in history," he said. "Castro has given them dignity, education and a little hope. I still don't like the system, but it has meant an improvement for the majority of Cubans.")

———

Air travel between Canada and Cuba got a boost in 1973 when the two governments signed an agreement on hijacking. Air piracy was such a persistent problem in the 1960s and the 1970s that the phrase "Take me to Havana" became a joke-phrase in North American popular culture. The problem had its roots in the early years of the Cuban-American stand-off. After the rebel victory in 1959, Cubans fleeing the Castro regime stole five Cuban planes and landed them in Florida. The aircraft were promptly seized under a court order by an American citizen claiming that the Cuban regime owed him money. Reacting angrily to the impound-ment of the planes, Fidel Castro announced that if anyone would like to hijack a U.S. plane, he would be happy to receive it. It was an intemper-ate statement, and one the Cuban leader would live to regret. It set off a spate of hijackings to Cuba that continued with varying degrees of inten-sity into the 1980s. The peak year for hijackings was 1968, when twenty planes were commandeered to Havana. Between 1963 and 1973, the total number of hijackings was eighty-three.

Although Cuba did not sign the 1963 Tokyo convention on air crimes, Castro took a dim view of hijacking. Contrary to the myth that the regime was soft on air piracy, most perpetrators were taken into custody by force, tried in Cuban courts and sent to prison. It was often Castro himself who greeted the passengers and crews of diverted planes on the tarmac of José Martí Airport. In at least one instance, in November 1972, he intervened personally in a hijacking case, reportedly assuring a Southern Airways pilot that the three perpetrators would spend the rest of their lives in "a four-by-four-foot cell." (It later came to light that the hijackers in this case had threatened to fly the plane into the Oak Ridge Atomic Center in Tennessee.) In 1969, the Cuban government passed a law under which air pirates would be extradited to their home countries, but only on the basis of "equality and strict reciprocity"—language that made the status of American hijackers uncertain. As a general rule, Castro allowed hijacked American planes safe passage back to the United States but did not deport the hijackers. In 1970, the Cuban government took the unprecedented step of allowing U.S. military officials to escort twenty-seven-year-old Robert Labadie, a U.S. Army private indicted on air-piracy charges, from Havana to Miami. Along with the return of hijacked planes Castro would send itemized bills to the airline for the cost of feeding and housing stranded passengers, a practice that galled Washington even though it was the standard policy for hijackings within the United States.

On Boxing Day 1971, a twenty-four-year-old New Yorker named Patrick Dolan Critton boarded an Air Canada jetliner at Thunder Bay carrying a gun and at least one hand grenade—weapons the regional airport had no equipment to detect. He forced Air Canada Flight 932 (en route to Toronto) to fly instead to Havana, where he was immediately taken into custody by Cuban authorities. The incident was the first successful hijacking of a Canadian airliner; two other attempts had been made within the previous year, but both had been thwarted by airline personnel. Three weeks after the incident, in mid-January 1972, the Canadian government made a formal request to have Critton extradited to Canada to face charges of kidnapping, armed robbery of an aircraft and extortion. (Hijacking was not yet a federal offence, so the warrant for Critton's arrest was issued by police in Mississauga.) Canada was then negotiating a bilateral hijacking treaty with Cuba, and so it seemed a timely request. However, when Cuban and Canadian officials finally signed the anti-hijacking treaty, on February 15, 1973, it was not made retroactive. Critton thus remained in a Cuban jail cell, and the Trudeau government quietly dropped its extradition request.

Since at least 1969, American aviation officials had been pressing for a similar hijacking treaty between the United States and Cuba. What they got instead was a five-year accord, under which both nations agreed to deport hijackers as criminals. (Significantly, ordinary exiles fleeing Cuba for the United States were exempted from its provisions, but it included a clause giving Cuba the right to prosecute raids by exiles on Cuban targets.) Not coincidentally, the Cuban-American accord was signed the same day as the Cuban-Canadian treaty. Fidel Castro would let the accord with the United States lapse in 1977, after the Air Cubana bombing tragedy. But, for the moment, the fact that Washington and Havana were prepared to cooperate in the prosecution of air piracy was taken as a promising sign that tensions between the two nations were easing.

———

On April 19, 1961, a short article appeared on Canadian wire services. Two pilots employed by the Montreal charter carrier World Wide Airways, it said, were "trapped in Cuba by the rebellion" at the Bay of Pigs. One of the men was identified as Ronald Lippert of Kitchener, Ontario.

Lippert, it turned out, was working for the CIA. In October, 1963, he was caught red-handed by the Cuban authorities flying small-arms ammunition and grenades (hidden in papaya fruit cans) to counterrevolutionaries. The same month, he pleaded guilty in a Cuban court to a charge of attempting to smuggle arms into Cuba, admitting that he had been receiving $500 a month from the CIA. He was originally sentenced to be shot, execution being the standard fate of counterrevolutionaries, but an intercession by Prime Minister John Diefenbaker got the sentence reduced to thirty years. The other Canadian arrested with Lippert, William Milne, was acquitted.

In February 1973, Lippert's story vaulted to the front pages of Canadian newspapers, where it remained for the better part of a year. The saga began when the pilot's seventy-eight-year-old mother, Genevieve, who was in failing health, wrote to Fidel Castro begging him to release her son so that she might see him "one more time before I die." At the same time, Lippert's daughter and one of his sisters began a public campaign to raise money so they could travel in person to Havana to plead his case. Thanks largely to Tory MP Tom Cossitt, who informed the

House of Commons of Lippert's incarceration and even offered to go to Havana himself, the case became a high priority at External Affairs. Cuban Foreign Minister Raúl Roa was petitioned for Lippert's release. The Lippert family, meanwhile, urged Prime Minister Trudeau to take the matter up directly with Fidel Castro. "Canadian officials here feel that a word from one man at the top to another man at the top could help Ron be back in Canada with his mother and his family," said his sister, Rosemary Lawrence.

In March 1973, Lippert's married daughter, Ruth Ann MacLean—identified in the press as a "pretty teen-ager"—was granted permission by Cuban authorities to visit her father. "This is the most exciting year of my life," she said. "First the baby and now this." Ronald Lippert was released from prison for a week in order to meet his sister and daughter. The three were reunited at the Deauville Hotel in Havana in early April, where, like the FLQ terrorists residing there, he was given free access to the bar, dining room and swimming pool. His sister described Lippert as looking "fit and well" but would not discuss with the press anything he said about his ten years in the Cuban penal system. By July, with the two women back in Canada and Lippert back in a maximum-security prison at Guanajay, twenty-five miles south of Havana, the family was not taking no for an answer. The Canadian government should "stop pussyfooting around and try something stronger to get him out of there," said Lippert's sister.

On July 6, Tom Cossitt moved for a vote in the House of Commons requesting that the prime minister intervene in the Lippert case directly. The motion was defeated. Not until mid-September, when Fidel Castro showed up in Gander, Newfoundland, en route from Hanoi, did the tide turn in the family's favour. Confronted by the Canadian press, which had by this time helped to make the Lipperts' case a national crusade, the Cuban leader agreed to look into the matter. (Joey Smallwood also offered to use his personal influence with the *Comandante* to get the pilot released.) "There have been many cases in which the revolutionary government has shown generosity to this kind of person who has committed crimes against our country," said Castro. In late October, a resolution in the House of Commons requesting that Cuba grant Lippert his freedom passed unanimously. The following week, when the new Canadian ambassador to Cuba, Malcolm Bow, presented his credentials in Havana, Fidel Castro told him that Lippert would be released. He gave no explanation, but the regime later issued a statement saying that the amnesty had been granted "in the interests of co-operation between Canada and Cuba and out of humanitarian regard for the Lippert family."

On November 5, 1973, to the jubilation of his family and the many Canadians nationwide who had been caught up in the drama, Ronald Lippert returned home to Kitchener. Photographs of his ecstatic reunion with his mother and daughter made headlines across the country. When the press descended on Lippert at Toronto International Airport, he was described as showing signs of strain from his prison ordeal and as guarded in his responses to questions. He was predictably emotional in the presence of his family. After ten years speaking only Spanish, he groped clumsily for the words in English to describe his joy and relief at being back in Canada. One journalist asked him whether he thought the CIA had let him down. "I didn't hear the question," he replied. When the question was repeated, he offered the same response.

Once he had settled into his old life, Lippert began to talk much more openly about his experiences, revealing more about the cruelties of the Cuban penal system under Fidel Castro than Canadians had ever previously known. In a feature interview published in the *Toronto Star* in November 1973, Lippert called his years in captivity "the golden years of terror." He was treated exactly like all other prisoners, he said, being forced to work in Cuban fields from dawn till dusk. Food was inadequate, especially in the first years of his incarceration. Prisoners were sometimes made to clean deep ditches of excrement with their hands. Severe beatings were a regular occurrence in the four prisons he experienced, including Cabana in Havana and the huge prison on the Isle of Youth where Fidel Castro had once been imprisoned by Batista. Lippert had a five-inch scar on his left arm, caused by a guard's bayonet. He likened moving through prison halls to running a gauntlet (a description that accords with Armando Valladares's prison memoirs from the same period). "There wasn't a time," said Lippert, "when there wasn't 100 to 150 guards who came in for whatever motive they dreamed up and beat everyone. They stationed themselves in stairways. You had to come down. And when you came down you got hit."

Lippert remained cagey about his involvement with the CIA. He had started out as a legitimate cargo pilot flying livestock from Canada to Cuba, he said, and as he got to know counterrevolutionaries in Miami and Cuba he grew sympathetic to their cause. He started out doing small favours for them, such as couriering letters. When he began running guns and ammunition, he claimed, his contacts were only with Cuban ex-patriots in Miami. The inference was that he never met any Americans, nor had any direct contact with the CIA. "If the Cubans were American citizens or not, I don't know," he said. In the 1970s, Lippert never divulged publicly whether the charge that he was on the CIA payroll was true, only that he signed his confession to Cuban authorities under duress. Not until the publication of his angry memoir, *Spy Bate*, in 2003 did he acknowledge that he had worked out of a CIA field office in Miami. The central claim of the memoir, in fact, was that the agency deliberately "compromis[ed] my covert activities, causing my capture and weakening the prevalent trade relations between Canada and the Castro government."

Speaking to the press in 1973, Lippert was highly critical of some Canadian Embassy staff in Havana. In 1965, he recalled, he had managed to send a letter to the Canadian ambassador criticizing Canada and other nations for buying the produce of Cuban prison farms—produce "virtually saturated with the blood of the prisoners," as he put it. He suggested that Canadian authorities enlist the support of the UN to press for improved conditions for prisoners in Cuba. Once when he was visited in prison by a Canadian Embassy staffer who was working on his release, he was harangued. "Christ, man—you did something to them, so don't cry now you're a prisoner," he was told. Other embassy staff, however, "conducted themselves marvellously," Lippert said. Their food parcels in particular were always welcomed by himself and the other prisoners with whom he shared them. (He never showed Embassy staff the injury to his arm, knowing that doing so would only make his life inside worse.) Lippert said that he was also deeply indebted to former prime minister Lester Pearson. Embassy staff had told him that Pearson had threatened to cut off wheat supplies to Cuba if he was shot. Given the number of summary executions he had seen while in prison, Lippert believed that only such a "severe threat" from the prime minister of Canada could account for his remaining alive. When asked what he intended to do with the rest of his life as a free man, he said he intended to dedicate himself to bringing down the Castro regime.

It appears that Pierre Trudeau never intervened directly in the Lippert saga. The available evidence points in the opposite direction, in fact. The prime minister appears not to have found the Lippert family's appeals compelling. (In his memoir, Lippert claims that "Castro's bitch," Trudeau, directed Liberal MPs to defeat Cossitt's motion of July 6, 1973.) Why this was so remains a matter of speculation but, that said, it would have been out of character in the extreme for Pierre Trudeau to go to bat for a CIA operative. As a liberal political theorist, the prime minister was deeply committed to the principle of the sovereignty of states. And as a liberal politician, he took pains not to meddle in the affairs of sovereign states precisely so that no one would meddle in Canada's. Trudeau also took a dim view of terrorism. It is not difficult to imagine how he would have reacted had Lippert been brought up on charges of running guns from Miami to the FLQ in Montreal. Trudeau also took a dim view of the covert operations of the CIA. He may even have agreed with the Embassy official who told Lippert that it was his own fault that he was stuck in a Cuban jail, though, of course, he would never have said so publicly. Trudeau would undoubtedly have done what both Diefenbaker and Pearson did—intervene personally to see that Lippert was not shot. (It is plausible that he did so behind the scenes.) But Ronald Lippert was no dissident, and in 1973 his cause was not that of a prisoner of conscience. He was a soldier of fortune, pure and simple, and thus it would have been most extraordinary had Trudeau expended his own diplomatic capital in the cause of getting him freed.

———

As remote as it seems from today's perspective, with the U.S. embargo approaching the half-century mark and President George W. Bush treating Cuba in much the same manner as Dwight D. Eisenhower, the normalization of relations between the United States and Cuba seemed imminent in the mid-1970s. Canadians and Europeans were so certain that the United States was going to make its peace with Fidel Castro, in fact, that they mobilized all of their diplomatic resources to protect their place in the sun. When the planning for Pierre Trudeau's state visit to Havana began in 1974, the main concern at External Affairs was to insulate Canadian trade from the looming onslaught of U.S. competition. "Internationally, the 'blockade' of Cuba seems to be coming to an end," observed a confidential memo written by Canadian Embassy staff in Havana for the minister of trade. A November 1975 memo listed "solidify[ing] Canadian-Cuban relations at the highest level in anticipation of an eventual Cuba/U.S. détente" as a priority of the visit.

The U.S. embargo against Cuba was Richard Nixon's inheritance when he took office in 1969, but it was evident that his efforts to tighten the economic screws on Castro were failing. In 1975, the U.S. Commerce Department conducted a study on the effectiveness of the thirteen-year-old sanctions. It confirmed the obvious. With each passing year, the embargo became more difficult to administer and more injurious to American business.

There were several reasons for the embargo's declining efficacy. For one thing, the Soviets were more successful in curbing Cuban ambitions with carrots than the Americans were with sticks. With $300 million in Soviet subsidies flowing to the island annually by the late 1960s, the Cuban regime had grown visibly, if grudgingly, obliged to Moscow. (The Soviets had become so exasperated by Havana's policy of exporting revolution throughout Latin America that at one point it reduced oil exports to Cuba to bring Castro into line.) In 1972, Cuba was invited to join COMECON, the Soviet foreign-aid organization, which gave the island developing-nation status within the communist bloc. This meant even more favourable terms for export subsidies and loans, but it also signalled a new willingness on Castro's part to play by the rules of détente.

In addition, America's competitors in western Europe and Japan were moving aggressively into Cuba. From their vantage point, the absence of American competition in Cuba was a godsend. "Never before had such a highly integrated and lucrative U.S. market simply been abandoned and thrown open for new business," observed one economist. In 1971, Britain sent its first trade mission to Havana since 1959. French, West German and Japanese delegations soon followed. Cuba's already sizeable trade with Spain was fattened by an $890-million contract in 1971. The following year, the foreign ministers of the European Economic Community (EEC) granted trade preferences to Cuba. In January 1975, high-ranking Cuban officials visited France for the first time since 1959 and received a $500-million line of credit. Six months later, the British followed suit with a £250-million credit deal. By 1975, Japan, the Americans' strongest Asian ally, had become Cuba's largest non-communist trading partner.

In March 1975, Canadian trade minister Alastair Gillespie hopped on the bandwagon and led a delegation of twenty-five business people to Cuba. The Canadian press accurately depicted the visit as a blatant attempt "to pre-empt an American incursion into flourishing Canadian-Cuban trade relations." At a reception for Gillespie and his wife, Fidel

Castro chatted openly with members of the Canadian delegation. He was asked about the likelihood that Cuban-American relations would be normalized soon. "We are really not impatient about it," he replied casually. "Sooner or later it will happen. When it does we will consider it a positive event." (The Cuban leader added, in anticipation of the forthcoming state visit, that Prime Minister Trudeau "will always be received with great satisfaction in our country.") Following the European example, Gillespie inked a deal extending $100 million in EDC (Export Development Canada) credit to Cuba. Canadian business leaders also reported new contracts. Cuban-Canadian trade, worth $144 million in 1974, was expected to hit $200 million by 1976. It was precisely because America's own allies were taking such advantage of the embargo that the U.S. Commerce Department redoubled its efforts to enforce the Trading with the Enemy Act in these years. Yet, by August 1975, a rising chorus of criticism had induced the Ford administration to drop the extraterritorial application of U.S. trade law altogether. "Increasingly our sanctions policy was damaging relations with traditional friends," Henry Kissinger later conceded.

President Nixon was under no illusions that Canadians and Europeans would fall in behind the U.S. embargo. But he had high hopes for Latin American countries, which were far more vulnerable to American pressure. Here, too, things did not go his way. Nationalism was on the rise throughout Latin America, most obviously in Salvador Allende's Chile and Juan Perón's Argentina, and so was anti-Americanism. Technically, by the terms of the 1964 Rio Declaration, the OAS embargo against Cuba remained in force. But it was widely known that Chile, Jamaica and Mexico were defying the OAS policy. Starting in the spring of 1972, Peru began a campaign at the OAS to reverse the Rio Declaration. Member states, said the Peruvians, should be allowed to restore diplomatic relations with Cuba if they liked. By late 1974, twelve OAS countries had come out in favour of lifting the blockade, two votes short of the two-thirds' majority needed to carry the organization. Undaunted, six of them (Argentina, Panama, Peru, Ecuador, Honduras and Venezuela) broke ranks and opted to restore relations with Cuba on a bilateral basis, a move that one Canadian pundit astutely called "the death knell of the inter American [*sic*] system."

Gerald Ford, who assumed the U.S. presidency in August 1974, did not share Richard Nixon's personal antipathy toward Fidel Castro. "If Cuba will reevaluate and give us some indication of a change of its policy toward the United States," Ford said in a major policy speech in February 1975, "then we certainly would take another look." A month later, Secretary of State Henry Kissinger extended the olive branch even further. "We see no virtue in perpetual antagonism between the United States and Cuba. We have taken some symbolic steps to indicate that we are prepared to move in a new direction if Cuba will." Pierre Trudeau could tell which way the wind was blowing. "A very short time after I went to Peking, President Nixon went to Peking," the prime minister observed. "A very short time after I'd been to Moscow, President Nixon went to Moscow. Statements of Henry Kissinger as regards Cuba, efforts which have been made, the lifting of the blockade of the OAS and so on, these are all indications that people are coming to terms with the reality of a Cuba directed by this type of leader and this type of government." After China and the USSR, détente with Cuba should have been a piece of cake. This was Trudeau's view. It was also Henry Kissinger's.

In April 1975, Kissinger undertook a personal tour of Latin American countries to consult with foreign ministers on the Cuban question. Perceiving that a united front against Cuba was no longer possible, he directed the United States to vote in favour of a "freedom of action" resolution in the OAS in July 1975. The resolution passed 16–3. Back in Canada, where there had never been much enthusiasm for either the OAS or for sanctions, there was smugness in certain quarters. The OAS decision, said one editorial, "puts a finish to a sorry era of United States domination—often downright bullying—of inter-American affairs."

—•—

The most significant evidence that U.S. sanctions were running out of steam came from within Cuba itself. In the 1960s, Cuba's successes in education and especially literacy had dazzled the world and shored up international respect for Castro, however grudgingly. Adult literacy training, which began in 1961 and focused on rural Cuba, was particularly successful. The Cuban illiteracy rate dropped from a pre-revolutionary high of 25 per cent (already one of the lowest in Latin America) to 12.9 per cent in 1970 and to 5.6 per cent in 1979. Health-care performance actually declined in the 1960s, as many of Cuba's medical professionals emigrated and the U.S. embargo cut off medical supplies. But, by the 1970s, Cuba had made up this lost ground. Infant-mortality and general-morbidity rates were reduced to the levels of the industrialized West, a remarkable achievement for so poor a country. Castro also delivered on his promise to the farmers who had backed him in the Sierra Maestra. Free high-quality health care was made available to Cuba's rural poor for the first time.

In general, the 1960s had seen the regime bungle the Cuban economy, something Castro admitted with striking candour many times over the course of the decade. Speaking to the Cuban Water Resources Institute in 1963, for example, he acknowledged that over-centralization and red tape had produced serious economic problems. "Since the administrators have their salaries assured," he said, sounding very much like his own North American critics, "they don't bother to attend to the public. That is neither revolution nor socialism, it is bungling." In the 1970s, the Cuban economy would finally stabilize, partly because Castro adopted a Soviet model for long-term economic planning, but mainly because of Soviet largesse. By the mid-1970s, direct subsidies from the USSR—above-world prices for sugar and nickel imports and below-world prices for oil exports—amounted to roughly 10 per cent of Cuban GDP. Cuba's economic growth rate came to rival the world's leading economies, generating near-full employment and providing staple goods to Cubans at low prices via rationing and subsidies. All Cubans, even the poorest, enjoyed a social safety net that included relatively high wages, reduced rents and free health care and education. Even Castro's most acerbic critics could not deny that he had by 1976 accomplished the main socio-economic goal of his Revolution, vastly decreasing the gulf between Cuba's rich and poor.

Not only was the Cuban economy booming, but the boom was being driven by trade with the West. Sugar was again king. In 1974 the world price for sugar reached a record high of thirty cents per pound, inflating Cuba's export earnings to unprecedented heights and giving it a trade surplus for the first time since the rebel victory. (In the 1960s, the world price for sugar had languished in the two-cent-per-pound range.) What was truly striking was that exports to the West now accounted for 41 per cent of Cuba's international trade, up from a low of 17 per cent in 1962. Cuba's overall economic growth rate between 1971 and 1975 averaged 14 per cent annually, the highest rate in Latin America. Industrial output, always the weakest link in the revolutionary economy, rose 35 per cent in these years. Equally important from the vantage point of Western investors was the fact that policy reforms in Cuba had introduced material incentives to the Cuban workforce—a dramatic departure from the "new man" ideal once espoused by Che Guevara, according to which people ought to work selflessly for the good of all. For the first time, workers could earn up to 25 per cent of their take-home pay in bonuses for high productivity. A related initiative was the government's expansion of housing and consumer goods (refrigerators, televisions), access to which was also based upon workers' "economic contribution." All of a sudden, Cuba's economy was embracing market reforms, and the shock waves were being felt across the island. Even the houses along the Malecón, which had fallen into dilapidation under the austerity measures of the 1960s, were glowing with renovations and fresh paint.

Accompanying these economic reforms were significant political reforms—significant, that is, when judged against the status quo that had prevailed since 1959 (and indeed since the Batista coup of 1952). The first

Congress of the Cuban Communist Party was convened in December 1975. It reorganized the Cuban state, issued statements on broad principles of policy and approved a draft constitution (ratified the following year in a national referendum). For the first time, the Cuban people had a party structure through which to participate in politics—no small departure from the earlier era, when "mass mobilization" in politics had literally meant attending Fidel Castro's rallies and shouting *¡Sí!* or *¡No!* on his policy statements. The constitution created a new National Assembly to serve as the legislative branch of government, as well as elected provincial and municipal "assemblies of popular power." With the introduction of these bodies, Cubans could for the first time debate and vote on solutions to specific local problems. Starting in 1974, in Matanzas province, elections for the assemblies began. These were the first elections held in Cuba since 1948. Such elections were, of course, far from open in the Western sense of the term. Only the Communist Party could run candidates, campaign or freely discuss issues. The assemblies thus remained subordinate to the executive, which was controlled by Fidel Castro. Yet the repression of opponents of the Castro regime—estimated at roughly one-fifth of the Cuban population—also declined measurably in the mid-1970s. Moderate ministers at the interior and justice departments, as well as moderate judges on the Supreme Court, were directly responsible for this trend, but they could have brought reform only with the tacit blessing of the party elite and Castro himself.

By late 1975, when Western leaders including Pierre Trudeau were mired in economic problems, Cubans were finally enjoying the fruits of a booming economy that the Revolution had long promised but only now delivered. There was no mistaking their excitement, or their newfound confidence. At an October 1975 ceremony commemorating the founding of the Banco Nacional de Cuba, President Osvaldo Dorticós gave voice to this new mood of optimism and strength. "Without going beyond the modest way in which we, the leaders of the Government, appreciate everything our country has accomplished so far," he said, "we are pleased to know that, after a whole period of isolation and defamation of the world of the Cuban Revolution, the truth is now known in many circles of world opinion that our country has reached the level of prestige which goes to explain the fact that such eminent representatives of world banking are here with us today." As even the Cuban communists know, when the world's bankers sit up and take note, you've arrived.

Fidel Castro would tell Pierre Trudeau during the state visit that, although the Cuban economy had had a good run, sustainability remained the regime's ultimate economic goal and this required continued austerity. "We must do without luxury goods," he said bluntly. Yet, after a decade of bungling the economy, Castro was clearly thrilled to have presided over the turnaround.

———

"U.S. Reacts Warmly to Castro's Wooing." So said a United Press headline for May 1975, accompanied in newspapers across North America by a photograph of Fidel Castro driving South Dakota Senator George McGovern around Havana in his jeep.

McGovern was not the first American politician to meet with Castro. In September 1974 Senators Jacob Javits and Claiborne Pell had met the Cuban leader in Havana—the first such visit since Cuban-American relations had been severed in 1961. All had returned to the United States recommending—"very strongly," in McGovern's words—that the embargo be lifted Castro told McGovern that a good first step toward normalizing relations would be the resumption of American exports of food and medicine to Cuba, a gesture that the senator supported. Another sign of Castro's new openness to dialogue with the United States was the fact that he had granted broadcaster Barbara Walters an interview in English, something he had not done since 1959. There was even talk of a Cuban-American baseball exchange. "There can be no mistake about the clarity of the signal sent to Washington during my stay in Havana," McGovern said. "Indeed, if all diplomatic signals were as clear as those which the

Cuban Government sent out during our visit, we could eliminate scores of intelligence analysts." In the wake of McGovern's visit, Castro literally put his money where his mouth was. He agreed to return to Southern Airways the $2-million ransom Cuban authorities had confiscated during a 1972 hijacking incident. To many Canadians watching from the sidelines, this unprecedented warming of Cuban-American relations was long overdue. "The mood has changed," observed one editorial, "perhaps in step with the painfully slow mellowing of the once-hysterical mood with which Premier Castro and his revolution were viewed by Cuba's neighbours."

Publicly, the Republican White House continued to express its reservations about Congress's growing willingness to end the embargo and make peace with Fidel Castro. What was happening behind the scenes, however, was a far different story. It remains one of the best-kept secrets of the era. Starting in June 1974, while Richard Nixon was still president, Henry Kissinger embarked on a series of top-secret talks with Cuban officials aimed at ending the embargo and normalizing diplomatic relations. This dialogue would ultimately fail, early in 1976, and so its existence was not made public. Even during the 1976 presidential election campaign, the talks remained "a deep dark secret." Not until Jimmy Carter was in the White House, in early 1977, did the *New York Times* break the story. Why the veil of secrecy was maintained is not much of a mystery. Kissinger's proclivity for secrecy—and his obvious delight in stunning the world with agreements negotiated behind closed doors— had by the mid-1970s become commonplace. Had the story of the secret talks been leaked, there would have been an anguished outcry in the Cuban émigré community which in the era of Vietnam and Watergate no Republican presidential candidate could afford. On the other hand, if the secret talks had been successful under Ford, with a *fait accompli* presented to the American people before the election of 1976, the backlash from anti-Castro forces, though undoubtedly dramatic, might have been of short duration.

The man doing Kissinger's bidding behind the scenes was William D. Rogers, assistant secretary of state for inter-American affairs. Fidel Castro selected his trusted confidante Ramón Sánchez-Parodi to speak for Cuba. The talks began in earnest in January 1975, when Rogers held a meeting with Cuban representatives in the cafeteria at Washington's National Airport. The following July, the same group met again at the Pierre Hotel in New York. Rogers presented an American wish list, making it clear (on Kissinger's instructions) that the Cubans did not have to deliver on all items all at once. It included the release of U.S. nationals held in Cuban prisons, a reduction in Cuban-Soviet military co-operation, a Cuban promise of non-intervention in the western hemisphere and the settlement of American claims to property nationalized by the regime. The Cubans responded with the position that was—and remains—central to Fidel Castro's thinking on Cuban-American relations: they would not negotiate the details of a rapprochement until the economic blockade was lifted. "It is not that Cuba reject[s] the ideal of improving relations with the United States," Castro explained on January 15. "We are in favour of peace, of the policy of détente, of coexistence between states with different social systems. What we do not accept are humiliating conditions—the absurd price which the Unites States apparently would have us pay for an improvement of relations."

The secret talks began to fall apart in December 1975. The Americans were disturbed by revelations of Cuba's involvement in Angola, but this development alone was not a deal-breaker. Kissinger insisted that the two sides persist with the dialogue. Two more meetings were held, in January and February 1976. In the end, according to William D. Rogers, it was the Cubans who let the talks lapse, presumably because Castro would not drop his demand that the embargo be lifted as a condition of continued negotiations. State Department officials were perplexed. It was a mystery to them why the Cuban leader would throw away this singular opportunity to heal the breach with the United States. It remained a mystery to Henry Kissinger even in 1999, by which time the former secretary of state had simply adopted the standard conservative explanation for Fidel Castro's behaviour. "Castro needed the United States as an enemy to justify his totalitarian grip on the country and to maintain military support from the Soviet Union," Kissinger wrote. "So long as he could claim that Cuba was threatened, he could insist that his island could not afford the luxuries of a more open system, politically or economically. Normalization of relations with the United States would have been difficult to reconcile with continued Communist rule."

Kissinger was probably correct about Castro's need for an enemy in the United States, a view shared by William D. Rogers. But he overstated Castro's refusal to move to a more open system, as a steadily lengthening list of U.S. allies doing business in Cuba could attest. By 1975, Fidel Castro had in fact opened Cuba politically and economically to an extent that would have seemed inconceivable just years earlier. Under the influence of the Soviet Union, he had also come around on détente and especially on the idea that his Revolution was compatible with traditional diplomacy and established international trade practices. Before Cuba's involvement in Angola precipitated an international meltdown in early 1976, only the United States and a handful of Latin American governments persisted in treating Cuba as an international pariah. Henry Kissinger may have been correct in his observation that Castro needed a perpetual American enemy to shore up the domestic political status quo in Cuba. But, as Kissinger knew, this argument cut both ways. The reason his own negotiations with Cuba had to be kept secret, even after they had failed, was the same reason why all future American attempts at *El Diálogo* had to be clandestine. The domestic political status quo in the United States required an enemy in Cuba.

———

As he prepared in 1974 and 1975 for his state visit to Havana, Pierre Trudeau must have felt the wind at his back. His main foreign policy goal when he became prime minister in 1968 was to reduce tensions between the West and the communist world, including Cuba. This meant not only recognizing China and doing what he could to advance détente with the USSR but also allowing Canada to serve as an example to its allies and adversaries alike. Trudeau put his own political capital on the line in pursuit of these objectives, believing that he and other proponents of dialogue were on the leading edge of a transformation of the Cold War world. The currents of history, as he reminded Canadians from time to time, seemed to be on his side. He went to Beijing, and Nixon followed. He went to Moscow, and Nixon followed. When he decided to go to Havana in 1976, he had every reason to believe that the U.S. president would follow him there as well.

When Richard Nixon became president in 1969, he saw the world in much the same way as Trudeau, though through a vastly different ideological lens. Hard-nosed anti-communists and students of *realpolitik*, he and Henry Kissinger did not for a moment buy the prime minister's claim that dialogue was an international ideal worth realizing for its own sake. They believed instead that the national security of the United States was better served by détente (and the Nixon Doctrine) than by any alternative international system. Détente may have been the velvet glove but *deterrence* remained the iron fist of U.S. policy, as it had for a generation.

To most outside observers and to an increasing number of Americans, détente between the superpowers ought to have precipitated a thaw in the Cuban-American stand-off. Yet it did not. Cuba remained a special case. Cuba was not in some distant corner of the globe like Vietnam but in the Americans' own backyard. Castro's Revolution was not only communist but a striking betrayal of the special relationship between the American and the Cuban people, something that Nixon's personal friendship with members of the exile community underscored. Fidel Castro still had the power to infuriate American leaders and citizens alike, and he appeared to delight in doing so. There was thus little political will on either side of the Cuban-American feud to take the decisive step to end it. But a unilateral suspension of the embargo by the Nixon administration some time between 1972 and 1974 might well have led directly to a negotiated settlement on the only outstanding issue that lay behind the sanctions in the first place, namely, compensation for nationalized U.S. assets in Cuba. "We are not enemies of détente or of peaceful coexistence between states with different social systems based on strict respect for the norms of international law," Castro said repeatedly in these years. "We would even be willing to maintain normal relations with the United States on the basis of mutual respect and sovereign equality, without renouncing any of our principles." Nixon and Kissinger believed that he was bluffing—that he could never make peace with the "imperialist" United States. They may well have been correct. But the fact remains that they alone had the power to call Castro's bluff, and they refused to do it.

The main point is this: A rapprochement with Cuba was still achievable politically in the final years of the Nixon presidency, at least in the sense that the anti-Castro exile community had not yet coalesced into the powerful lobby that would in 1981 become the Cuban American National Foundation (CANF). By the time of the 1976 presidential primaries, Ronald Reagan's hawkish pronouncements on Cuba would put Gerald Ford (and Henry Kissinger) on the ropes, especially in Florida. It is true that Jimmy Carter would take one last stab at *El Diálogo* in 1977–78, but by then it was already clear that the window of opportunity to normalize relations and end the embargo had closed. (Carter's insistence that human rights take centre stage in U.S. foreign policy turned out, ironically, to undermine his dialogue with Castro, since it added the plight of Cuban dissidents to the list of American grievances against Cuba, where it remains.) Seen in retrospect, Nixon and Kissinger thus missed the best (and perhaps the only) opportunity since 1961 to put Cuban-American relations on a normal diplomatic footing, though they clearly had no way of knowing this. What they did know was that the old strategy was not working. Nixon's hardline policy against Castro appeared to have no measurable impact on Cuba, it divided the OAS, and it antagonized many of America's closest allies and trading partners. Had Nixon not been so personally antagonistic toward Castro, he and Kissinger could have normalized relations with Cuba in 1973 or 1974, just as they had with China and the USSR. It would have been, as more than one official at the State Department told Kissinger, a piece of cake.

As it turned out, no American president would ever get so close again.

5

Trudeau's Gamble
The Angolan Crisis

"The world wasn't a very nice place at the start of 1976," the *Toronto Star* told its readers on New Year's Day. Civil war, airline disasters, poverty, famine and recession—these were just some of the problems that "continued to plague mankind" as it lurched into the final quarter of the twentieth century. Canadians hardly needed to be reminded. By any measure, 1975 had been an abysmal year. The Canadian economy had stalled almost completely for the first time since the Second World War. *Stagflation* had entered the economists' lexicon, suggesting that the failing economic promise of the postwar era, once thought temporary and therefore not so serious, had now become chronic. In 1975, returns on the Toronto Stock Exchange had not even kept up with inflation. In many ways, January 1976 also marked the high-water mark of a distinctive seventies *Zeitgeist*. The pet rock and the mood ring were making millions. The Bay City Rollers were topping Toronto's CHUM chart, and *One Flew Over the Cuckoo's Nest* was dominating the box office. Kidnapped newspaper heiress Patty Hearst was on trial in the United States for armed robbery. The Concorde jet took its first commercial flight. And Pierre Trudeau went to Havana.

———

As journalist Richard Gwyn observed, the prime minister's public profile was higher in January 1976 than at any time since the days of Trudeaumania. He had to sell Canadians on his controversial wage-and-price controls, and this meant putting himself at the disposal of the national media, a task he did not relish. In keeping with the severity of the times, Trudeau adopted a new, decidedly sobre public persona. With austerity the watchword in Ottawa, he even looked austere. Gone were the roses in his lapel, at least when he was on television talking about his economic policies. Gone as well was the sugar-coating with which he had recaptured the hearts of the Canadian electorate in 1974. "The time has come when we must adopt a new life style," he told Canadians. "We are being forced to do this not merely by our own economic situation, but by the worldwide evolution of mankind." They did not thank him for this wise counsel. "We now have in Canada a prime minister who is not only uncaring, but is also incompetent, a man who mistakes undergraduate platitudes for philosophy and whose government's actions flatly contradict whatever substance you can find in his moral lectures to the people of Canada." The words were NDP leader Ed Broadbent's, but they were widely shared. When Trudeau went to Havana, more than one political cartoonist caricatured him as escaping the pressures of Ottawa for a little respite in the sunny Caribbean.

If the public mood in Canada was grim in January 1976, in the United States it was abysmal. The American bicentennial might have been an

occasion for celebrating the rise to world power of the United States, but the long shadow of Vietnam and Watergate made this difficult. In April 1975, two years after the withdrawal of American forces from Vietnam, the North Vietnamese had rolled into Saigon and pronounced their revolution victorious. A year before that, President Nixon had been forced to resign the White House amid charges of dirty tricks that extended to both the FBI and the CIA.

In the wake of Watergate, powerful congressional committees put the U.S. intelligence community under their microscopes for the first time. Their probes revealed—in the words of Senator Frank Church— that the CIA "may have been behaving like a rogue elephant on a rampage." In November 1975, Church's Senate committee published its interim report, which confirmed that the CIA had, among its many other misdeeds, engaged in a systematic program to assassinate foreign heads of state, including Fidel Castro. (Castro himself contributed an eighty-six-page dossier to the committee, detailing the twenty-four known CIA plots to kill him, which Senator George McGovern personally carried to Washington after his trip to Havana in May.) The national campaign in the

United States to root out co-conspirators left almost no one untouched. In January 1976, three of the most prominent American journalists in the United States, including CBS news anchor Walter Cronkite, were forced to publicly deny allegations that they had worked for the CIA. The same month, under extreme public pressure, Richard Nixon agreed to answer written questions under oath about the role of the CIA in obstructing the election of Salvador Allende in Chile in 1970.

The popular response to the revelations of the Church Report—both in the United States and among its allies—was to deepen the already considerable malaise of the mid-1970s. The idea of a freewheeling, unaccountable CIA doing the dirty work of an imperial presidency worsened anti-Americanism wherever it had already taken root. But more than this, it called into question the entire logic of the Cold War. If the CIA was indistinguishable from the KGB, then little remained of the moral high ground that had guided the anti-communist West for a generation. Popular culture reflected this new paranoia. In fiction, James Bond, the dashing symbol of Western espionage in the 1960s, now had to compete on the bookshelves with the likes of Yurasis Dragon, the psychopathic ex-Nazi who ran an ultra-secret counter-intelligence organization for the U.S. government in the best-selling *The Eiger Sanction*. Hollywood contributed a spate of conspiracy thrillers that drew directly on the revelations of black ops in the Church Report. Sydney Pollack's *Three Days of the Condor* epitomized the genre. Released in the fall of 1975 and starring Robert Redford, the film follows a naive, low-level CIA researcher as he attempts to find out why "the Company" gunned down all of his co-workers and sent an assassin out after him.

Politically, the impact of the Church Committee's findings was to strengthen the already considerable post-Vietnam resolve of the U.S. Congress not to allow the president—*any* president—a free hand in the conduct of American foreign policy. Early in 1976, President Ford issued an executive order prohibiting political assassination. Later the same year, his soon-to-be successor, Jimmy Carter, appealed to Americans to "set a standard within the community of nations of courage, compassion, integrity, and dedication to basic human rights and freedoms." Gentle and soft-spoken, Carter seemed to personify the catharsis through which the United States was passing. "I was deeply troubled," he later recalled, "by the lies our people had been told; our exclusion from the shaping of American political and military policy in Vietnam, Cambodia, Chile, and other countries; and other embarrassing activities of our government, such as the CIA's role in plotting murder and other crimes." Henry Kissinger, on the other hand, who as secretary of state bore much of the brunt of Senator Church's exposé, never saw the committee's work as anything but tragic. It exaggerated both the recklessness and the lack of accountability of U.S. intelligence, he claimed. It soured morale in the intelligence community and "blighted" the lives of many "distinguished public servants." And above all, it severely constrained America's ability to act in the world. "The intelligence investigations were but one act in the drama by which, starting with Vietnam, the United States struggled to come to grips with an imperfect world it could neither abandon nor dominate," Kissinger reflected in 1999. The result was institutional paralysis and "self-flagellation."

The depth of the paralysis in U.S. foreign policy described by the Henry Kissinger was demonstrated decisively on December 19, 1975. On that day, in a vote of 54–22, the Senate rejected President Ford's request for $28 million to sustain America's covert-action program in Angola. The margin of loss in the House of Representatives was even larger, at 323–99. After Vietnam, said many senators, they were not about to sanction yet another secret war in a part of the world that had nothing to do with the national interests of the United States (and that most Americans could not find on a map). "The war in Angola represents the first test of American foreign policy after Vietnam," said Democratic Senator Birch Bayh. "Unfortunately, our performance to date indicates that we have not learned from our mistakes. Rather than recognizing our limitations and analyzing our interests, we are again plunging into a conflict in a far cor-

ner of the world as if we believed it was still our mission to serve as police-
man of the world." Senator Edward Kennedy agreed. "If ever there is a
'domino effect,'" he observed, "it is how covert activities can easily fall
into overt involvement and long-term commitments. The American people will not tolerate this. The United States must avoid this in Angola."
Here was the first and most decisive assertion of the new mantra in U.S.
foreign policy: no more Vietnams.

———

In marked contrast to Cold War milestones like the fall of Saigon in 1975
and the Soviet invasion of Afghanistan four years later, the conflict in
Angola remains largely unknown in North America. Like much of Africa,
Angola was a place of no apparent consequence to most Westerners until
the mid-1970s, and hence one that Western media had no interest in
covering. Not until thousands of Cuban combat troops were discovered
in Angola in November 1975, in fact, did North Americans begin to take
a serious interest in the civil war there. And when the crisis appeared
to have blown over just four months later, Angola fell off their radar
screens once again. Yet the importance of the Angolan crisis to the Cold
War world was enormous. It represented the death knell of détente, for
one thing. For another, it fundamentally altered Cuba's relations with
the West, demonstrating to a thunderstruck world that Fidel Castro was
hardly the paper tiger he had seemed in the early 1970s.

Only recently, with the declassification of State Department documents under the Freedom of Information Act, have historians been able
to piece together what actually happened in Angola in 1975–76. And as
Professor Piero Gleijeses of Johns Hopkins University has shown in his
masterful book, *Conflicting Missions*, Fidel Castro's version of events was
much closer to the truth than Henry Kissinger's.

In April 1974, a military coup in Portugal overthrew the government of Prime Minister Marcello Caetano. The victorious junta moved
immediately to decolonize Angola (along with Portugal's other African

territories), which opened the country up to a local three-way power struggle. The Popular Movement for the Liberation of Angola (MPLA) was led by Agostinho Neto, a medical doctor and poet who espoused "an eclectic interpretation of Marxism" and who would personally inspire Fidel Castro's solidarity with Angola. Arrayed against Neto's MPLA were the National Union for the Total Independence of Angola (UNITA), led by Jonas Savimbi, and the National Front for the Liberation of Angola (the FNLA), led by Holden Roberto. In January 1975, Portugal signed an agreement with all three organizations, the Alvor Accord, through which Angola would be governed by a Portuguese high commissioner until November 11, 1975. A transitional coalition government was to have been organized in the meanwhile, a constituent assembly elected and a president named. But the accord was doomed from the start. Within months of its signing, Angola dissolved into civil war.

The Cubans had dabbled in Angola in the mid-1960s. Che Guevara spent many weeks in sub-Saharan Africa in late 1964 working with liberation movements there. But after Guevara's death in 1967, Cuba's interest in Africa had waned. The American presence in Angola also dated back to 1964, when a consular office and a CIA station were opened in the capital Luanda. At that time, the United States placed Holden Roberto of the FNLA on a $6,000-per-year retainer for intelligence-gathering purposes, a salary that rose to $10,000 per month by mid-1974.

In July 1975, Henry Kissinger's "40 Committee" (a subcommittee of the National Security Council that advised the president on clandestine programs) designed a program of covert action against Neto's MPLA. President Ford approved the operation, code-named IAFEATURE, authorizing $6 million in aid for Roberto and Savimbi on the grounds that they were "sympathetic to the West." Another $18.7 million followed before the end of the summer. The first shipment of American arms arrived in Angola in late July, along with the CIA's own military experts, sent to train FNLA and UNITA officers. In early August 1975, South Africa, which was also hostile to the MPLA, sent troops thirty miles inside Angola ostensibly to protect a hydroelectric project it had financed. (The Americans worked alongside officers from the South African intelligence force, although they denied it.) At roughly the same time, the Soviets began shipping arms to the MPLA. Britain, France, Zaire, Zambia, China and North Korea made their own contributions to the various factions in the civil war, turning Angola into "a cockpit of covert operations," as journalist Murray Marder put it.

Believing that American funding of the enemy FNLA was "massive," Agostinho Neto asked Fidel Castro several times over the spring of 1975 for one hundred military officers to help train his MPLA troops. Castro was slow to respond but in July offered 430 such officers, telling Neto that anything less could not accomplish the task of training thousands of Angolans in mere months. Castro also appealed to Leonid Brezhnev for increased Soviet support of Neto. Brezhnev, then in the midst of disarmament talks with the United States, was lukewarm on the idea. The Cuban advisers arrived in Luanda and other Angolan cities in early October 1975, where they immediately established four Centros de Instrucción Revolucionaria (CIRs). One group of Cuban officers was unexpectedly drawn into combat almost immediately, helping the MPLA fend off an FNLA attack at Morro da Cal.

Even with the backing of the United States, the FNLA and UNITA continued to lose ground to Neto's MPLA on the battlefield. Independence day in November drew closer. Facing the prospect of an MPLA victory, South Africa invaded Angola on October 14. Calling its invading army "Zulu," the South Africans pressed northward toward Luanda, meeting only minimal resistance. Cuban officers were again involved directly in the fighting. MPLA claims that South Africa had invaded went unheard or disbelieved in the West, in some measure because press coverage of the fighting was so poor. (The South African government used its strict security laws to forbid the national press from reporting that its troops were advancing into Angola.) By the first week of November 1975, Zulu was within striking distance of Luanda. It was then, on November 4, that Fidel Castro decided to send an artillery regiment and a 652-strong battalion of Cuba's elite Special Forces to Angola.

In late November, President Ford approved another $7 million for IAFEATURE, which brought the total U.S. commitment to approximately $32 million. The new money cleaned out the CIA contingency fund, which meant that the president now had to consult the U.S. Congress for additional funding. As noted above, when Ford did so in mid-December 1975, he was stonewalled. The South Africans, who fully expected to be backed by the United States, were stunned by the Senate vote to cut off funding. So were the French, who were also providing aid to the FNLA and UNITA. Meanwhile, the North American press had by this time fully exposed both the CIA's clandestine war in Angola and South Africa's secret invasion, weakening Ford's position even further. American policy makers had bungled Angola, most commentators agreed, not only by completely underestimating the Cubans but by positioning the United States as "the collaborator" of racist Pretoria. Fidel Castro took full advantage of the debacle. In a major speech before a million cheering Cubans on December 22, 1975, he said that Cuba was "fulfilling an elementary internationalist duty" in supporting the MPLA. "We shall defend our African brothers," he shouted. "Let the South African racists and the Yankee imperialists know it!"

By late December 1975, there were thirty-five hundred to four thousand Cuban troops in Angola, a number roughly equal to the three thousand South Africans. In one of the most dramatic and decisive engagements of the conflict, the Cubans stopped the South African advance into Luanda toward the end of the year. The Ford administration was incredulous. Neither Henry Kissinger nor the U.S. intelligence establishment had even entertained the possibility of Cuban intervention in Angola. They simply assumed that the South Africans, in company with U.S.-backed FNLA and UNITA forces, would roll into Luanda before the world had even noticed. Facing stiff resistance from the Cubans in the field and the apparent abandonment of the cause by the United States, South Africa decided to withdraw. By early February 1976, it had retreated almost to the southern border of Angola. Both UNITA and the FNLA were on the verge of collapse. In mid-February, France and then most other Western nations, including Canada, officially recognized the MPLA as the government of the People's Republic of Angola. In March, the last of the South African troops pulled out of Angola, just as the UN Security Council voted 9–0 to name South Africa the aggressor in the conflict.

Throughout the four-month drama, the U.S. State Department painted the Cubans as puppets of the Soviets—a characterization that accorded with what was known or suspected in the West about Russian support for Third World revolution. America's allies, including a great many Canadians, accepted this interpretation of Angola unquestioningly. The idea that Cuba had gone to Africa on its own seemed inconceivable.

———

The Angolan crisis brought new and unforeseen pressures down on Pierre Trudeau, peaking as it did just weeks before he was scheduled to become the first Western leader to visit Castro's Cuba in late January 1976. When officials at External Affairs and at the Canadian Embassy in Havana began planning the trip in 1974, it appeared that Cuba's readmission into the international community was only a matter of time. Their working premise was that Trudeau's journey to Mexico, Cuba and Venezuela would strengthen Canada's relations throughout the Caribbean and Latin America—an objective that had long been "associated with the advent of the Trudeau government," as one of them put it. In light of Trudeau's earlier move to normalize Canada's relations with Beijing, his announcement that he would visit Havana seemed almost anti-climactic.

When the Angolan crisis burst onto the world's front pages late in 1975, however, the diplomatic implications of the prime minister's forthcoming trip grew suddenly momentous. External Affairs officials acknowledged that Fidel Castro's intervention in Angola imperilled the goodwill that had been building on both sides of the Cuban-Canadian relationship in the Trudeau era. Faced with the prospect of cancelling a visit that had been on the books for almost two years, something they had good reason to believe the prime minister would be reluctant to do, Trudeau's normally circumspect aides adopted a blunt strategy of telling reporters that if the visit went ahead as scheduled it would in no way represent an endorsement of Cuba's "African adventure." Angola had become a "touchy issue," one official observed just days before Trudeau was scheduled to depart. "But there will be no attempt to duck it. We disapprove of this type of involvement."

Canada's ambassador to Cuba, James Hyndman, who had a bird's-eye view of the Cuban perspective on the upcoming state visit, believed that cancellation would be unfortunate for both Canada and Cuba. Castro had said almost nothing in public about Angola, and thus the precise nature of the Cuban involvement in the conflict remained an open question as far as the ambassador was concerned. "Was Russia behind the Cuban action," he wondered, "or was Russia reluctantly involved in something which was very much Cuban?" Posted to Havana in November 1975, Hyndman had served for several years prior to that as Canada's ambassador to the USSR. Even before he left Moscow, in fact, he had begun trying to clarify the Soviet role in Angola. (His own suspicions that the USSR was not behind the Cuban intervention were later confirmed. "It turned out that this was primarily Fidel's doing," he recalled, "and that it caused a lot of worries in Moscow.") As a seasoned veteran of the Canadian diplomatic corps, Hyndman knew that there was a risk in expressing his own views too forcefully to his colleagues back in Ottawa, especially on the question of whether to cancel the state visit. "It occurred to me that my trying to have a direct impact on that decision would be resented in Ottawa," he recalled. Not wanting to fuel a backlash from the prime minister's political opponents, Hyndman sought instead to impress upon his colleagues just how important Trudeau's visit was from the Cuban perspective. "In doing so I was perhaps making it a little less easy to back out."

That Trudeau's timing could have been better did not escape the notice of his critics, or even of his allies. "Few of Prime Minister Pierre Trudeau's recent trips have been as ill-considered as his journey to Cuba this week," announced the normally supportive *Toronto Star* just days before the prime minister's departure. In view of the crisis in Angola, "Trudeau will have no choice but to tell the Cuban leader that this is dangerous mischief-making that is already hurting world peace." The *Star* accurately distilled the dilemma. Trudeau would either have to risk "sharp frictions" with Cuba by asserting Canada's disapproval or "gloss over" the issue of Angola and thus betray "both his own foreign policy and the Canadian public." The risk to Canada was that protesting the Cuban role in Angola would offend Castro and end up damaging relations with Cuba. The risk to Trudeau himself was far greater—as later events would prove. However much the raison d'être of the visit was consistent with the recent thaw in Cuban-American relations, it was evident that Trudeau might well get caught out on a limb. He might end up welcoming Castro back into the international fold at precisely the moment when the rest of the Western world was again writing him off.

Meanwhile, back in Havana, as the official visit of the Canadian prime minister loomed, Fidel Castro was doing his best to brief himself on the man who would be his guest for four days. Cuban authorities knew, probably from Canadian sources, that Pierre Trudeau had visited Cuba at least once in the early years of the Revolution, and also that he had once cut cane in the Cuban countryside. But, because their information was sketchy, Castro's aides appear to have conflated Trudeau's 1949 and 1964 trips, concluding that he had come to the island in the mid-1960s as part of a Venceremos Brigade. Cuban intelligence operators had been involved in the organization of these brigades, maintaining detailed files on all of their North American participants, and so Castro requested of both his G2 security police and his Dirección General de Inteligencia (General Intelligence Directorate, or DGI) that they dig out their files on Trudeau. When his security personnel reported that there were no such files, the *Comandante* expressed his displeasure in no uncertain terms.

There is no question that Pierre Trudeau recognized the gravity of his decision to visit Castro's Cuba. The state visit would be the first by the leader of a NATO country since the imposition of the U.S. embargo in 1960. The eyes of the world seldom fixed their gaze on the travels of Canadian prime ministers, but for three days in January 1976 they would. The Angolan crisis alone had upped the ante. Trudeau embraced the paradox. He knew that he was doing something extraordinary but, in typical fashion, he insisted on camouflaging the high drama of the moment with nonchalant understatement punctuated by his famously casual shrug. He knew that he was about to spend three days walking the razor's edge but he did not let on.

On Friday, January 23, the Canadian prime minister, his wife and baby son, his chief foreign policy adviser and various other members of his inner circle boarded an Armed Forces Boeing 707 and set their course for the Caribbean. It would be a wild and woolly ride, even by Trudeau's standards.

PART TWO

THREE NIGHTS IN HAVANA

6

¡Bienvenido!
Pierre and Margaret in Latin America

When the Trudeaus left Ottawa, the city was bitterly cold. The weather in central Canada had been unusually severe in the weeks before the state visit. Ontario had seen freezing rain, heavy snow and temperatures so low that they were threatening to freeze the ducks that populated the province's many waterways and ponds. The Trudeaus' plane was delayed because minus-thirty-one-degree temperatures had caused the fuel line to freeze. "Bloody cold," Pierre remarked to reporters as he boarded, accompanied by Margaret, Michel and their nanny. The baby, destined to be the media star of the trip, was already the centre of attention. On board the plane with Michel in his arms, Trudeau turned to the press and gave an uncharacteristically warm smile. "Trudeau Carries the Baby" announced the headlines the next day.

By 1976, when she accompanied Pierre on his state visit to Cuba, Margaret was drifting beyond the point where she believed she could reclaim Canadians' affections. More than this, though it was not known publicly, she and Pierre both felt that their marriage was faltering. Thus, as if it were not sufficient to try to bring some semblance of normality to Fidel Castro's relations with the Western world, Pierre Trudeau set for himself a second goal of marital reconciliation. He would allow Margaret to accompany him to Havana and there, in one of the world's sexiest cities, they might rediscover their passion for one another.

—•—

As Pierre Trudeau noted in his *Memoirs*, 1970 was "the year I fell in love with a beautiful girl." He added, "On March 4, 1971, we were married in Vancouver. The romance took the press by surprise, which is the way we wanted it." That was about as much as he ever said publicly about his love life. His bride, on the other hand, said plenty.

Margaret was the fourth of five girls born to James and Kathleen Sinclair. Her father, a no-nonsense Rhodes Scholar and strict disciplinarian, had served as fisheries minister in Louis St. Laurent's cabinet. Much would be made of Margaret's dyed-in-the-wool Liberal pedigree, as if somehow her marriage to Pierre Trudeau was arranged by the backroom power-brokers in the party. But there was nothing partisan about their first encounters, or about her parents' dim view of their budding relationship. ("Don't be the mistress of a politician twice your age," she recalled her mother warning her. "Pierre will never marry you.") Margaret and Pierre met by chance when she was on vacation with her family in Tahiti over Christmas 1967. He was water-skiing, she was sunning herself on a raft. She later described the encounter as an intellectual exchange, in which they discussed "student rebellion and Plato and revolution." But the truth seems far less lofty. She was a beautiful young woman in a bathing suit and he, quite famously, had a weakness for beautiful young women. The extent of her political worldliness can be gauged by the fact that, when she returned to the beach, her mother had to tell her that she had been chatting with the Liberal justice minister. Later in the same holiday, Pierre asked Margaret, with characteristic shyness, if she would go deep-sea fishing with him. She said she would, and then casually stood him up. He was smitten.

At the time of this first chance encounter, Margaret was an undergraduate student at Simon Fraser University (SFU). She was a charter member of "the class of '65," a cohort of students caught between the staid, conformist world of their parents and the radical youth counterculture that was just about to explode on North American campuses. At sixteen, she had represented her high school on the teen-fashion council of the local Bay store, where she spent Saturday mornings listening to catalogue models talk about "grooming and poise and charm." As a first-year student at SFU in 1965, she remained a model of "middle-class respectability," as she later put it, dating a football player and dutifully attending classes. In her second year, things began to change. She dropped the jock in favour of a long-haired, bearded teaching assistant who exposed her to radical politics and classical music, and set her on a path of open rebellion against her father, the "Establishment" and other symbols of authority. She smoked pot, listened to the Beatles, experimented with sex and hallucinogenic drugs, and set about—in the parlance of the day—to find herself.

In this quest, she failed. She remained an aloof observer of the student-power movement that was then turning Simon Fraser inside-out, and she was indifferent to the Vietnam War. In truth, Margaret was incapable, then and later, of exorcising the pre-feminist straightjacket of her formative years. Well into her adult life, she could be fiercely competitive and catty where men were concerned, preoccupied with clothes and beauty, and hostage to her own fairy-tale fantasies. On a post-grad soul-searching trip with some hippies in Morocco, she recalled feeling "square, critical and much, much too clean." When she returned to the churning, dynamic Canada of the late 1960s, she became confused and, as she admitted herself, depressed. She had a foot in each world but felt at home in neither, too bourgeois for the hippies and "too hippy" for her family and friends. It was inevitable that she would carry this inner turmoil into her marriage with Pierre Trudeau. And to anybody with an even passing acquaintance with him, it was equally obvious that Pierre was ill-equipped emotionally to help her resolve it. He, too, had a foot in both worlds, part Outrement establishment, part bohemian freethinker. But in typical fashion, he revelled in these contradictions and navigated them with ease. The result, practically from the moment they wed until the day that he died, was a deeply passionate but tumultuous love affair that transcended rather than bridged the great gulfs between them, one that did nothing to bring Margaret the inner peace she so desperately longed for.

———

By the time he met Margaret, Pierre Trudeau had grown obsessive in his need for privacy and solitude. As a statesman, he accepted social obligations only when they were unavoidable. As a husband, his insistence on privacy was so absolute that he placed "an embargo" on Margaret. "I was absolutely taboo," she later recalled, "not only for his office, but for everybody. No one was to come near me, no one was to pester me, or ask me questions. I was to give no interviews." Trudeau disdained prying, abhorred gossip and refused to discuss the people he knew even with Margaret. Indeed, she has said, "I learned far more about him from his family and the old friends he made in his university days than I ever learned from him." His best friends—Jacques Hébert and Gérard Pelletier, for example—respected his privacy and kept their personal relationship with him out of the public eye. Canada's ambassador to Cuba, James Hyndman, who had known Pierre Trudeau since his student days, recalled his public persona as sphinx-like. In conversation he would sit in extended silence, betraying no emotion or information, so much so that he made others uncomfortable in the extreme.

Pierre was "destined for eternal solitude," Margaret would later say. Not only did he prefer his own company to a gregarious social life but, in contrast to his public persona as a tough politician, he was deeply concerned not to hurt people. His reputation as a playboy was myth. As a bachelor, he enjoyed the company of women but he was never casual about his romantic liaisons and even less casual about sex (in part because, as a devout Catholic, he abhorred birth control). His love for solo athletic challenges, especially canoeing, enhanced both his love for solitude and his ascetic streak. He claimed to be indifferent to material wealth. "I want to be as little as possible a slave to material things," he once said. "To be able to appreciate a meal, a good book, a holiday, is marvellous. But to suffer, if one is deprived of them, is to be a slave to material things."

The most striking theme in *Beyond Reason*, Margaret Trudeau's 1979 memoir, is Pierre's indifference to her isolation and loneliness. It began even before they were married, he working the long hours of the prime minister, she working a dull job in the Manpower and Immigration Department and cultivating virtually no friendships in Ottawa. At dinner parties, not only would Pierre's invited guests not include Margaret in their conversations but they would converse in French, a language she did not speak. Why Pierre did not make a greater effort to include her is not clear. She seemed to believe that he was oblivious to her discomfort partly because he could be so intense and partly because she was so good at disguising it. What is certain is that, from their courtship forward, Pierre showed absolutely no inclination to treat her as his intellectual equal. They never discussed his work as prime minister. "I don't even know the work he does most of the time," Margaret once acknowledged. "We don't discuss politics and his day at the office and I never look at his papers or his boxes, or, we leave each other alone when we're working." She was invited to participate in political life only once, during the election campaign of 1974, when it was thought that she would soften his public reputation as "arrogant and aloof."

It is never easy to see what makes the chemistry between lovers. In the case of Margaret and Pierre, this seemed to be something of a mystery even to themselves. It was commonly said of Trudeau at the time that he had seduced Margaret, mainly because he wanted children. She confirmed that there was some truth in this. He had reached age fifty, achieved every conceivable career goal he set for himself and was "saddened every time he looked around at his friends and saw them with children already grown up or even with small grandchildren around." She described Trudeau as "confused" when he proposed marriage, the only time she ever saw him "out of full control." Even so, he treated their engagement as a negotiation. Some of his conditions were non-negotiable. "I had to convince him," Margaret recalled, "that I would be a good, faithful wife to him; that I would give up drugs, and stop being so flighty." Pierre also insisted on learning everything about her past, in case he was ever blackmailed about it in the future. Margaret agreed to it all. "I didn't care where, how or when we married," she recalled. "I just knew I wanted to be with him."

Margaret believed that, in marrying Pierre Trudeau and realizing her own naive fairy-tale dream, she could make herself his confidante. "I would marry Pierre and turn his cold, lonely life into a warm, happy one," she said. "I would listen to his problems, and understand him when no one else did." After their marriage collapsed, she was extremely hard on herself for this rationalization—and so were many Canadians. And yet her instincts about their relationship were correct. She was—most obviously at his deathbed and at the death of their son Michel—Pierre Trudeau's refuge, a vital source of comfort and solace during the handful of times in his life when the world dealt him a cruel blow and he lost the ability to control events. This was true even before they were married. The most moving passage in Margaret's memoir recounts the agonizing grief Trudeau felt when Pierre Laporte was murdered by his FLQ kidnappers in October

1970. Faced with the numbing realization that his hardline approach to the terrorists had ended in the murder of an innocent man, Trudeau wept openly. "Tears pouring down my own face," she recalled, "I tried to comfort him. I knew that my strength for him lay in my innocence, my ignorance of politics. I couldn't understand the political implications, but I could love him." For all of her later recriminations, she had hit upon the key to their lifelong love. She provided him with the one thing he could not provide himself and would never ask of anybody else: sanctuary.

Thus, while Pierre could be astoundingly indifferent to Margaret's isolation, and callous in his disregard for her anxiety about being the wife of the prime minister, it is also true that he could take great delight in her spontaneity and warmth, even when it took the form of diplomatic faux pas or an ill-considered lapse in judgment. During the 1974 campaign, for example, Margaret gave an impromptu speech to a crowd at Humboldt, Saskatchewan, dispensing with what she called the "tedious" themes of the speech that had been written for Pierre. She spoke freely and easily, pleasing the crowd. But she incurred such hostility from the Liberal entourage that they did not speak to her all the way back to Ottawa. Pierre, however, "just laughed." He thought her speech "wonderful." There were also times when Margaret found herself in a position to make a genuine contribution. In 1973, for instance, while touring a Beijing maternity hospital, she discovered that the Chinese knew nothing of the inoculation for RH incompatibility between mothers and their babies—a simple but life-saving shot that she had received at the birth of Justin. She mentioned this to the Canadian deputy minister of health, who was also part of the Canadian delegation, and he subsequently had the vaccine sent directly from the RH Disease Centre in Winnipeg to Beijing.

———

In the wake of the 1974 election, Margaret's behaviour became increasingly erratic under the influence of what she later called "severe emotional distress." Out of the blue, she announced to Pierre that she was flying to Paris. She told him that she wanted to brush up on her French, but in fact she went in search of an old lover. From Paris she ventured to Greece and then to New York, where she claimed to have met and fallen in love in one night with an American. When she returned home, she confessed her affair to Pierre in a fit of exhaustion and rage, tearing off her clothes and threatening to stab herself with a kitchen knife. "You're sick," she recalled him saying. At Pierre's urging, she checked herself into the psychiatric wing of a Montreal hospital. There, with the help of a sympathetic doctor, she dampened her suicidal impulses and regained her equilibrium. In the aftermath of the episode, about which she spoke publicly and without inhibition, she was praised by mental-health sufferers and their advocates for her honesty and openness.

Margaret Trudeau's many critics were hard on her not only for what she did but for who she was. It is true that she would leave Pierre and her three young sons in 1977 to find herself, a decision for which she fully expected to pay a high price in public condemnation and, not surprisingly, did. What is unfair about the steady stream of scorn she faced as her mental health declined and her marriage dissolved is how little acknowledgement was made of the impossible circumstances in which she found herself. When she left Pierre, in 1977, she was only twenty-eight. She had gone in scant months from flower child to Canada's "first lady." When she and Pierre went on official state business, she was always the youngest "wife" by a long measure—usually the age of the other wives' daughters. She recalled visiting France in 1974, for example, and attending a reception held by Mme. Chirac, the prime minister's wife. "The guests were all women, the wives of cabinet ministers, diplomats and members of parliament, and, oh boy, did they condescend to me," she wrote. "I was the youngest by twenty-five years, and they made me feel like a stupid, ill-informed, clumsy, illiterate child." Political power was concentrated almost exclusively in the hands of male presidents and prime ministers, and political wives were consigned the monotonous routines of cutting ribbons and serving as their husbands' haute couture social ornaments. Margaret declared bluntly that she was fed up with this ornamental role—and she was not alone. "Frankly, I just wasn't interested in dental hospitals, or zoos, or centers for adult education," she said. "They bored me almost to tears. They bored all the other wives too. I cannot see a picture of a prime minister's wife opening a new hospital or civic center today without conjuring up for myself the murderous thoughts that must be going through her head under the widebrimmed hat." Try as she might, she seldom pleased the foreign leaders with whom she and Pierre had so much obligatory contact. She never mastered the protocols of being the prime minister's wife. And above all, being young, inexperienced and female, she failed to persuade her many Canadian detractors that she was anything other than a precocious flower child who was completely out of her depth.

———

The decision to include Margaret and Michel on the state visit to Latin America was, in fact, urged on Pierre by Margaret herself. Michel, not yet even four months of age, had become a complicating factor for the trip planners at the Canadian Embassy, since he was breast-feeding and in need of round-the-clock care. Documents at External Affairs suggest that he and Margaret were included on the trip only grudgingly, and only because Pierre, once persuaded himself, could not be talked out of it. Some of Trudeau's biographers have suggested that, by the time of the state visit, little remained of his affection for Margaret. James Hyndman disagrees. "What struck me as important," he has recalled of their relationship at that time, "was that Pierre was very, very sensitive to her, doing a great deal to cope with the pressures that were on her, and to keep the two of them together. He was still in love with her." For her part, Margaret's only worry was that Michel might get sick in Latin America. She was assured by her pediatrician that as long as he was breast-feeding he would be at little risk. Pierre insisted that Margaret be allowed to take a nanny. She selected a woman named Diane, "the most hippy member of our staff," she later recalled, "who I felt was just the kind of friend I needed in Latin America." After baby Michel, Diane's hot pants would prove to be the most newsworthy aspect of the state visit in some quarters.

The Trudeaus' first stop was Mexico City. When they arrived, the sun was shining and the temperature was a balmy twenty-four degrees Celsius. Margaret, who had been feeling isolated and depressed in Ottawa, later recalled feeling unexpectedly euphoric upon arriving in Mexico. "It was like coming home," she said, "magic and drugs, all my old stomping grounds."

The Trudeaus were welcomed with an elaborate formal reception on the airport tarmac. As they disembarked from the plane, they were serenaded by sombrero-clad mariachi musicians and well-wishers throwing flower petals. Roughly three thousand children and public servants had been drafted by Mexican President Luis Echeverría Álvarez to welcome the prime minister and his family. Banging drums and tambourines and chanting "Can-a-da, May-hi-co!" they formed a jubilant gauntlet through which Pierre, Margaret and Michel passed. The pathway over the tarmac was sprinkled with red and white carnations. A presidential guard had been assembled. Six army field guns fired a deafening salute overhead. Pierre—decked out in a dark suit with a massive white rose in his lapel—was mobbed by Mexicans. He beamed as he shook hands and exchanged pleasantries with some of the people in the crowd. The prime minister, who had been brushing up on his Spanish in advance of the trip, spoke almost no English or French on the day of his arrival.

President Echeverría was then, in January 1976, a highly respected statesman, part reformer and part nationalist. Among his achievements as president were the introduction of programs to modernize Mexican agriculture and public works, and measures to strengthen Mexican control of the national economy. He had served as Mexico's secretary of the interior in the 1960s, establishing a reputation for uncompromising toughness in his handling of student demonstrators during the 1968 Olympic games in Mexico City. This toughness would later be his undoing: in 2003, Echeverría was named as a conspirator in a cover-up of the government's responsibility for the killing of some of those demonstrators. Trudeau had first met Echeverría in 1973, during the president's state visit to Canada. At the time of Trudeau's return visit three years later, it was widely rumoured that the president's aggressive promotion of a "new economic order" for the Third World was at least partly motivated by his ambition to become secretary general of the UN. Echeverría would leave the Mexican presidency in December 1976.

The Trudeaus left the airfield in a limousine accompanied by Echeverría, after which the president and the prime minister shared a formal lunch. Trudeau toasted his host, saying that he looked forward to strengthened relations between Canada and Mexico. He spoke of Canadians' sympathy for the aspirations of Latin America and the developing world in general, and praised Echeverría's idea of a new economic order. He spoke as well of the need to limit the proliferation of nuclear weapons—one of the priority objectives of his Latin American tour—asserting that "a failure to overcome them may well seal the fate of mankind." Throughout the visit, Echeverría made it clear that collaborating with Canada to divert trade away from the United States was one of his top priorities. Trudeau agreed, underscoring Canada's interest in *contrapesos* (counterweights) to its dominant trading relationship with the United States. But whether a dramatic expansion of Canadian-Mexican trade was plausible at that time remains in doubt. Most Canadian critics of the visit took the view that, despite Trudeau's best efforts, Mexico's state-run economy and notorious red tape would remain serious impediments to Canadian business. When Echeverría's public criticisms of the United States got to be too much for his Canadian guests, Trudeau was forced to do damage control. Canada intended to maintain "very strong and friendly relations" with the "friendly but enormous giant that exists next to us," he told the press with uncharacteristic obsequiousness.

Echeverría and Trudeau tacitly agreed to steer clear of controversial subjects in foreign affairs, but the issue of Angola could not be avoided. Here Echeverría got the upper hand, stating firmly that Mexico was opposed to the intervention of any outside forces in the conflict—a reference to the Cuban role in the war. "Leave the people of Angola alone," Echeverría said. "Leave all of us alone in our independent situations." Forced to respond to the Angolan situation in light of his imminent visit to Cuba, Trudeau reiterated that Canada did not support Castro's policy of intervention in Angola. He defended his decision to go through with the meeting with the Cuban leader, in fact, on the grounds that it was "more advantageous" to the West to maintain relations with Cuba than to "see it settle exclusively and uniquely in the Soviet orbit."

While Pierre Trudeau was buried in formal talks with the president, Margaret was delighted to spend virtually all of her time in Mexico with his wife, Maria Esther Echeverría. Of all of the wives of heads of state she had met, Margaret recalled, Señora Echeverría was the first "who was not only charming and motherly but an extremely hard worker." She was especially impressed by the "fleet of mobile health units" Señora Echeverría managed herself. As much as Margaret detested the ornamental role "political wives" were expected to play on official visits, she was on this occasion eminently gracious. On Saturday, the second day of the visit, while Pierre was touring Mexico's state-owned Petroleum Institute with the president, Margaret accompanied Señora Echeverría on a visit to a government-run home for girls, telling the press how impressed she was. Later, at a state luncheon, Margaret gave an impromptu speech in which she sang the praises of her hostess, reminding the assembled dignitaries of the important role she had played earlier that year at the International Women's Year conference in Mexico City. Although Pierre later expressed his "surprise and delight" that Margaret had spoken so freely at the luncheon, it was obvious that some of his aides were mortified by her casual indifference to diplomatic protocol.

On Sunday, the third and final day of the Mexican visit, the Canadian entourage was taken to Cancun for what Trudeau aides called "rest and recuperation" before undertaking the "gruelling" Cuban leg of the tour. There, the Trudeaus were scheduled to explore the Mayan ruins at

Palenque on the Yucatan peninsula. Pierre was so enthusiastic about this excursion that he had personally added it to his itinerary months earlier. On the highway from Mexico City to Palenque were rows of posters exclaiming, "*¡Bienvenido Pierre Trudeau!*"

When the Trudeaus got to Palenque, Margaret did something unusually reckless even for her. Two young people, old friends of hers whom the media labelled "a pair of hitchhiking hippies," had heard about her official trip to the ruins and managed to persuade security personnel to allow them access to her. She was "overjoyed" at seeing her friends and, according to the press, eager to introduce them to Pierre. What Pierre did not know was that Margaret had deliberately left her bag unattended, and one of her friends had stashed a baggie of peyote mushrooms inside it. Her bodyguard witnessed the drop and approached Margaret immediately. "I think you should know, Mrs. Trudeau," he said, "that that girl has slipped something into your bag." Margaret casually removed from the handbag some cookies she herself had packed, saying to the guard, "Thank you so much. Those must be the cookies she told me about." Later the same evening, she treated herself to a "secret taste" of the mushrooms. This was, without question, an extraordinary risk for the wife of a visiting head of state to take. If discovered, the embarrassment to Trudeau, to the government and especially to the Canadian people would have vastly outweighed whatever secret pleasures the hallucinogenics had afforded.

By Monday, January 26, the day the Trudeaus departed Mexico for Havana, the Mexican stopover was being openly characterized by Canadian officials as frustrating. Prime Minister Trudeau and President Echeverría issued the obligatory joint communiqué agreeing to expand Mexican-Canadian cultural and trade relations. At their final press conference, both leaders affirmed their commitment to amicable relations with the United States. Trudeau's aides were annoyed with the ceremony because Echeverría upstaged the prime minister with "long-winded answers and policy statements." One official complained that the president had conducted himself in a similar manner during the private talks with Trudeau, boring him to tears with a one-hour harangue about how the United States "stole" Texas from Mexico. By the time the Trudeaus were actually in Havana, Canadian aides were speaking even more bluntly. The Canadian delegation had been "exploited" by Echeverría's "grandstanding," said one official, which had the effect of putting Trudeau on the defensive and of making him extremely leery of being played in a similar fashion by Fidel Castro.

The big story coming out of the Mexican visit had nothing to do with diplomacy or trade. Journalists seemed only too happy to report on the every move of baby Michel Trudeau, claiming that he had completely stolen his father's thunder. No detail of the baby's daily ministrations was beneath their notice—the Canadian ambassador's wife giving him a bottle, the skimpy clothing of his nanny, the spectacle of Trudeau's RCMP bodyguards running around with cribs and baby chairs. While Pierre was exploring the Palenque ruins in private, reporters descended on Margaret and Michel on a Cancun beach. Margaret was cast in her usual role, part cranky matron, part superficial flower girl. Unable to get away from the camera-wielding press, Margaret exploded at them. "You make me so bloody mad," she fumed. "I feel like punching you right in the nose."

———

On the last evening of his stay in Mexico, when the Trudeaus were relaxing in Cancun, the prime minister met with Canadian journalists to prep them for the Cuba leg of the trip. He acknowledged that the Cuban visit would be historic but insisted that it not be construed as signalling a radical shift in Canadian foreign policy nor, more to the point, as any sort of compromise of Canada's obligations to its friends and trading partners. The truth was, Trudeau ventured, that in the era of détente, with the ideological stalemate between East and West at a postwar low, his going to Cuba was really not such a big deal. "The category of people that would be shocked by this have long since been shocked by my visits to China and the Soviet Union," he said. "That happened several years ago and I don't think Canada has veered notoriously toward Communism since—and I don't think it will happen now." Trudeau was asked about how the visit might affect Canada's relations with the United States and other Western allies. "I have visited other countries before which weren't particularly American lovers," he replied, "and this didn't affect our policy."

Pierre Trudeau knew the delicacy of the situation, of course, and he understood that every nuance of the visit would be gauged against the Americans' much different approach to Cuba. There was no anti-American agenda connected with his trip, he emphasized. "Obviously people must have known that Cuba wasn't a country that was exactly in love with the United States. In the world today you don't only seek links with countries that are your exact mirror. You seek links with every-one." When pressed, Trudeau acknowledged the possibility that Fidel Castro might attempt to seize the moment to advance his own diplomatic rehabilitation. He also conceded that Angola had emerged as a thorny issue, and not one on which there was likely to be a meeting of minds. He told reporters that he would be raising the issue of Angola with the *Comandante*, and that he would be expressing Canada's displeasure with his policy. "We'll likely agree to disagree," he said with a shrug.

———

The Trudeaus flew into Havana's José Martí Airport in the late after-noon of Monday, January 26, 1976. Stepping out of the plane, they were immediately engulfed by the steamy, fragrant heat that has always made Cuba a favoured destination for Canadians in mid-winter. In the back-ground lurked the ominous forms of Soviet MIG-23 fighter jets, sitting idle on a nearby runway after escorting the prime minister's plane into Cuban airspace. (The MIGs, the most technologically advanced in the Soviet arsenal, had been presented with great fanfare by General Dimitri Krutskikn on the same tarmac exactly four years earlier.) Pierre wore a smart taupe pin-striped suit and tie, Margaret a bright and billowy yel-low dress with matching wide-brimmed hat. Baby Michel was decked out in a matching two-piece outfit, the same colour as his mother's. Fidel Castro himself was on hand to meet the Trudeaus as they descended from the plane, clad in his famous green fatigues, boots and combat cap. He wasted no time in ingratiating himself with Margaret, plying her with what she called "a stream of romantic and flowery English." (Later that evening he would tell her, "When I saw you come down the steps of the plane I told myself, 'Oh, the prime minister of Canada has a very pretty wife.'") Ambassador Hyndman was also present on the tarmac, accompanied by his charming wife, Michelle Asselin. The prime minister greeted his old friend with a familiar "Hi, Jim"—a salutation that did not escape Castro's notice.

Once they had descended the steps from the plane, Trudeau and Castro exchanged pleasantries in Spanish and then proceeded to review a Cuban military unit on the airport tarmac. The Cuban "Invasion Hymn" was played by a military band. By prior agreement, and in accordance with diplomatic tradition, only the two leaders were supposed to review the guard. Margaret, however, decided that she, too, would join in the review—a spur-of-the-moment decision that clearly embarrassed Canadian officials.

Fidel Castro's charm was beguiling to the Trudeaus from the outset. He eschewed diplomatic formality, opting instead for the casual intimacy with which he might have treated his closest friends. From the moment of the Trudeaus' arrival, the *Comandante* fawned over Michel, exuding the warm, magnetic affection for children for which he is famous in his own country. "I am very glad to have the distinguished prime minister of Canada and his lovely wife and his intelligent entourage," Castro joked during his speech at the airport. "But I want you to know that as far as I am concerned, as far as the people of Cuba are concerned, the most important visitor today is Miche." The Cuban leader had special VIP badges made for the baby and insisted on holding him whenever the opportunity arose. Twenty-four years later, when he ventured to Montreal for the funeral of Pierre Trudeau, Castro would reiterate sadly that it was his genuine fondness for baby "Miche" (pronounced Mee-chay) that had allowed him and the Trudeaus to quickly cut through the thicket of diplomatic niceties and establish a warm and familiar acquaintance. That he was pained personally at hearing of the death of Michel Trudeau in 1998 was obvious.

As the entourage left the tarmac, the Trudeaus were welcomed through a receiving line of Cuban dignitaries and then escorted to their limousine, a large Russian-built imitation Cadillac. A motorcade carried Castro and his guests into the heart of Havana. The route was flanked by two hundred and fifty thousand cheering Cubans, the largest crowd ever assembled for a visiting dignitary other than Soviet premier Leonid Brezhnev. (Castro, who certainly knows how to stage-manage a political spectacle, actually had the crowds trucked in.) Press footage captured the genuine excitement of the motorcade, with the prime minister standing in the limousine and waving to the Cuban people. On Trudeau's right stood Castro, a good five inches taller. On his left was President Osvaldo Dorticós, at one time a person of great influence in the regime but now "treated as junior" to Castro.

Once in downtown Havana, Pierre Trudeau discovered that giant-sized posters of himself had been plastered all over the city. His likeness was more in evidence than that of either Castro, José Martí or even the iconic Che Guevara. Cuban radio adopted Canadian themes as well, punctuating discussions of Canadian politics with Atlantic Canadian folk songs and Anne Murray hits.

The Trudeaus were accorded top-flight hospitality by their host. They were invited to stay in a newly expanded state guesthouse nestled in a row of mansions once owned by Havana's pre-revolutionary millionaires. The house, built of wood and stone and surrounded by dense tropical gardens, was cooled by built-in canals of flowing water. Between the warm reception Castro had given them and the idyllic setting in which they were now ensconced, Margaret was completely smitten. "This is the answer to Utopia," she enthused. "If this is revolution, it is truly marvellous."

(Canadian journalists were not so lucky. They were billeted in the dilapi-
dated Havana Libre hotel, formerly the Havana Hilton, which they took
every opportunity to criticize.) A grand state reception for five hundred
followed the Trudeaus' installation in their guesthouse. It lasted until midnight and was described as "a glittering occasion" even by North American
standards. Cuban authorities eased their usual uncompromising security
standards and allowed guests at the reception to mingle freely. No doubt
tired from the day's hectic pace, Pierre and Margaret ended up relaxing
by the swimming pool with their host until retiring. Castro continued to
charm Margaret shamelessly. "You are not only pretty," he told her poolside, "you are too intelligent for your own good."

Margaret thought Fidel Castro "a ridiculously romantic man [who]
obviously worships women." Yet at no time during the Trudeaus' visit
would he be accompanied by his own "political wife." Castro has always
refused to discuss his private life publicly, maintaining that his only true
devotion is to the people of Cuba. He is careful never to be seen in the
company of women (the only significant exception being his interpreter,
Juana García). Thus, much of what is rumoured about his romantic life
amounts to little more than gossip. What is known for certain is that in
1948 Castro married Mirta Díaz-Balart, and was divorced from her six
months later. Since then, he has had many amours—hardly surprising for
a man of eighty. He is believed to have eight children and eight grandchildren, most of them with Dalia Soto del Valle, a woman he started
seeing in the 1960s and may have married in the 1970s. Despite his reputation as a Don Juan, people close to Castro have observed that in the
company of women he is a gentleman almost to the point of prudishness.
Exactly the same thing was said of Pierre Trudeau.

What can be said for certain is that Castro has always been a great
admirer of strong, capable women and that his Revolution embraced
feminist principles long before they had become *de rigueur* in North
America. "It is clear that women need to participate in the struggle
against exploitation, against imperialism, colonialism, neocolonialism,

racism," Castro told an international women's conference in Havana in 1974. "But when the objective of national liberation is finally achieved, women must continue struggling for their own liberation within human society." Tellingly, the most important woman in his life, according to Ann Louise Bardach, author of *Cuba Confidential*, was not Mirta or any of his other romantic liaisons. She was Celia Sánchez, a fierce and courageous revolutionary he first met in 1956 and loved until her death from lung cancer in 1980. Sánchez organized anti-Batista resistance groups for Castro in the 1950s, fought in his guerrilla war, and ended up running the logistics of his entire rebel army. After the victory of the Revolution, she remained his closest confidante and protector, and one of the few people who could openly challenge his views.

Western observers speculated that Castro had staged his extraordinary welcome for the Trudeaus in an attempt to turn the state visit to his own diplomatic advantage. He had much to gain from the perception abroad that Cuba's isolation was ending. *Toronto Star* reporter Bruce Garvey described Castro as "animated" and "solicitous" around the Trudeaus, a clear sign that "he desired from the outset to imprint the visit with his own—as well as Cuba's—warmth and hospitality." Yet it appears as well that Castro's initial reaction to Pierre Trudeau and his family was one of genuine warmth, and that the normally aloof prime minister recognized it as such. Trudeau and his entourage had not forgotten Echeverría's bold manipulation of the Mexican visit, and thus they had arrived in Cuba with a good deal of apprehension that Castro might attempt an even more dramatic hijacking of the state visit. Yet, even before the official talks had begun, Trudeau was visibly awestruck by the reception he had received in Havana. "Trudeau and his wife were content to relax in the gush of Cuban hospitality," said one report, "and enjoy the immense personal charm and charisma of their host, the tall, towering figure of Castro." Within hours of their arrival, in short, the Trudeaus knew that their stay in Cuba was not likely to follow the standard, stodgy diplomatic script. Like the many Canadians who have since been seduced by the homespun charms of Havana and the warmth of Cuban hospitality, Pierre and Margaret sensed that they were in for a very special three days.

———

In planning the visit in the preceding months, Ambassador Hyndman had made it clear to the prime minister that Fidel Castro intended to be by his side for the entirety of the state visit, thus providing an opportunity for "continuous dialogue." The *Comandante* was as good as his word. ("Prime Minister Castro practically lived with his guest throughout the visit," an External Affairs memo observed after the fact.) No sooner had the Trudeaus awakened from their short night's rest than Castro himself appeared at their door to chauffeur them around Havana personally. The morning tour included a visit to the national monument to Cuba's revolutionary war dead, where the prime minister placed a ceremonial wreath. He was casually dressed in a light suit, gold tie and white running shoes—a striking contrast with the dark suits of the Cuban security officials accompanying him. Mid-morning, Trudeau, Castro and a dozen top-ranking Cuban and Canadian officials were sequestered for a formal two-hour meeting at the Palace of the Revolution. These talks, which had been on the official itinerary for months, would turn out to be the only formally scripted conversation the two leaders would have. In the many hours of private talks that followed, they would dispense with official constraints and let their conversations wander freely.

The formal session began with a symbolic gesture. Castro removed his sidearm and announced that he was ready to talk. The *Comandante* began by expressing his gratitude for Trudeau's politically risky decision to keep his promise to visit Cuba in light of heightened international tensions—a reference to the crisis in Angola. Castro also alluded to John Diefenbaker's demand in the House of Commons that Trudeau postpone his trip, the irony of which was obvious to all, since Diefenbaker had been prime minister when Canada first refused to follow the U.S. embargo. Trudeau offered Castro the same response he had been giving his Canadian critics, that Canada did not have to agree with all policies of the countries with which it maintains relations. The subject of Angola was avoided by mutual agreement during the formal talks, postponed until the two leaders could discuss it in a more private setting. Instead, the two delegations kept to a prepared agenda, reviewing recent exchanges between the two countries, Canadian tourism in Cuba, bilateral trade relations and the law of the sea. Trudeau outlined the objectives of Canada's Third Option policy, which Castro used as an entree to criticize U.S. policy. In contrast with Canada, the *Comandante* fumed, which had contained its "empire" within its legitimate borders, the United States was trying to "destroy and starve" Cuba through its embargo and its "CIA murder plans." The CIA was "worse than Hitler," he railed. "Cuba does not feel obliged to respect [the] USA at all."

The problems of the developing world were also discussed at some length, including impediments to North-South trade. Castro noted that Cuba was poor, and that it therefore had to be careful not to give money to regimes that were corrupt. He then criticized Canada for sending aid all over the world indiscriminately and for doing little to see that aid money trickled down to the neediest people. At this affront, Trudeau interjected directly and forcefully. Canada was indeed careful about distributing its aid, he told Castro, and it was especially concerned to see that the aid got to the people for whom it was intended. The prime minister then introduced a representative from CIDA to elaborate. Castro subsequently "backed away from his earlier remark," recalled Ambassador Hyndman. "It was an example of how Pierre was not letting anything go by without a quick rejoinder." This exchange between Trudeau and Castro, observed the ambassador, "was all part of the jockeying between them." Having set the record straight, Trudeau put the matter behind him. At his final press conference before leaving Havana, Trudeau would praise Castro's internationalism. "He receives aid of course, from countries like Canada and he is grateful for it, but Cubans under his government are also helping other parts of the world who are even less developed than they are."

After the closed-door session, Pierre and Margaret resumed their guided tour of Havana, with Castro himself at the wheel of their jeep. The Cuban leader, wearing his black horn-rimmed glasses and smoking a cigar, insisted that an automatic rifle be kept ready for his own personal use on the floor of the jeep. (Cuban authorities later confirmed that threats had been made on the life of the Canadian prime minister.) The day was extremely hot, with temperatures well over thirty degrees Celsius, so the Trudeaus donned broad white sun hats and airy lightweight clothing. They looked every bit the pair of Canadian tourists. Castro insisted that his guests be allowed to meet ordinary Cuban folk, something that Canadian Embassy officials had expected and on which the prime minister had been briefed. Here, too, in this very public setting among his own people, Castro took every opportunity to hold Michel and show him off to reporters. Photographers caught him "clucking and cooing" at the baby. More than one Canadian journalist remarked on his obvious love of children. Some linked his attentiveness to Michel to his well-known declaration that the welfare of Cuban children was the highest priority of the Revolution.

Highlights of the day's sightseeing excursion included a visit to a new housing development outside Havana, a tour of a textile factory and a visit to an agricultural project run by Fidel's brother, Ramón Castro. At one point during their tour, some Cuban children presented the Trudeaus with souvenir blankets memorializing "Comrade Che." A Cuban journalist asked Trudeau to comment on the changes he perceived in the country in the twelve years since his last visit. "In truth," he answered, "the previous visit was one where I had much more occasion to walk around and see the cities and meet a great deal of people. From all observations that I have heard and the statistics I have seen there has been immense progress in the ten years or more since I have been here in areas like education, like health, like agricultural development. I remember visiting an agricultural farm, a cattle farm, in the early sixties and compared to the one I visited on this trip there was immense visible progress. I can also make a comparison in the kind of schools and housing developments because in both instances I visited housing developments, and there is no doubt in my mind that the type of housing development that I saw the day before yesterday was of immensely superior quality to the one I had seen some ten or twelve years ago."

Fidel Castro could not have been more pleased.

7

Cayo Largo

The Origins of an Unlikely Friendship

Cayo Piedra, a Caribbean key that sits ten miles off Cuba's southern shore, has been described as Fidel Castro's "real home." With its helicopter pad, modest four-room house and guesthouse, it is a place where Castro can let his guard down and enjoy the rare pleasure of solitude. His other private retreats include a house on the Isle of Youth where he spearfishes, and a military compound in western Cuba where he hunts. On the occasion of Pierre Trudeau's state visit, Castro extended his customary hospitality and invited his guests to an undisclosed location for private talks. This component of the state visit, designed to be intimate and informal, had in fact been part of the official itinerary for many months. It was agreed that only Ivan Head and Ambassador Hyndman would accompany the prime minister, and that Castro would bring only his key advisers. Perhaps because Castro's security forces feared an attempt on Trudeau's life, the location he chose for their retreat was none of his usual spots but a tiny coral key near Cayo Largo, off Cuba's southern shore.

Ambassador Hyndman had been uniquely sensitive to the needs of the Canadian press while the state visit was being planned. He had seen first-hand the Cubans' obsession with security, and he knew that they would be adamant about controlling journalists' access to Castro. "We may still have great difficulty getting [a] detailed program from Cubans much prior to the visit itself," he wrote in one pre-visit missive from Havana, "since [the] Cubans keep program details to themselves until the last minute for security reasons." Hyndman also knew that the Canadian press would want as much access to Castro as possible. After all, "he was the one who could make good copy." Sensing that the two groups were on a collision course, the ambassador did what he could to smooth the way for the thirty or so Canadian journalists who accompanied Trudeau to Cuba. As it turned out, it was a mostly wasted effort. The Cubans took matters entirely into their own hands. Before the end of the visit, tensions between Cuban security personnel and the Canadian press corps would erupt in a scuffle at the ambassador's residence, producing the visit's only bona fide diplomatic incident. The irony that it should be his own living room that was trashed during the melee was not lost on Hyndman.

It went without saying that the press would be excluded from the private tête-à-tête between Trudeau and Castro. Hyndman had thus recommended that reporters be present for the prime minister's arrival at the secret site, and that they be provided with a "special program" during the time he was "incommunicado." It was not to be. Unbeknownst to anyone, the Cubans had hatched a plan to ditch the Canadian press toward the end of the Trudeaus' tour of Havana. In the late afternoon, as the official motorcade was en route from one of its scheduled stops, the long train of vehicles broke in two. "Suddenly, in the leading cars, we veered off the road and the rest of the caravan kept on," Hyndman recalled. This deft manoeuvre sped Castro and Trudeau off to the army helicopters that would take them to Cayo Largo, and left the oblivious journalists trailing off toward what they assumed would be another photo op. Ambassador Hyndman was not surprised by this subterfuge, but he knew it would have repercussions. Far more "embarrassing and difficult," from Hyndman's vantage point, was that the Cubans would not tell the Canadian security personnel exactly where they intended to take Trudeau. "The rejoinder from the Canadian side," the ambassador later recalled, "was this. 'Can you visualize for one second the Prime Minister of Canada not being able to communicate with the government of Canada?' There has to be constant access and communication between Canada and the prime minister." In the end, the Cubans never did reveal the destination, but they assured the Canadians that Trudeau would never be out of communication with Ottawa.

The wild card in all of the preparations for the private excursion was whether Margaret would go. "It was a touchy issue in Ottawa because there was a possibility that there would be a confrontation between Margaret and External Affairs on the question," Hyndman recalled. The key on which the two heads of state, their advisers and Cuban security personnel would spend the night was tiny—160 by 60 yards at most. "It's unbelievable," Hyndman later recalled. "It's so small!" The only dwellings were a two-bedroom bungalow and a small shed, the "sort of thing you might find in a Canadian fishing camp." Portable generators provided the only power. Castro and his advisers were naturally worried about the baby's welfare in such a rustic setting. Cuban officials signalled strongly to Hyndman that they preferred Margaret to stay in Havana, where they had put together a full itinerary for her. The day of the retreat, Trudeau asked Hyndman his opinion on the matter in private. "I want to be frank, Pierre," the ambassador replied. "I think they were very much hoping she would not go." The prime minister replied, "Well, in that case, the proper thing is that Margaret will not go. She can stay in Havana and attend to her programme there."

In the end, Margaret could not be talked out of going. Pierre acquiesced. "My own feeling is that this was a reflection of the fact that Pierre really had a strong love for Margaret," Hyndman later commented. For her part, Margaret recalled that the reason she had been encouraged to remain in Havana was that Ivan Head thought she "would only embarrass our Cuban hosts." She also claimed that it was Castro who insisted that she join him and Pierre. "I am not inviting any press up there tonight," she recalled him saying. "You shall be our photographer and, of course, you must bring Miche because there's no one else who can fulfill his needs." Not knowing for certain what Margaret would end up doing, the Cubans prepared for every contingency. They outfitted one of the bungalow's two bedrooms with baby clothes, a change table, a crib and a bed for the nanny. The other they prepared for Pierre and Margaret. This arrangement meant that all of the other participants—the Cuban and Canadian ambassadors, the senior advisers including Ivan Head, Castro's security people and members of the RCMP—would spend the night crammed into makeshift barracks in the shed. "It was really very funny," Hyndman recalled. As for Fidel Castro, he would end up sleeping on a motorboat.

The entire entourage arrived at the island late in the afternoon via helicopter. A security perimeter had already been established by Cuban gunships. Castro and Trudeau immediately donned diving gear—including spearguns—and set out to catch the evening meal. They were accompanied at all times by heavily armed Cuban security agents, some of whom dived with them. Margaret later recalled her surprise at seeing Pierre participating in spearfishing. "Pierre is such a pacifist that he won't kill anything, not even insects," she observed, whereas Castro had "no qualms about killing anything." But on this occasion the prime minister speared fish alongside his host, and took delight in making such a primordial contribution to their communal supper. (That he was proud of his effort can be gauged from the fact that he included a photograph of himself spearfishing in his *Memoirs*.)

A delicious multi-course fish dinner was prepared on open fires by the Cubans. Chilean wines were brought in for the occasion. The informality of the meal gave it a special charm. A single long table with benches was set for all of the guests, including Margaret's nanny and Castro's security crew. Dinner was eaten picnic-style, under garlands of twinkling lights. Distinctions of rank and status were ignored, everybody participating in the various conversations freely. Fidel Castro and Pierre Trudeau conversed in Spanish, as did the Cuban staffers and Ambassador Hyndman. At one point in the dinner conversation, Margaret literally stopped Fidel in mid-sentence by thrusting the baby into his arms. Whether or not her inclination to fantasize got the better of her on that evening, Margaret later recalled that "it was as well that Castro and I were not alone." She found the *Comandante*'s constant flattery bewitching. "You know, my eyes are not very strong," he told her, "so every day to make them stronger I force myself to look at the sun. I find it very hard. But do you know what I find harder? That is to look into the blue of your eyes."

———

The exact content of Pierre Trudeau's conversations with Fidel Castro on that idyllic evening has been lost to posterity. The planned informality of the meal, the fact that conversation was intended to range freely as the two leaders dived, fished and dined, signalled a willingness on both sides to allow their discussions to remain off the record and therefore unguarded. The Canadian officials who were present remain disinclined, for security reasons, to disclose the details of the two leaders' conversations. Exactly what was said, therefore, must be gleaned from second-hand sources, and gauged against the information each man is known to have carried with him to Cayo Largo.

Pierre Trudeau and Fidel Castro had known each other for only twenty-four hours when they went spearfishing, but it is clear that each man had already taken the measure of the other and formed a highly favourable opinion. Castro had spared no effort to make the Trudeaus' visit hospitable, which had clearly impressed the prime minister. As Trudeau had intimated to the Canadian press even before his arrival, he was predisposed to think highly of the social policy achievements of the Revolution, which he had seen first-hand in the mid-1960s and on which he remained well briefed. In their closed-door session, Castro had tested Trudeau's mettle and discovered what Canadians had long known of their prime minister. Not only was he a man of deep conviction but he was not about to let an adversary gain the upper hand through even the slightest misstep. Trudeau could be gracious, Castro discovered, but he was no pushover. For his part, of course, the *Comandante* had the home-court advantage, impressing Trudeau not only with his charm as a host but with his extraordinary grasp of all things Cuban. Castro's knowledge of history and politics has always been impressive, but his command of minutiae—his ability to cite statistics from memory, for example, or to explain how this or that machine functions—has invariably struck his visitors as a tour de force. So it was with Pierre Trudeau. By the end of their first day's tour of Cuban homes and factories, the prime minister's genuine interest in the rhythms of life in Cuba—what Richard Gwyn once called his "insatiable interest in the way the world works"—had already established a spirited dynamic between him and the indefatigable Castro.

At Cayo Largo, the two leaders extended their discussion of Cuban, Canadian and world politics openly and extensively. Canadian officials later told the press that during their "long talks" together the Cuban leader was "well-informed, eager to debate issues, and very frank." He and Trudeau compared their nations' relative social and economic achievements and failures. Castro took an especially keen interest in Trudeau's description of the Canadian parliamentary system and in his characterization of Canadians' political beliefs. The prime minister, for his part, asked many "pointed, trenchant questions," as Ambassador Hyndman later put it, on Cuba's social and economic policies. When Trudeau met the press the next day, he was effusive in his praise for "the achievements of the revolutionary Cuban government"—clear evidence not only that he had been impressed by what he saw in Cuba but that he accorded Castro a good deal of credit. The *Comandante* has never been reluctant to extol the achievements of the Revolution, or to explain in meticulous detail the origins and development of his own political philosophy. That he impressed Trudeau with his passion for improving the lives of even the poorest Cubans is beyond question. Castro enjoyed an "intense rapport with the Cuban people," Trudeau said later, and he was largely responsible for the island's "immense progress" since 1959. The prime minister would also tell the press that the great advancements the Revolution had brought Cubans in education, health care, agriculture and housing—despite the U.S. embargo—were astounding, so much so that they might serve as a model for economic and social policy reforms in other developing countries. "What is happening in Cuba is of great importance to the world," said Trudeau. "The Cuban experience has attracted interest from near and far because of its undoubted dedication to bettering the lives of Cubans."

———

As expected, the main topic of conversation at Cayo Largo was Angola. Neither the Cubans nor the Canadians had expected that there would be a meeting of minds on the subject. Trudeau's own expectation that he and Castro would probably "agree to disagree" spoke to this. The prime minister knew that there was a good deal of political capital riding on his promise to Canadians that he would not only raise the matter of Angola with Castro but inform him in no uncertain terms that Canada was unhappy with Cuban intervention there. Yet it is also apparent that he and the other Canadian officials were keenly interested in learning what they could about the Cuban role in Angola. All they knew for certain was that several hundred Cuban officers were stationed in Angola at a training school. The true number of Cuban combat troops there, then estimated in the North American press to be upwards of twelve thousand, remained unknown. Margaret would later write in her memoir that Castro was "far less than honest with Pierre" about Cuba's involvement in Angola, and that the prime minister learned only two weeks after returning to Canada that he had sent large numbers of troops. In his own *Memoirs*, Pierre wrote that Castro "minimized the number of troops he had there," giving him "a very low number."

Ambassador Hyndman believes that the context for the two leaders' discussion of Angola was more nuanced. While Castro might have been cagey about the numbers, the ambassador has suggested, it was a matter of no small importance to him that he be seen by the Canadians as forthcoming. Trudeau's opinion of him would have been irreparably harmed had he spoken deceitfully, which it never was. The key issue from the Canadian vantage point—indeed, the key issue as far as the entire Western world was concerned—was not so much the numbers as the principle. Were the Cubans acting as Soviet proxies in Angola, or were they not? "The nature and future of the Trudeau-Castro relationship, and of Canada's attitude toward Cuba," Hyndman observed, "could have been affected by Angola if it turned out that it was driven by Moscow, and Fidel was really doing Moscow's bidding." The Canadian view was that, if intervention in Angola was Castro's policy alone, Canada might have some influence on that policy. Hyndman does not believe that Trudeau had "any illusions" about his capacity to influence Castro on Angola during his state visit. Rather, by registering his displeasure, he thought that Canada might have some influence on the question over the longer run.

Pierre Trudeau would later tell Canadians that he spent three hours discussing Angola with Fidel Castro and that their conversation was "brutally frank." Ambassador Hyndman has recalled that the conversation may have run even longer and agrees that the talks were "very, very wide open." As his Canadian guests had expected, Castro took the high road, explaining in painstaking detail the events of 1975 and stressing that Cuba had intervened in Angola only after South Africa had sent its columns toward Luanda. At one point, Trudeau accused him of "meddling in the internal affairs of a foreign country." As the prime mister himself later recalled, Castro "explained that this was a different situation—very different from the Americans in Vietnam—and that he was doing it only to assist the legitimate government of Angola, which was trying to protect itself against guerrillas backed by South Africa and some NATO powers." The *Comandante* offered Trudeau the same principled justification for his intervention in Angola that he had presented to the First Party Congress just weeks before. "The imperialists are irritated with us," he had said then. "Some of them wonder why we help the Angolans, what interests we have there. They are accustomed to thinking that whenever a country does something, it is in pursuit of oil, or copper, or diamonds, or some other natural resource. No! We are not after material interests, and, logically, the imperialists do not understand this, because they are exclusively guided by chauvinist, nationalist, and selfish criteria. We are fulfilling an elementary internationalist duty when we help the Angolan people. We are simply practicing a policy of principles."

Castro's impassioned appeal to Trudeau rang true because, as historians have since demonstrated, it was true. It is clear from all available sources—Cuban, Soviet and American—that Castro acted as he did because he believed deeply in the cause of resisting the South African invasion. As Cuban troops were preparing to leave for Angola, for example, the *Comandante* made a point of speaking in person to the men of the Special Forces unit. "He spoke above all about the South African invasion," one soldier later recalled of Castro's talk. "He said that some of the Cuban instructors had died, that it was a difficult situation, that we must stop the South Africans before they reached Luanda, and that many of us would not return. He said that it was very hard for him to say this and not go with us." Other Cuban units to ship out to Angola later in 1975 and 1976 were either briefed by Castro in person or were played recordings of this first speech. The mission was strictly volunteer. No one was compelled to go.

Historians have also confirmed that Agostinho Neto had not asked the Cubans for these troops. Castro acted on his own, without even consulting his own political bureau, believing that if he did not, Luanda would fall. He surmised that the United States must be in league with the South Africans, and that Washington would not engage the Cubans directly in Angola. He was correct on both counts. Castro also did not consult the Soviets. He opted instead to present the Cuban troops in Angola as a *fait accompli* that Moscow would have little choice but to accept and support. It is now known that the Soviets distrusted Neto, and that they backed Cuba's intervention in Angola only after it became obvious that his MPLA was going to win. It is also known that U.S. intelligence understood at the time that the Soviets were not pulling the strings. In early January 1976, for example, American officials claimed publicly that up to twelve thousand Cuban troops had been ferried to Angola via Soviet airborne transports. But confidential State Department documents showed that only seventy-five hundred Cubans were in Angola at that time, and that all of them had got there on Cuban ships and planes. (The Soviets contributed ten transatlantic flights to ferry Cuban troops to Angola in mid-January, but this was, as Henry Kissinger himself noted, a temporary measure.) Only on January 16 did the Soviets agree to provide $25-million worth of arms for the Cubans fighting in Angola, and only late in January did they become available for Cuban use. On February 5, 1976, the *New York Times* leaked a report that Henry Kissinger believed Cuba had acted "on its own initiative" but he would not say so publicly. Kissinger's official line—that the Soviets were responsible—prevailed.

In April 1976, on the fifteenth anniversary of the Bay of Pigs, Fidel Castro spoke to the Cuban people at length about Angola. He laid out the details of the Cuban involvement exactly as they are now known to have happened. He stressed that "Cuba alone" bore the responsibility for intervening in Angola. "Ford and Kissinger lie to the people of the United States and to world public opinion," he said, "when they try to place the responsibility for Cuba's action in solidarity with Angola on the

Soviet Union. Ford and Kissinger lie to the people of the United States when they hide the fact that the fascist and racist troops of South Africa criminally invaded Angolan territory long before Cuba sent any regular unit of soldiers there."

Fidel Castro has much to answer for but, on the Angolan crisis at least, history has absolved him. As the *Washington Post* observed in mid-February 1976, "the Cuban intervention, which turned the tide of battle in Angola, is an extraordinary event in postwar history. There is little precedent for it in the past behavior of either Latin American countries or Communist countries."

———

Just days after Trudeau had returned to Canada from his Latin America tour, Southam newspaper columnist James Ferrabee would make an extremely perceptive observation. Before going to Havana, Trudeau had been talking a tough line on Cuba's intervention in Angola, and he would do so again after his return. But at times, particularly during his final press conference in Havana, he seemed to equivocate. "Something seemed to happen to the tone and emphasis when the prime minister was asked about his talks with Castro on Angola."

Ferrabee was correct. During joint press conferences, when Castro was compelled to defend his Angola policy, Trudeau was forceful in his objections to Cuban policy. Sending troops to Angola violated the very principle that Castro defended in Latin America, he said, namely, the right of the region to settle its affairs without intervention by outsiders. Trudeau also criticized the Cuban policy as destabilizing, and inimical to the efforts being made in the era of détente to bring an end to proxy wars being fought by the superpowers and their allies. These were important criticisms, and the prime minister was not reticent in expressing them. Among those observers who would praise him for his tough talk on Angola was NATO Secretary General Joseph Luns, who affirmed in early February that Trudeau's visit to Cuba had done NATO no harm and that his forceful critique of Castro's intervention in Angola "might have done some good."

But Trudeau also came away from Cayo Largo with what he called "a better insight into socialist reasoning" on Angola. Clearly, as he intimated to reporters during his final press conference in Havana, he had come to accord Fidel Castro's rationale for intervening in Angola a legitimacy he had not anticipated. "There was very extensive exploration not only of Angola but of the whole balance of power in Africa," Trudeau said of their private talks. "I found Premier Castro extremely well informed on Africa. It was obvious to me that Premier Castro had made this decision [to send troops to Angola] with a great deal of thought and of feeling for the strategic situation in Africa. I can't say that I have changed my mind on the importance of non-intervention, and I think it would be foolhardy to assume that I changed Premier Castro's mind. But I certainly came out of the talk with a much greater knowledge of the assessment of the African situation viewed from the particular socialist point of view of Premier Castro, and I hope that he benefited from some of the arguments and ideas that I put forth." Such a casual acknowledgment of the complexity of the Angolan situation was entirely consistent with Trudeau's view of the world. But this is not how his critics judged the matter, James Ferrabee among them. "What happens to the country's self-respect," asked the columnist, "when it appears the prime minister is saying one thing in Cuba, for Cuban consumption, and quite another in Canada for Canadian consumption?"

Perhaps the most striking element in Trudeau's comments after Cayo Largo, at least when judged against Fidel Castro's reputation in the West as a firebrand, was his insistence that the Cuban leader was balanced and objective in his view of the world. "He is certainly a man who has a feeling for international affairs," said the prime minister. "As I was saying in answer to the question on Angola, he has assessed very well the qualities and weaknesses of the various leaders and countries of Africa. He did not seem like a fanatic when he was talking about South Africa, for instance, but he identified some world leaders whom he would describe as fanatics, and I would agree with him—people who seek extreme solutions. He did not seem that way to me. On South Africa, I would not like to state his policy for him, but he was not what I would describe as an extremist." Trudeau would later tell journalists that he viewed Castro as "unquestionably a leader of world stature, with a feeling for world affairs and extremely realistic views on many world problems." Coming from the Canadian prime minister at the height of the Angolan crisis, this was high praise indeed.

———

It is clear from their mutual praise that the two leaders had discovered in each other a level of intellectual virtuosity—a command of language, history and philosophy—that was unexpectedly refreshing and perhaps even disarming. Both Pierre Trudeau and Fidel Castro were, of course, capable of communicating with ordinary folk. This aptitude is a prerequisite for political success. But both were also men of commanding intellect and rhetorical skill, accustomed to having the upper hand even in casual conversation. By practice if not by temperament, they seldom conceded the role of highest authority to anyone but themselves. Fiercely competitive in debate, utterly convinced of the superiority of their own ideas, and obsessed with precision and elegance in the use of language and reasoned argument, neither man knew many intellectual equals, and perhaps even fewer that they would have recognized as such. It is clear that Trudeau and Castro both revelled in their intellectual jousting at Cayo Largo and also that it was for both men a rare and unexpected pleasure. This is what Trudeau acknowledged when he told reporters the next day that "he and Castro had acquired a deep respect for each other."

Pierre Trudeau and Fidel Castro obviously liked each other as well. It is never easy to fathom what draws friends to one another—even less so when they are highly circumspect heads of state and men of legendary discretion. The general contours of their mutual affection can be discerned, however. They were men of remarkably similar temperament, quite apart from their unique intellectual gifts. They were perfectionists, men of extraordinary self-discipline who judged themselves and their accomplishments against the stratospheric standards of their own performance. They were also self-contained, not only in the sense that they liked and often preferred their own company, but in the broader sense that they seemed, even to their closest friends, not to need other people. This insularity manifested itself socially in their similarly shy demeanour, intellectually in their aloofness and, perhaps not least, romantically in their reputed incapacity for intimacy. And yet both men had achieved their greatest glory as consummate political actors. To paraphrase a memorable line from Trudeau's friend Leonard Cohen, their ability to fashion larger-than-life public personas, to rank among the world's most charismatic and inspirational leaders, was not entirely devoid of the con. It cannot have escaped their notice that they had these traits in common, though it seems equally certain that they would never have deigned to discuss them explicitly.

It is also apparent that each man recognized and appreciated in the other some of the values he had so painstakingly cultivated in himself. Chief among these was courage. On the few occasions when Trudeau or Castro spoke about the character of the other, the virtue of courage figured prominently. Their established reputations for political toughness preceded their 1976 introduction, each man being well briefed on the biographical details of the other. But at Cayo Largo, when they had the opportunity to take the measure of each other as men, each recognized that the reputation of the other for a deep, principled moral toughness was deserved. Introducing Trudeau at Cienfuegos the day after their private talks, Castro spoke openly of the courage Trudeau—and by extension Canada—had shown in even venturing to Cuba. "We will never forget," Castro asserted, "that in the most difficult years of the Revolution, when almost every single country and state joined the [American] blockade, only two countries in this hemisphere maintained relations with us,

Mexico and Canada." Only Pierre Trudeau, he said, had shown the courage to risk his reputation at home and especially in the United States to decide for himself whether revolutionary Cuba was worthy of the community of nations. "When Prime Minister Trudeau visited Latin America he did not forget Cuba, or exclude Cuba," said Castro. And he had done so "in spite of the efforts of some others to block legitimate relations between Canada and Cuba." Trudeau returned the compliment on the same occasion when he praised Cuba's record of social progress under the Revolution. "This record," said Trudeau, "both in its achievements and its shortcomings—which you, Prime Minister, have analyzed in public courageously—will long be studied by students of social and developmental processes."

Courage, of course, has a highly personal aspect. By the time Trudeau met him in 1976, Fidel Castro was acknowledged even by his enemies to be a man of almost superhuman fearlessness, defying assassination plots, living always on the move, fortifying himself with a vigilant security apparatus and yet habitually putting himself in harm's way to converse with the people of Cuba. As an athlete, and especially as a warrior, there could be little doubt about Castro's personal courage. Though he had never been tested in war, Trudeau's penchant for personal courage was comparable. As a young man, he had deliberately courted risk in order to hone fearlessness in himself. He had sought out the world's trouble spots as a personal challenge. Physical courage was also of the essence in his favourite leisure pursuits, especially canoe-tripping. Castro had been impressed by Trudeau's attempt to paddle a canoe across the Straits of Florida, and even more so by his earlier sojourn in Cuba hacking sugarcane. And he was not an easy man to impress.

But courage for statesmen also has a political aspect. However much Trudeau might have been awed by Castro's bravery and bravado, and vice versa, it was in the realm of politics that each man came to value the courage of the other. The reason for this is obvious. Each man found himself in political circumstances with which the other could instinctively identify. Though each man imagined himself to be destined for great-ness—and there were aspects of the megalomaniac in both of them—the fact remains that they headed up nations that, in the context of the Cold War, could only be called second-tier. Thus, they faced the same conun-drum. Each was a fiercely independent and original thinker and a leader of great vision. Each believed deeply in the destiny of his own country, and hence in the importance of charting an independent national course. Each also believed in the crucial example he was called upon to set inter-nationally, both as a means of asserting national autonomy in a world polarized into two hostile camps and also—perhaps more obviously—as a means of demonstrating to the other peoples of the world that they could live according to their own lights and let others live by theirs.

And yet, however visionary and independent each man sought to be, both found themselves constrained by the hard reality that they led nations whose de facto status on the world stage was that of an economic and stra-tegic satellite. Trudeau might have wanted to be assertive in distancing himself from the United States and its predominance even in multilateral organizations like NATO, but his options, as he well knew, were bound by Canada's subordination to American strategic prerogatives. How to render Canada both an independent nation and a good ally to the United States has been the challenge of every Canadian prime minister, without exception. But for Trudeau, a man for whom compromise never came eas-ily, the challenge was especially daunting. For Castro, the tensions were even greater. To Cuba's complex historic status as a satellite of the United States had been added, under his leadership, the unprecedented challenge of a strategic alliance with the Soviet Union. Neither Trudeau nor Castro cared in the least for their nations' subordinate status vis-à-vis the super-powers, yet both acknowledged, sometimes bitterly, sometimes blithely, that this was the hand they had been dealt. The irony was not lost on them. However important their conversation at Cayo Largo may have seemed, and however profound their desire to use their limited means to advance the cause of their nations' destiny, they knew that the real conversation,

DETENTE AND MINI-TENTE

the one that the world acknowledged as the only one that really mattered, was between the White House and the Kremlin.

Political courage in this context, the quality that Trudeau and Castro came to respect so profoundly in each other, meant walking the tightrope. It meant having the fortitude to challenge continually the limits imposed on their nations by history and circumstance, without destroying the delicate strategic balance that was absolutely essential to their self-preservation. After their diving expedition at Cayo Largo, everything that each man said about the other, even including Castro's remarks at Trudeau's funeral, can be read as an homage to this particular brand of political courage—the courage to insist that nations like Canada and Cuba must be free to chart a course not only on the basis of the world as they find it but also on the basis of the world as they wish it to be.

The morning after the Cayo Largo retreat, a reporter asked Trudeau his opinion of Castro as a politician. He replied, "I'd rate him A–1. All kinds of superlatives. I'm really impressed." Castro, he went on, had "superb self-control," the quality for which Trudeau was himself justly famous. "He's controlled, he's cool, yet with a great intensity, a man of pride who does not forget easily the hurt that he has suffered or the aid he had received." When he was asked whether Canada might broker some kind of rapprochement between Cuba and the United States, Trudeau said it was out of the question. The prime minister acknowledged that the unexpected warmth of his relationship with Castro would likely be seen by American critics of the regime as "going a bit far." But, as he would assert repeatedly in the aftermath of the state visit, he had initiated similar openings with other communist governments, and the United States had followed suit. "World events are changing," he mused, "and international relations have a knack of imposing themselves on the rest of the world."

———

Because they had established such an amicable rapport at Cayo Largo, the last full day of the state visit, Wednesday, January 28, was coloured by both leaders' new-found confidence in each other and in their mutually reinforcing visions of their nations and the world. It was, without question, a heady day, and both men—operating on little sleep—were swept up in the emotional intensity of the moment.

Trudeau had been invited by Castro, as part of his official itinerary, to give a speech at the southern port city of Cienfuegos. Whether Trudeau had come to Cuba with some sense of the content of this speech is not clear. Margaret later recalled that he excused himself from the late-night talks at Cayo Largo in order to work on the speech, evidence that his appreciation for Castro had directly affected its tone and substance. The "mass rally of friendship," as the Cubans called it, began at noon at the vast Cienfuegos shipping terminal, after a brief motor tour of the city. Castro saw to it that an estimated twenty-five thousand Cubans were assembled to cheer the Canadian prime minister on, many of them children waving Canadian and Cuban flags. Some had waited up to six hours "in the blazing sun" to see Trudeau, something that he joked would have been inconceivable back in Canada. The prime minister said later that he was "moved by the enthusiasm and warm response of the crowd." Margaret, so casually dressed in a white T-shirt, sneakers and faded jeans that she mortified Pierre's aides yet again, was nonetheless said to have captured the hearts of the people of Cienfuegos.

After the playing of the Canadian and Cuban national anthems, Castro took to the stage to introduce the prime minister. His remarks, clocking in at a relatively modest forty-five minutes, took the form of enthusiastic praise for Pierre and Margaret, for baby Michel and for Canada in general for refusing to accede to American pressure and allowing the Cuban-Canadian relationship to flourish. The subtext of the *Comandante*'s remarks, which he made no effort to conceal, concerned the long and bitter history of counterrevolutionary violence directed at Cuba from the United States. "We've never had to lodge a protest against the Government of Canada for conspiring against the Cuban Revolution, encouraging subversive activities or encouraging counterrevolution in our country." Castro carefully outlined the logic of his regime's long history of good relations with Canada. "Canada had no colonies," he observed, "no Manifest Destiny, no urge to annex Latin-American territory; Canada never adopted any policy of aggression against the peoples of Latin America. And, really, there have never been any contradictions between Canada and Cuba or between Canada and other countries of Latin America." When Castro announced to the crowd that Trudeau would be giving his speech in Spanish, people "cheered wildly."

Trudeau then took the stage. After thanking Fidel Castro and the people of Cuba warmly for their hospitality, he acknowledged their recent economic successes and political reforms. "For Cuba this year holds forth many changes," said Trudeau. "You will be voting on a new constitution and electing representatives to a national and to local assemblies; you will be undertaking a new phase of economic development; you will be changing even the political-administrative divisions within the country. I wish you well in these endeavours." Trudeau next spoke of the importance of dialogue between nations with fundamental differences. "Countries which have different social systems, in some instances very different and even opposite systems, countries which make different and at time radically opposed judgments about how best to serve peace and development in the world are learning to speak together and work together toward the solution of common problems." He enumerated Canadians' political convictions, including pluralism and respect for human rights, noting that he and Castro had agreed to disagree on some matters. "We have talked of many things since my arrival, Mr. Prime Minister, and we shall talk of many more before I depart. In those discussions we have found that we are not able to agree on every issue. We have found instead something more important—that we can disagree honourably and without disrespect."

Trudeau's twenty-five-minute speech climaxed with the enthusiastic cheer of friendship that would be heard round the world. "*¡Viva Cuba y el pueblo cubano! ¡Viva el Primer Ministro Fidel Castro! ¡Viva la amistad cubano-canadiense!*"

The evening of the Cienfuegos rally would be the Trudeaus' last in Cuba, and true to form, in a visit that had been full of surprises, it would prove to be a strange one.

Ambassador Hyndman had been jousting with Ottawa for many weeks prior to the state visit over the question of his hosting a formal reception. External Affairs had agreed to a luncheon at the ambassador's residence for twenty-five or thirty guests, but in light of the fact that the Cubans had welcomed the Trudeaus with a grand reception, it was obvious that the Canadians would have to reciprocate with something on a larger scale. What to do about the Canadian press corps was an additional headache for Hyndman. (The Cubans had invited an ABC-TV film crew to cover the Trudeau visit and, at Castro's request, they, too, were expected at Ambassador Hyndman's soiree.) The press had spent three thankless nights in Havana and, far from gaining access to the star of the state visit, Fidel Castro, they had been deliberately kept at a distance. It was clear to the ambassador that some accommodation would have to be made for them, though without spending the kind of money that they could report back in Canada as lavish.

In the end, it was agreed that the Hyndmans would host an evening reception and that the Canadian journalists would be invited. (The ambassador later noted that his home in Havana, a lovely Spanish villa regarded as one of the nicest of all Canadian missions abroad, was too small to house all of the invited guests indoors but that there was not sufficient time to come up with a contingency for rain! Luckily, the skies were clear.) A buffet supper was served in the garden, a collaborative effort by the Canadian chefs and those whose services had been donated by other foreign diplomats living in Havana. Cuban security showed up well in advance, of course, as did Fidel Castro's food tasters. The plan was that Trudeau, Castro and a small group of advisers would dine in the living room—a space easily secured by the Cubans—while everybody else, including the press, would eat outside. The journalists, Hyndman recalled, were "bloody mad" about this arrangement because they wanted access to the two leaders. Meanwhile, Castro, who had agreed to give a press conference at some point in the evening, changed his mind and, in Hyndman's words, "was not budging." The ambassador knew that this, too, would be a problem for the press. Even Pierre Trudeau agreed that the optics were bad. Denying the press access to him and Castro would not play at all well in Canada.

As Trudeau and Castro were chatting amicably over dinner, Cuban security personnel were becoming more assertive in securing the perimeter around their leader. They showed little regard for diplomatic protocol or the sensibilities of their Canadian hosts. Under established diplomatic tradition, the homes of foreign diplomats are treated as sovereign soil by host nations, and thus are supposed to be strictly subject to the prerogatives of the ambassador. Yet on this night, Hyndman recalled, "Cuban security were controlling access into our house." They threatened members of the Canadian press, shoved some Embassy personnel and guests, and even strong-armed the normally unflappable Ivan Head when he tried to make contact with Trudeau. The scene was so chaotic—and the Cuban security force so uncompromising—that Ambassador Hyndman was said to be "almost frantic with worry." The tension was diffused only after Inspector Barry Moss, a Canadian Mountie, was able to persuade Castro's chief of security that the *Comandante*'s safety would not be compromised if the cordon of bodyguards was relaxed within the residence. (In the course of this conversation, the Canadians learned that Castro had become acutely concerned about threats to his life since the publication of the Church Committee findings on CIA plots against him. They learned as well that Castro was also worried about the possibility of a CIA attempt on the life of Trudeau. "You can't really blame them for being uptight," one Canadian official later remarked. "If someone was trying to assassinate you, so would you.")

It was Trudeau himself who finally persuaded Castro to allow the Canadian reporters some time with him. Hyndman agreed to a press conference in his living room, a concession to Castro, who insisted that he be able to "pick and choose the questions, and do this in a disorganized way, which would enable him to avoid having to answer things he didn't want to answer." The ambassador knew what he was in for, in light of the already strained relations between the press corps and Cuban security. Sure enough, it was chaos. "There you had 30 people in my living room, getting on my furniture, climbing on with their cameras, breaking things," he later recalled. "All hell broke loose!"

Just before midnight, Fidel Castro began his impromptu press conference by launching into the most detailed public account he had yet given on Cuba's policy on Angola, thus reinforcing the appearance that Pierre Trudeau had catalyzed Castro's sense of obligation to his own people and the rest of the world. Cuban troops, he said, had been dispatched to Angola to drive out "the dogs of war," by which he meant South African troops and mercenaries from neighbouring Zambia. He characterized the Cuban policy as reactive, emphasizing the fact that he had sent combat troops only after Angola had been invaded by South Africa. "We cannot do anything fairer than to help the Angolan people," he said. Castro was also openly critical of U.S. policy in the region, accusing Americans of engaging in a "criminal war" and of placing themselves on the wrong side of history. The U.S. involvement in Angola, he said, "is real madness. And it tends to win enmity for the United States in black Africa. They hate apartheid. A few corrupted governments have submitted but the African masses deeply hate apartheid. To work with the South Africans is very bad for the prestige of the U.S." He conceded that the refusal of the U.S. Congress to continue to provide aid to the invading forces in Angola demonstrated that there were at least some "sane" Americans who were capable of drawing "lessons from experience." Castro was asked about Trudeau's position on Cuba's Angola policy. "I respect Prime Minister Trudeau's position," he replied, "and I think he respects our position." (For his part, Trudeau was not interested in hearing it all again. He waited in the wings for a few minutes, and then retired. "I'll read all about it in the papers tomorrow," he remarked.)

The Trudeaus left Havana for Caracas the next day, receiving a warm and emotional send-off at José Martí Airport. As he had for the previous two days, Castro insisted on driving the Trudeaus to the airport himself. Pierre extended to Fidel Castro an invitation to come to Canada sometime over the next year. "It is a duty practically," Castro replied. "I can't do anything but accept it." The *Comandante* gave Pierre a big bear hug, Margaret a kiss and Michel a cuddle. He presented Margaret with a collection of colour photographs as a souvenir, a gesture he would repeat twenty-four years later at the funeral for Pierre. He also presented her with a necklace, a box of cigars and three matching cowhide children's chairs for Justin, Sacha and Michel. Margaret recalled being "tearful" as she said farewell to Castro, partly because she had been made to feel so welcome in Cuba, and partly because she knew she would shortly have to return to Ottawa to resume the lonely, stultifying life of the prime minister's wife. "The Cuban visit," she later recalled, "showed up more sharply than ever before the contradictions between what I felt happy doing and what I was actually expected to do. The two, I was beginning to see, were just not compatible." Pierre must have known the hidden meaning of her tears. "I'm glad you're still with me," he told her. "I thought you would ask for asylum."

As the Trudeaus' jet flew off to Venezuela for the third and final stop of the tour, Castro, clad as always in his fatigues, stood at attention, a final gesture of the deep respect with which he had come to view the Canadian prime minister.

8

A Song for Blanquita
Controversy in Caracas

The Trudeaus arrived at Simón Bolívar International Airport outside Caracas, Venezuela, on Thursday, January 29, 1976. They were met by President Carlos Andrés Pérez and his wife, Blanca Rodríguez de Pérez, and welcomed with the customary military review. Already Pierre was on the defensive about his unexpectedly warm friendship with Fidel Castro. He was asked by a Canadian journalist whether he would "change the nuance or the friendliness" of his approach to Castro now that he had left Havana. "I don't see why I would," Trudeau replied tersely, as if he were being interrogated about a love affair. "Nothing incorrect happened between us, I can assure you."

The itinerary for the first day in Caracas saw Pierre Trudeau lay a wreath at the tomb of Simón Bolívar, the famed Latin American patriot, and attend a state reception at the Canadian Embassy. His official talks with Pérez and other Venezuelan officials began the next day and, according to aides on both sides, the discussions were amicable and productive. Trudeau's aides emerged with obvious optimism about forging extensive new commercial ties with Venezuela. Pérez himself was effusive. "This is a historical happening in our hemisphere," he told the press. "We view the presence of Canada here as a historic moment in the life of Latin America." Pérez agreed to send a trade delegation to Ottawa before the spring. He and Trudeau also agreed to establish a permanent joint commission to facilitate Canadian-Venezuelan trade. Canadian officials were especially pleased by Pérez's willingness to settle the nagging question of Canada's trade deficit with his country, the direct result of Canada's massive imports of Venezuelan crude oil. The president accepted an invitation from Trudeau to visit Canada, joking happily of going on a "buying spree" in Canada to rectify the trade imbalance.

In talks the next day, the same positive tone prevailed. That evening the Trudeaus attended a lavish state banquet at which President Pérez gave a toast to Pierre that included an invitation to create some kind of formal economic association with Latin America. Trudeau responded warmly, telling his host that he was pleased to commit Canada to a "Latin connection." Canadian officials later elaborated on the proposed link, suggesting that Canada would perhaps be invited to negotiate a tie with the Latin American trading bloc, SELA, something like the negotiations then taking place with the European Economic Community.

The biggest story to come out of the prime minister's Venezuelan visit concerned Margaret and would end up having repercussions well beyond the trip itself. According to even her own version of the story, Margaret arrived in Caracas with a sizable chip on her shoulder. The planning of her Venezuelan itinerary had fallen to Patricia Schwarzmann, the wife of Canadian Ambassador Maurice Schwarzmann, and a woman with whom Margaret fully expected to get along. As Margaret discovered upon her arrival in Caracas, however, Mrs. Schwarzmann was a Cuban émigré and, like most Cubans who had fled the Revolution, she had no love for Fidel Castro. Fresh from her own idyllic experience of Cuba, Margaret was keen to sing the praises of Castro and Cuba's socialist miracle. Predictably, this put her on a collision course with Patricia Schwarzmann, who responded to her pro-Castro enthusiasms with "not just deaf, but decidedly chilly ears." Margaret later claimed in her memoirs that she had had no idea of the depth of some Cuban exiles' hatred for Castro. Thus, she made no apology for failing to curb her enthusiasm for the Cuban leader in light of Mrs. Schwarzmann's politics. (If, in 1976, Margaret Trudeau was genuinely unaware of the anti-Castro sentiments of many exiled Cubans, then she was even more politically naive than either she or her husband knew.)

Petulance, like euphoria, came easily to Margaret during the Trudeaus' tour of Latin America. She had been grateful to Patricia Schwarzmann for her meticulous planning in the months leading up to her Caracas trip, but she became a severe critic of her once she was in Venezuela. "We weren't destined to get on," Margaret later wrote, adding that she was in no mood for the many formal lunches and cocktail parties Mrs. Schwarzmann had laid on for her. "I took refuge in the guesthouse we were staying in—a charming, luxurious little house run by a friendly girl about my age—and brooded on the contrast between this social hell and my good times in Cuba." For the remainder of their stay, Margaret was by her own admission openly disdainful of Mrs. Schwarzmann. Her saving grace came in the form of President Pérez's wife, Blanca, known affectionately to Venezuelans as Blanquita. She was, Margaret later recalled, "a delightful warm figure with a great sense of humour and sparkling eyes." Margaret was especially impressed by the daycare program she ran in one of the poorest sections of Caracas. Contrary to Mrs. Schwarzmann's insistence that Señora Pérez would never visit "the slums" herself, Margaret discovered to her great delight that, "far from never visiting her centres, [she] went there five days a week, and kept the

whole thing going by cajoling rich Venezuelans to part with their dia-
mond earrings and ruby necklaces." Her dedication to the children, who
all seemed to know her, was all the more impressive because it took place
without publicity or self-aggrandizement. Having expected the worst
from the wife of the president in such a class-bound society, Margaret
was literally overwhelmed with Señora Pérez's humility and charity.

Overcome by her own affection for Señora Pérez, Margaret decided
that she would compose and sing a short song in her honour. The venue
was to be the dinner meal on Sunday, February 1, planned as an intimate
affair attended only by the president and Señora Pérez, Pierre and herself.
When she told Pierre that she had planned this homage to Señora Pérez,
he was "all for it."

As it happened, the dinner for four had been shelved by Canadian
and Venezuelan officials in favour of a "glittering state banquet" attended
by 130 guests. The revised dinner program included an exchange of
toasts between Pierre and the president. No mention was made of
Margaret's song and, as events would subsequently reveal, nobody other
than Pierre and one or two aides had any inkling of her wish to sing for
Señora Pérez. Margaret later claimed that she would have preferred
to abandon her plan to sing but that Pierre had urged her not to. (She
even speculated in her angry memoir that he might have let her go
through with it out of malice.) One Canadian official tried in vain to
save her from yet another diplomatic gaffe, even going so far as to hide
her purse from her because he thought the lyrics to her song were in
it. The idea of a song, they told her bluntly, was "nutty." It was all
for naught. She astounded her hosts and the assembled dignitaries by
standing up and, without an introduction, announcing that she would
like to sing a song she had written in Señora Pérez's honour. Though
Margaret was tanned and wore a long, low-cut peach-coloured gown,
her elegant appearance could not hide her stage fright. She apologized
in advance for her amateurish singing voice, and then proceeded to sing,
in Spanish, the following verse:

Señora Pérez, I would like to thank you.

I would like to sing to you.

To sing a song of love.

For I have watched you

With my eyes wide open.

I have watched you with learning eyes . . .

When she finished, there was a moment of awkward silence, and then Señora Pérez, obviously charmed by the gesture, stood up, embraced her and gave her a gentle kiss. The guests then burst into applause.

How her performance went over with the assembled guests has been the subject of differing interpretations. Canadian press reports of the incident, for example, which made front-page headlines the following day, interpreted Margaret's gesture generously. They emphasized the honest sentiment she had expressed and quoted Trudeau's aides to the effect that "many of the guests had tears in their eyes when the song ended." Margaret's own recollection of her audience's response was far less forgiving. "Half the guests were so embarrassed they kept their eyes riveted to their plates," she recalled. "The Canadian delegation, to a man, was horrified." She knew that, for Ivan Head, this was "the last straw." He could not hide his contempt. Another guest affirmed that when she stood up and announced her intention to sing "just about every Canadian in the room was trying to slide under the table." At least one Trudeau aide was a little more diplomatic. "When she got up I almost groaned," he recalled, "but then realized that perhaps she's not on the same wavelength as some of us and has different ways of expressing herself. She sang very, very sweetly, and the Venezuelans in the room were obviously very touched and moved."

———

It was all in a day's work for the unflappable Pierre Trudeau. He would return to Canada the next day to face a torrent of criticism about everything from his "*¡Viva!*" cheer in Cienfuegos to Margaret's impromptu song in Caracas. Whatever he thought or felt about the ten extraordinary days he had spent in Latin America, he was not letting on. Someone asked him whether he thought the trip had been successful. "There has been no breakthrough," he replied with a shrug, "nor did I expect one."

Trudeau had spent more time in the region than any prime minister before him, shoring up Canada's trading relationships, promoting nuclear disarmament and North-South dialogue, and endearing himself and his family to the many Mexicans, Cubans and Venezuelans who turned out in person to see him. Fully aware of the pitfalls of venturing so boldly into a region understood to be within the American sphere of influence, he had taken pains to keep to the standard diplomatic script. He refused to criticize the United States, for example, and more than once he was forced to douse the anti-American rhetoric of his hosts with fawning statements aimed directly at Washington.

Yet he was, as Canadians well knew, a man who loathed scripts of any kind. Throughout his Latin American tour, and in Cuba especially, he remained every bit his own man. He established a warm personal acquaintance with Fidel Castro, even as it appeared that Cuban troops in Angola might unravel détente and the Cold War thaw he and others had worked so hard to achieve.

The razor's edge, it turned out, was no place for Pierre Trudeau. And Canadians would not be squeamish in telling him so.

PART THREE

AFTERSHOCKS

9

Stranded in Havana

Pierre Trudeau and the New Cold War

Within days of Pierre Trudeau's return from his 1976 state visit to Latin America, it became apparent that he was on the wrong side of history, both personally and politically. Margaret had not been back in Canada twenty-four hours before her many breaches of diplomatic protocol exploded into a national *cause célèbre*, presaging her flight from 24 Sussex and, ultimately, from her marriage to Pierre. The prime minister's own diplomatic gamble—to follow through with his visit to Cuba even as Castro's troops were pouring into Angola—also proved to be a grave miscalculation. Within days of his return, Canadians let him know in no uncertain terms that, however laudable his talk of dialogue, cuddling up to Castro was not winning him any converts at home.

The broader implications of Angola for the Cold War world, already apparent at the time of the state visit, came into full view over the following months, eventually hobbling détente, discrediting dialogue and cementing Fidel Castro's outlaw status. No one, not Pierre Trudeau or even Henry Kissinger, emerged unscathed. By the spring of 1978, when estimates of the number of Cuban troops in Angola ranged between twenty and forty thousand, the prime minister himself would concede that Castro was undermining international stability. In the face of souring public opinion in Canada and relentless attacks from his political opponents, Trudeau decided to pull the plug on Canadian aid to Cuba.

By the time Jimmy Carter assumed the presidency in 1977, Republican critics of détente—Ronald Reagan foremost among them—had already begun to build the momentum that would give them the White House in 1980 and send the Cold War into its second deep-freeze. Carter would do more than any U.S. president before or since to ease tensions with Cuba and to engage Fidel Castro in *El Diálogo*. In this sense, perhaps, Trudeau's visit to Havana delivered on the promise that Canada might once again serve as an "icebreaker" for the talks between Americans and their communist adversaries. Carter would sponsor a secret dialogue with Castro in 1977–78, and without question it would produce tangible results, including the release of thousands of Cuba's political prisoners. But it would also serve to consolidate Cuban-American opposition to *El Diálogo*, establishing the anti-Castro exile lobby in Miami as the de facto arbiter of U.S. Cuba policy. Henceforth, Cuban-Americans like Bernardo Benes who advocated negotiation with the Castro regime would not only be shunned in South Florida but targeted for violence. By the 1980s, the idea that the United States might lift the embargo while Castro was in power could no longer even be whispered in Washington, since it virtually guaranteed the electoral loss of Florida. Bill Clinton, the first Democratic president since Franklin Roosevelt to be elected to two terms, was an outspoken proponent of dialogue with communist governments in China and Vietnam. Yet even he could not afford to run afoul of the Cuban-American vote. Only with great reluctance would he sign in 1996 the Helms-Burton Act, which tightened the embargo against Cuba and made it impossible for the president to end it without the approval of Congress. "Supporting the bill was good election-year politics in Florida," Clinton would concede in his 2004 memoir, "but it undermined whatever chance I might have if I won a second term to lift the embargo in return for positive changes within Cuba."

Pierre Trudeau had gone to Havana in January 1976 in the belief that he was only one jump ahead of Henry Kissinger and possibly even President Ford. The lifting of the U.S. embargo seemed imminent—so much so that Canadians feared the prime minister would arrive in Cuba too late to protect their business interests from the onslaught of American competition. His visit, Trudeau believed, would accelerate the restoration of normal diplomatic relations between the United States and Cuba, just as his visits to other communist countries had done previously. He fully expected to find himself on the cutting edge of a new rapprochement in the western hemisphere.

Instead, he ended up stranded in Havana.

———

Pierre Trudeau said little over the years about his relationship with Fidel Castro. His *Memoirs*, for example, devoted only three paragraphs to Castro and Cuba, and they were squeezed in between his recollections of Chou En-lai—"a fascinating personality in his own right"—and Indira Gandhi—"quiet and untalkative." With the exception of Angola, the emphasis in the *Memoirs* was on the personal rather than the political. Trudeau described Castro's prowess as a skin diver and spearfisher, noting his ability to hold his breath for long periods even though he was a heavy cigar smoker. As for Castro's famous charisma, Trudeau acknowledged that it was the genuine article. "In private, in contrast to his public speeches, he was so quiet-spoken that you had to lean forward to understand him. He was very thoughtful and didn't overindulge in monologues; he would throw out questions and be prepared to have an exchange of views with you. This was a very different man from what the public sees, but both sides of his personality were quite magnetic—the powerful orator and the soft-spoken, subdued revolutionary with only the beard as a reminder that he was a radical." Castro got not so much as a mention in *The Canadian Way*, a weighty tome about foreign policy co-authored by Pierre Trudeau and Ivan Head. Clearly, by the time Trudeau was in retirement and turning his thoughts to his prime ministerial legacy, Castro had become a liability.

In the immediate aftermath of the state visit, by contrast, Trudeau spoke of the trip as "a significant diplomatic achievement." And while he never claimed to have set out to rehabilitate the *Comandante*'s reputation in the West, the prime minister believed he had "contributed significantly to bringing Castro into the mainstream of responsible world diplomacy." As he had said frequently during his trip, Trudeau was impressed by Cuba's record of social progress under the Revolution. "He probably does accept the premise," Richard Gwyn observed, "that for underdeveloped countries, socialism may be the best route to take, though naturally, he is far too pragmatic ever to say so in public." Trudeau had never made a secret of his belief that governments had a responsibility to ensure that the worst inequalities of laissez-faire capitalism were tempered for the benefit of all citizens. Cuba may have inspired in him an even firmer conviction in this respect, coming as it did in the wake of his New Society remarks in late 1975. Certainly, it was his and Castro's mutual interest in social justice that grounded their friendship and continued to draw Trudeau to Cuba after he left office.

Not surprisingly, Fidel Castro took full advantage of Pierre Trudeau's warm response to the Revolution. *Granma*, the Communist Party newspaper, covered the visit extensively and missed no opportunity to quote the prime minister's praise for Cuban social reforms. As some of his North American critics had predicted, the regime turned Trudeau's remarks on Angola to its own advantage. "Prime Minister Trudeau said that Fidel was an exceptionally well-informed leader as regards African and Middle Eastern matters and the world situation," reported *Granma*. The text of Trudeau's Cienfuegos speech was published in full, as was the Cuban-Canadian joint communiqué. Far more telling than this dry copy, however, were the many photographs published in *Granma* showing Trudeau and Castro in close contact and obviously enjoying each other's company. One front-page photo caught them locked in a two-handed handshake. "The strong handshake between Fidel and Trudeau," said the accompanying story, "a sign of the friendship sealed, brought to an end the encounter of the last four days, during which the governmental delegation of Canada had the opportunity of examining closely the hospitality, the work spirit and the constructive effort on the part of our people, and the recognition for that North American nation which maintained an independent policy and did not join the criminal blockade against this Caribbean island."

In mid-February 1976, two weeks after the Trudeaus had returned to Canada, Fidel Castro and a thirty-seven-member Cuban entourage stopped in Gander en route to an international conference in Moscow. The Cuban leader toured the city by car, gave a lengthy radio interview and enjoyed a banquet arranged by External Affairs officials who had flown up from Ottawa. Over dinner, Castro expressed his "extreme gratification" for Trudeau's state visit and asked that his warmest regards be conveyed to the prime minister and his baby. "On Angola," a confidential External Affairs memo later noted, "he was unrepentant and evidently pleased about the victory scored by the MPLA with the support of Cuban troops." But Castro was also highly sensitive to Canadians' criticism of his Angola policy. "He wanted to assure the Canadian Government that neither the Angolans nor the Cubans had any aggressive designs toward other countries of Africa. He repeated this twice. Again he threw the whole blame for Cuban intervention on South Africa."

Coincidentally, while Pierre Trudeau was touring Latin America, the first volume of John Diefenbaker's memoir, *One Canada*, reached number two on the Canadian best-seller list (stalled behind Peter C. Newman's irrepressible *The Canadian Establishment*). Two more volumes would follow in as many years, and they, too, would be widely read by Canada's growing ranks of political junkies. That Diefenbaker's prime-ministerial legacy was back in the limelight just as Pierre Trudeau was hobnobbing with Fidel Castro was a delicious irony. The juiciest parts of Diefenbaker's memoir concerned his stormy relationship with Kennedy. And Cuba, as everyone knew, had been at the eye of that storm. Pierre Trudeau knew serendipity when he saw it, and he made the most of it.

The opposition Tories had been demanding for weeks prior to Trudeau's Latin American tour that he cancel or at least postpone his visit to Havana. Angola was a gift to Conservatives who did not care for Castro in the first place, and they took every opportunity of attacking the Liberals' Cuba policy in light of it. With their unofficial leadership campaign to replace Robert Stanfield in full flight, some Tory hopefuls took the opportunity to grandstand while Trudeau was away in Latin America. Conservative MP John Franklin suggested that the House should hold a non-confidence vote to bring down the government. Fellow Tory MP Sinclair Stevens demanded that the government terminate CIDA grants to Cuba if Castro persisted in meddling in foreign wars. Tom Cossitt, the Tory MP who had gone to bat for imprisoned Canadian Ronald Lippert in 1973, demanded that the House dissociate itself from Trudeau's "¡*Viva!*" cheer and from any other comments that might be construed as critical of free enterprise.[nx] (Cossitt also asked that External Affairs Minister Allan MacEachen address "the reported invasion of the Canadian Embassy in Havana by some 30 or more Cuban security police" while the prime minister was "inside the music room cuddling up to Castro.")

Trudeau's lieutenants were loath to speak for him while he remained in Latin America, of course, and they said as much. Thus, the stage was set for a major battle when the prime minister returned to the House of Commons on Tuesday, February 3, 1976. During Question Period, Opposition leader Robert Stanfield would repeat virtually all of the charges that had been made against the prime minister during his trip, starting with the question of why he went to Cuba at all. Trudeau offered his standard reply. The Angolan crisis had developed long after the decision had been made to visit Cuba, he said, and in any case the government of Canada had condemned Cuba's intervention openly and unequivocally. "Since there could be no misunderstanding on the part of anybody, let alone the Cuban government, about our position," Trudeau shrugged, "the trip should proceed as scheduled." At this point, the prime minister fired his first shot over Diefenbaker's bow. "I venture to say that if we had postponed the visit, it might have been postponed a long while, and without making any certain predictions I thought it important that Canada show its desire to continue the peaceful exchanges with Cuba which had begun in the days of the right honourable member for Prince Albert and that my visit to Cuba should precede any possible visit of a high level official of the United States."

Stanfield was not impressed. He correctly noted that the timing of the visit had presented the prime minister with an opportunity to register the strongest possible diplomatic protest. He noted as well that Trudeau's equivocations on Angola while he was in Havana had sent mixed messages about Canada's earlier condemnation of Cuban involvement. "Why was it not appropriate," asked Stanfield, "for the Prime Minister to follow the time honoured and very acceptable diplomatic practice of deferring his visit rather than giving the Canadian people the impression, regardless of what was said between the Prime Minister and Fidel Castro, that regards as tolerable or does not take very seriously this kind of intrusion into Angolan affairs which, despite whatever protests honourable members opposite may make, is the general perception of this event?"

The prime minister responded to this rambling question by asserting that the government's position had been "stated very clearly" before and after the visit. Any "misinterpretation" of the kind suggested by Stanfield, he added, "can only be willful and malicious." Trudeau then listed the many trade and cultural linkages Canadians and Cubans had forged over the years, again crediting Diefenbaker with initiating Canada's present Cuba policy. "That policy was established by the right honourable member for Prince Albert when he was prime minister and has been followed ever since by every other government, and with regard to these two countries it has established a feeling in the world that Canada indeed follows its own foreign policy, and is able to disagree with other countries and still have civil and commercial exchanges."

Stanfield knew that, with this invocation of Diefenbaker's legacy, he had been outflanked. "The general perception abroad is that [the visit] was great for Fidel Castro," he remarked before taking his seat. "What did it do for Canada?"

Prodded by Trudeau's remarks about his own record on Cuba, Diefenbaker plunged into the debate.

"The Prime Minister mentioned that during my period of administration we had relations with Cuba and that is right," he told the House. "We traded in non-strategic materials but we did not cuddle up to Castro."

"Mr. Speaker," Trudeau replied playfully, "I realize that in the right honourable gentleman's day there was no cuddling up to Cuba, probably because the right honourable gentleman was never very good with the Latin connection."

Unfazed, Diefenbaker demanded that Trudeau restate for the record precisely what he had said in private to Castro.

"What did he say in regard to Angola?" Diefenbaker pressed. "Did he say to Castro 'You should get out of Angola?' What did he say? Instead of evading the subject, just tell the House, even though the language be brutal."

Trudeau was evasive.

"There was no noticeable cooling off in the relations between his government with Cuba after Cuba had accepted missiles which were pointed right at the heart of the United States," remarked the prime minister. "If the right honourable gentleman was so concerned with the effect of my visit, he might have shown a little bit of that concern in those dark days of 1962."

Such a provocation from Trudeau was more mischievous than malicious, since it was well known that he had supported Diefenbaker's position on the Cuban Missile Crisis. Diefenbaker would not relent. He demanded to know whether, in his informal conversation with Fidel Castro, the prime minister had suggested that Cuba withdraw its troops from Africa. After all, he said, mocking Trudeau's own words, "Castro displayed a good deal of thought and feeling for the situation."

"I have the feeling that he has a good knowledge of Africa and a good feeling for the realities there," Trudeau acknowledged.

"And no knowledge of democracy," retorted Diefenbaker.

"Certainly no experience of democracy," Trudeau said, "but you cannot blame Mr. Castro for not having learned that in his childhood under Batista."

Pressed repeatedly by the Opposition to come clean on what he knew of Castro's rationale for intervening in Angola, Trudeau stayed on the ropes.

"Mr. Speaker," he said, "if I were to recite faithfully the arguments put forward by Premier Castro in defending his own position I am sure it would emerge as though I were being an apologist for his argument."

"He has not got a better apologist anywhere," snorted Diefenbaker.

Stanfield, by now visibly frustrated by Trudeau's prevarications, threw in the towel. "Mr. Speaker," he remarked, "could I ask the Prime Minister in connection with this brutal and frank encounter who wrestled whom to the ground?"

"It was a draw," Trudeau replied.

When the prime minister rose to table the joint communiqué he and the Cubans had signed during the course of his trip, members of the Opposition shouted him down.

"No, no!" they cried.

"Then let me just say," Trudeau responded, "*¡Viva Canadá y Cuba, viva la amistad entre Canadá y estos países!*"[2]

———

Perhaps not surprisingly, Margaret Trudeau's impromptu song for Señora Pérez proved to be more controversial than Pierre's warm words for Fidel Castro. Even the *New York Times* and the *Washington Post* covered the story of the Canadian prime minister's wife flouting diplomatic protocol.

What might have been dismissed as a minor breach of etiquette erupted into an international brouhaha mainly because Margaret insisted on confronting her critics personally. The furor began the morning of Monday, February 2, the day after the Trudeaus returned home from Venezuela. Margaret was awakened at 9 a.m. by her clock radio, set as always to CKOY talk radio in Ottawa. Much to her surprise, the subject of the morning call-in show was whether her indecorous behaviour— serenading presidents' wives, wearing jeans and T-shirts to state functions, having public tantrums—was bad for Canada. Most of the callers were exasperated with Margaret and said so. "I think she is an absolute disgrace to this country," said one. "She is a disgrace to every Canadian woman. She has no right to sing ridiculous songs in official company." After fielding several more irate calls, the radio host took a shot in the dark. "I doubt you are listening, Margaret Trudeau, but if by any chance you are, why don't you give us a call?"

She was, and she did. The station manager at first thought her call a hoax but called her back via the switchboard at 24 Sussex. She proceeded to speak on the air for half an hour, defending her right to be her own person, whether or not she was on official state business. "I'm not going to be locked away again like in the past and told I'm not allowed to do anything," she insisted. And she certainly was not going to be "a rose on my husband's lapel." Margaret had not exaggerated when she said she had

2. "Long live Canada and Cuba, and long live the friendship between Canada and all countries!"

felt like her old self again in Cuba. Having had a taste of the kind of free-dom and adventure that had always made her happy, and facing a return to the stuffy protocol and lonely isolation of her life in Ottawa, she returned home more determined than ever to follow her own lights. "I learned an awful lot when I was in Mexico and Venezuela and Cuba," she said. Even in the face of Canadians' derision, Margaret made no apologies. She was feeling "freer" now than at any time since she married Pierre Trudeau. "I'm talking about the freedom that comes from inside," she said. "In the end, it's the only thing." The radio host asked her whether her behaviour was damaging to her husband's reputation. Pierre is "a very beautiful per-son," she replied. "When I shine, he shines."

The day after her stint on talk radio, Margaret repeated her song of homage for Señora Pérez at a tea party attended by five hundred Ottawa women. Her audience burst into applause when she finished. "She really seemed to me to be a sort of flower child," said one woman in attendance, "just doing her thing in her own little world." Other Canadians also rose to her defence. "The infamous escapades of Mrs. Trudeau that scandal-ized the country's Anglophones," observed *La Presse* columnist Lily Tasso, "were just what won the heart of the Quebeckers, conquered by her spon-taneity, youth and charm." A union organizer who had heard her on the radio sent her a personal letter praising her courage and lamenting the sorry state of the world when it could not hear "a little song of love" with-out cynicism. He advised her to follow her husband's example and offer her critics the reply of "Fuddle duddle."

Margaret said in her many radio and television appearances that she was "well"—an allusion to her struggles with depression. In mid-February, for example, she was interviewed by Dan Turner on a CBC-TV news show out of Ottawa. She not only said that she was "in great shape" but pointed to her head and added that she had been pronounced "fine" by her doctor. Turner, whom Margaret had known for years, joked that he found her recent behaviour somewhere between "eccentric and a little loony." She replied that he need not worry. She had put her "fear and lack of confidence in myself" behind her. She also entertained her host with a comical impersonation of Fidel Castro's heavily accented English. "He's a very gentle and delicate man and he certainly loves my child," she said of the Cuban leader.

Margaret continued in the weeks after the state visit to describe her marriage as charmed. However much she may have annoyed Canadian officials during the trip, it was obvious that she and Pierre had enjoyed their time together. The gulf between them had been at least temporarily bridged by the intense social activities of the trip—which played to her strengths rather than his—and by their time away from the Ottawa fishbowl. Given her candour about her mental health and the frustrations she was experiencing in the role of prime minister's wife, there is no reason to doubt that she would have been equally blunt about tensions in her marriage. As she told the press repeatedly, the time she was taking to herself in the aftermath of the Latin American tour she regarded as a "gift" from Pierre—and also from her mother, who had agreed to look after her sons. When asked whether her newly awakened desire for freedom and independence would adversely affect her husband, she insisted that he was a great believer in such inner voyages. "Pierre understands—because he is such a thinker," she explained. "He understands intellectually so well the basic idea of freedom and what it means, and respect for the individual and for the individual's right to creativity. He understands that very well intellectually. You know, I think I don't understand that—I'm not so much of an intellect—I probably understand that more in basic, earthy kind of terms. So I think that we make a very good couple. We have a happy marriage."

Typically, Pierre Trudeau never commented in public on the state of his marriage. A reporter asked him about Margaret's new-found freedom and her decision to take paid work. "I always believe in the maximum of independence for the maximum number of people," he replied dryly.

Margaret's hope that she could reconcile her need for personal independence with her marriage to Pierre proved to be wishful thinking. Within months of their visit to Cuba, Pierre would reach the limit already long passed by the likes of Ivan Head. Margaret later recalled of their state visit to Israel in the summer of 1976 that Pierre was "incensed" at her "atrocious behaviour." By then, there was more to his frustration than her flouting of diplomatic protocol. "At this stage," she admitted, "Pierre and I had both realized that something had gone seriously wrong with our marriage."

———

Predictably, the prime minister's enthusiasm for Fidel Castro "raised eyebrows" in the United States, as the *Washington Post* put it. After seeing a photograph of the two leaders embracing at José Martí Airport, the conservative columnist William F. Buckley commented, "The wonder is that Trudeau was not leaning over kissing Castro's behind. One wonders whether Trudeau would say that a great deal of thought and feeling had been put into a move by Fidel Castro if he sent troops to Quebec to liberate the people from Canada." A *New York Times* editorial also took him to task for his flattery of the Cuban leader. "It seems a pity," commented the paper sardonically, "that Prime Minister Trudeau will be unable to extend his goodwill trip to Angola." External Affairs officials were sufficiently worried about negative press in the United States that they took pre-emptive measures to "spin" the state visit to Trudeau's advantage. A large file containing press clippings and transcripts of the prime minister's statements was sent to Canadian diplomats in the United States, along with a three-page memo coaching them on how to answer questions American reporters might raise.

They need not have worried. As Trudeau himself had anticipated, the agitated reactions of the U.S. press had little impact in Washington, where it was generally agreed that having a trusted ally at Fidel Castro's dinner table could only advance American interests. On January 28, the day after Trudeau's Cayo Largo conversation with Castro, a subcommittee of the U.S. House Foreign Affairs Committee held a two-hour hearing on Canadian-American relations. The chair of the session happened to be Dante Fascell, a representative of Dade County, Florida, now more than ever the hotbed of anti-Castro politics in the United States. As an official at External Affairs later noted, Fascell conveyed a "positive" view of the Canada-U.S. relationship throughout the hearings, even when discussing the prime minister's Cuba visit with Deputy Assistant Secretary of State Richard D. Vine. Trudeau's decision to follow through with the trip was perfectly reasonable, said Vine, given the long lead time, the forceful statements of disapproval the prime minister made on Angola, and the fact that he had "gone to great lengths" to demonstrate that his being in Havana meant no compromise of Canada's partnership with the United States.

As Trudeau had also expected, his conversations with Castro were of more than passing interest to the Ford administration. (In the aftermath of the visit, the FBI's field office in Mexico sent Washington a full report on the prime minister's activities, adding to the already bulky file J. Edgar Hoover had started on Trudeau after his 1952 trip to the USSR.) Coincidentally or not, the prime minister's Latin American tour had come only days before the Cubans scuttled their secret talks with William D. Rogers. As soon as the Canadian entourage was back in Ottawa, Rogers himself flew to Ottawa to be briefed by Ivan Head on Castro's conversations with Trudeau. (Here was further evidence, as Ambassador James Hyndman put it, that the Americans appreciated Canada's unique capacity to "feed in some valuable information about what was going on in Cuba.") Rogers wanted the Canadian view on whether Castro's intervention in Angola signalled a return to his early 1960s policy of "exporting revolution." Cuba had recently agreed to train Jamaica's police forces and was reportedly "increasing its political contacts with black revolutionary elements elsewhere in the Caribbean basin." Head recounted for Rogers the talks at Cayo Largo, emphasizing Castro's firm dedication to the cause of anti-imperialism in Angola. Pierre Trudeau may have come away from that conversation with "a better insight into socialist reasoning," but Rogers was not persuaded. Nor were Gerald Ford or Henry

Kissinger, both of whom were by then knee-deep in accusations that they had bungled Angola and, with it, détente.

———

On January 21, 1976, just days before Pierre Trudeau was sitting down to his picnic dinner with Fidel Castro, Henry Kissinger was in Moscow being humiliated by Soviet General Secretary Leonid Brezhnev. At least this is how Peter Rodman, White House assistant to Kissinger, remembers it.

The Americans were in the Soviet capital to hammer out a new strategic-arms-limitation treaty. Kissinger also wished to discuss Angola with the Soviet leadership, and he believed he had a good case to put before Brezhnev. The original SALT treaty, signed at the Nixon-Brezhnev summit in 1972, had been premised on mutual "restraint" abroad. Soviet and Cuban involvement in Angola violated this principle and therefore had the potential to destabilize superpower relations well beyond the confines of west Africa. The Soviets, Kissinger reasoned, were no keener than the Americans to see Angola derail détente. "We've been given a clear promise that there would be a significant modification in the Soviet position," he said confidently before leaving Washington.

What the U.S. delegation encountered in Moscow, however, was an utterly defiant Brezhnev. At a press conference prior to the first day of talks, an American journalist asked the Soviet leader if he was willing to discuss Angola.

"I have no question about Angola," Brezhnev replied gruffly. "Angola is not my country."

"It certainly will be discussed," interjected Henry Kissinger.

"You'll discuss it with Sonnenfeldt," replied Brezhnev dismissively, referring to one of Kissinger's own aides. "That will ensure complete agreement."

The Soviets' refusal to even consider a quid pro quo on Angola was enormously damaging to the Republican White House. President Ford, who had said in early January that it would be "unwise for a President—

"THE MESSAGE SAYS, 'TURN ... BACK ... OR ... DETENTE ... WILL ... BE ... ENDANGERED.'"

me or anyone else—to abandon détente," ended up himself abandoning détente just two months later.

Leonid Brezhnev may have humbled Henry Kissinger in January 1976 but it was California governor Ronald Reagan who forced President Ford to backtrack on détente and adopt a hard line against Fidel Castro. Point man for an increasingly powerful coalition that would before long be called "neo-conservative," Reagan was Ford's only serious rival for the 1976 Republican presidential nomination. During the primaries, Reagan's sense that Ford was vulnerable on foreign and defence policy (and not on domestic issues) was confirmed by polls that showed that one in two American voters were "worried about the state of U.S. military power and consider it a major issue." He thus went after Ford on arms control, Angola and Cuba. Détente, said Reagan in one of his famous one-liners, gave the Soviets the opportunity to establish military dominance and the United States "the right to sell Pepsi-Cola in Siberia." He also accused the Ford administration of sacrificing American superiority in cruise-missile technology during the current round of arms-control negotiations, just as it had sacrificed America's anti-ballistic-missile superiority during SALT I.

President Ford narrowly defeated Ronald Reagan in the New Hampshire primary on February 24, 1976, taking only 51 per cent of the vote. This near miss was, without question, a wake-up call for the president. The Reagan camp announced that it would pull out all of the stops for the Florida primary on March 9, effectively forcing the Ford camp to reciprocate. Ford spent two days in Florida on a "grassroots tour," making three major speeches and treating Floridians to a presidential motorcade. Speaking at the Dade County Auditorium, where roughly eleven hundred Cuban émigrés were being naturalized, Ford went after the exile vote with a tough anti-Castro message. "My administration will have nothing to do with the Cuba of Fidel Castro," the president said, sending the crowd into an ecstatic cheer. "It is a regime of aggression." (He did not mention that Castro had been in secret talks with his administration just weeks earlier.) Ford took 53 per cent of the vote in the Florida primary, decisively halting whatever momentum Ronald Reagan had built in New Hampshire. But he would go on to lose the White House to Jimmy Carter. Seen in hindsight, the fact that Reagan and his conservative coalition could push Ford toward a hard line on Fidel Castro in 1976 was a portent of things to come, anticipating Reagan's presidential victory four years later and foreshadowing the rise of the Cuban exile lobby as a major force in U.S. politics.

A more ominous sign of the exiles' growing assertiveness was the dramatic increase in violence directed against anyone advocating dialogue with the Castro regime. Gerald Ford's and Henry Kissinger's public statements in early 1975 that "we are prepared to move in a new direction if Cuba will" ignited the worst two-year period of terrorism by cuban exiles on record. Roughly one hundred members of the Cuban-American community thought to be soft on Castro were attacked, most of them in Miami. One of the most notorious of these incidents was the murder in February 1975 of Luciano Nieves, who was shot down in broad daylight in a hospital parking lot after visiting his eleven-year-old son. Publisher Rolando Masferrer was killed in a bomb blast six months later, while Miami radio news director Emilio Milián lost his legs in a car bombing in April 1976. In a single day in December 1975, eight bombs exploded in U.S. government buildings in Miami, including the state attorney's office and the FBI office. In April 1976, two Cuban fishing boats were attacked by Miami-based speedboats, killing a young fisherman named Bienvenido Mauriz Díaz, whom Fidel Castro later eulogized as a martyr to the Revolution. Over the summer of 1976, the Cuban Embassy in Portugal was bombed, killing two officials; the Cuban mission to the UN in New York was bombed; a time bomb intended to blow up an Air Cubana flight out of Kingston, Jamaica, exploded instead in an unattended luggage cart; the Barbados and Panama offices of Air Cubana were bombed; and two Cuban diplomats were kidnapped in Argentina (and never heard from again).

Then came the incident Fidel Castro calls "the crime off Barbados." Air Cubana Flight 455 left Caracas, Venezuela, on the morning of Wednesday, October 6, 1976, bound for Havana. The flight made two scheduled stops in the afternoon, at Trinidad and Barbados. At 1:15 p.m., the plane left Seawell International Airport (now called Grantley Adams International Airport) in Bridgetown, Barbados. Ten minutes later, the pilot radioed the Barbados control tower, saying, "we have an explosion on board, we are descending immediately!" He attempted to turn the plane around, hoping to return to Seawell for an emergency landing, but went into a steep nosedive. Some eyewitnesses later said that a second explosion blew the aircraft apart just before it hit the Caribbean. Others said that, although the plane was trailing smoke, it appeared to have been intact when it struck the water. There were no survivors.

The attack on Cubana Flight 455 marked the first time in history that a civilian airliner was downed by terrorists. Seventy-three people were killed on Flight 455, including twenty members of Cuba's national fencing team and five of their coaches. The doomed plane was one of two DC-8s on lease to Cubana from Air Canada. It had been serviced and refuelled by an Air Canada maintenance crew at Montreal's Mirabel International Airport only three days before the disaster, after a regularly scheduled flight from Havana to Montreal. Canadian personnel occasionally crewed for Cubana flights but not on this occasion. As it happened, there were no Canadians on board.

The circumstances of the attack were not a mystery for long. Comandos de Organizaciones Revolucionarias Unidas (CORU) took credit for the atrocity in a dispatch to the Associated Press in Miami, identifying the explosive device as a "magnetic bomb" and claiming responsibility for other recent airport bombings in Barbados, Jamaica and Trinidad. The modus operandi of the attack made easy work for the Cuban, American and Venezuelan investigators assigned to the case. Because the bombs on Flight 455 were detonated in the plane's baggage compartment, the obvious suspects were two Venezuelans, Hernán Ricardo and Freddy Lugo, who had checked bags bound for Havana but got off the plane without luggage in Barbados. The two were arrested the next day in Trinidad, where they had flown from Barbados the same day as the bombing. One week later, two Cuban exiles with long histories of anti-Castro violence, Orlando Bosch and Luis Posada Carriles, were charged with conspiracy for their role in masterminding the attack.

The downing of Air Cubana Flight 455 was an almost unparalleled tragedy in the history of revolutionary Cuba, and it remains so. Nine days after the attack, on October 15, 1976, Fidel Castro gave a lengthy eulogy for its victims before one million Cubans in Havana's Revolution Square. Calling the bombing "a brutal act of terrorism," Castro spoke of the young athletes who had been killed—"healthy, strong, enthusiastic, devoted young compatriots"—and of the courage of the pilot, who had attempted to avert the disaster after the first explosion. He provided a detailed account of what was then known about the perpetrators, including an accurate description of the founding of CORU. He listed the many terrorist acts in the months leading up to the Air Cubana disaster for which that organization had claimed credit. He reviewed the findings of the Church Committee, accused the CIA of training and backing emigré terrorists since the Bay of Pigs, and chastised the U.S. government for failing to explain or apologize for any of its actions against Cuba. Castro concluded his speech by announcing that his government would cancel the 1973 hijacking agreement with the United States "this very afternoon." (Similar agreements with Canada, Mexico, Colombia and Venezuela, he noted, would remain in force.)

As noted above, the worst of the émigré violence against Cuban targets in Canada took place before the CORU bombing spree of 1975–76. Threats against Prime Minister Trudeau had been made prior to his state visit to Havana and were taken extremely seriously by the Cubans, including Fidel Castro. There continued to be threats made against Canadian diplomats in the Cuban capital after the prime ministerial visit, but they produced no violent incidents. In September 1976, just two weeks before the downing of Flight 455, CORU claimed responsibility for the drive-by bombing of the Cuban Consulate in Montreal. The same building was bombed again in 1980. These were, however, comparatively isolated incidents, at least when measured against the terrorist violence clustered in the late 1960s and the early 1970s. Despite understandable worries in Canada that Pierre Trudeau's friendly visit with Fidel Castro would unleash a third wave of violence against Canadian targets, it never came. Cuban-American militants appeared to have lost interest in Canada.

The most plausible explanation for Canada's diminishing value as a target for anti-Castro terrorists is that the Cuban-American community of which they were a part was circling the wagons at home. Throughout the 1960s and early 1970s, there had been few serious challenges in the United States (or within the OAS) to the policy of isolating Fidel Castro and strangling the Cuban economy. As one of only two nations in the western hemisphere to maintain diplomatic relations with Cuba, Canada was thus singled out both for legitimate political pressure, which peaked in the Diefenbaker years, and for violence, which peaked in the early

Trudeau years. By early 1976, in contrast, everything had changed. The OAS had agreed to lift sanctions against Cuba, Europeans were pouring onto the island, and the Ford administration appeared to be moving toward a rapprochement with Castro.

All of a sudden, Canada's unique relationship with revolutionary Cuba had ceased to be unique.

———

Seen in retrospect, the exiles' apparent loss of interest in Canada was but one indicator of a seismic shift that took place in Cuban-Canadian relations after Pierre Trudeau's state visit. For almost two decades, Canada had taken a principled stand against those who would undermine Cuba's right to self-determination, and Canadians had given Fidel Castro the benefit of many, many doubts. No longer. By the summer of 1976, the Cuban leader would be viewed by many in Canada as a lost cause. That Canada was giving up on Castro just as the United States was resuming *El Diálogo* was a curious irony. It was not lost on the Americans, Jimmy Carter among them, whose concessions to Castro would carry a high political price.

Ambassador James Hyndman tells a comical fish story about Fidel Castro. The Cuban leader showed up unannounced at the ambassador's residence in Havana one Sunday morning in February 1976, two weeks after the Trudeau state visit. As always, he was preceded by his security forces, who swept the area thoroughly prior to the leader's arrival. When Castro made his entrance, he was carrying a large red snapper. The fish, he told Hyndman, had been speared by him and Pierre Trudeau simultaneously during their fishing expedition at Cayo Largo. Castro had decided, therefore, to present the fish as a gift to the Canadian prime minister, and requested that Embassy personnel deliver the snapper to Ottawa with his compliments. He remained at the ambassador's residence for almost two hours that Sunday morning, enjoying a glass of Canadian whisky and discussing Jimmy Carter's presidential prospects with Hyndman. "I thought it was important that Fidel should realize that perhaps a new wind might be blowing in the United States," the ambassador later recalled. After listening intently to Hyndman's views, Castro requested that he provide copies of some of the press clippings he had on hand, particularly those from the *New York Times*. The ambassador sent the clippings off the next day.

Whether Pierre Trudeau ever got the red snapper is not a matter of the public record. Intended as a personal memento of the Trudeaus' visit to Cayo Largo, the appearance of a two-week-old fish at the PMO must have struck Canadian officials as unintentionally poignant. Despite his virtuoso performance in the House of Commons upon his return from Havana, Pierre Trudeau had already begun to distance himself from Fidel Castro. At the suggestion of External Affairs officials, for example, he agreed to waffle on his suggestion that the Cuban leader make an official visit Canada. They advised Trudeau to cite the Montreal Olympics as a pretext for postponement if the necessity arose, but apparently it never did. (In July 1976, Ramón Castro visited Canada, and Trudeau agreed to meet with him at the urging of Ivan Head. Cuban officials did not press for a state visit by Fidel, however.) By the summer of 1976, Embassy officials were reporting from Havana that the Cubans suspected a "loss of interest" in Cuba on the part of the Canadian government. One year later, former Cuban ambassador to Canada José Fernández de Cossío told Ambassador Hyndman that Cuban officials had grown "quite concerned and worried" about criticism of Cuba in Canada.

There were several reasons for this sudden chill in Cuban-Canadian relations, and the Cubans were well aware of most of them. The most obvious was post-visit fatigue. The prime minister had devoted an inordinate amount of time to the Cuba file in the weeks leading up to the state visit. Not surprisingly, he felt compelled upon returning to Canada to turn his mind to other things—the sputtering Canadian economy foremost among them. Canadian journalists who had accompanied the prime minister to Havana went through a similar process of withdrawal. With the exception of the Angolan crisis, Cuba dropped off their radar screens almost entirely. The Canadian media virtually ignored the downing of the Air Cubana jet in October 1976, for example—a striking departure from their past interest in the misdeeds of Cuban-American terrorists.

A second concern was strictly practical. Trudeau's visit had been hyped in Canada with the promise of vastly expanded trade with Cuba. This prognostication had been premised on the continuation of the breathtaking success of the Cuban economy in the early 1970s. But, as so often happens in the island's economic life, things took an unexpected turn for the worse. In 1976, the growth rate of the Cuban economy dropped to 4 per cent—a far cry from the 14 per cent it had averaged in the five previous years. Cuba went from having one of the best hard-currency debt-to-export ratios in Latin America to having one of the worst. Ambassador Hyndman's final report to External Affairs before leaving his post in Havana, dated July 1977, made detailed note of the country's mounting economic difficulties. "As a result," he concluded with characteristic understatement, "possibilities of substantial industrial contracts had not materialized and the volume of our trade was likely to be affected for some time."

A third reason for Canadians' cooling ardour for Cuba came in the form of a spy scandal that rocked Ottawa in early 1977. External Affairs informed the Cuban ambassador on the evening of Sunday, January 9, that four Cubans—three of whom were diplomats with consular status—were being expelled from Canada. A fifth, who was temporarily away from Canada, was told he could not return. "It has been determined," said an External Affairs official, "that an intelligence operation was conducted in Canada involving Cuban nationals in contradiction of their status." In accordance with diplomatic protocol, External Affairs would not say precisely what the Cubans had done to warrant expulsion. But the RCMP Security Service, which had long since viewed the Cuban presence in Canada as subversive, happily revealed that the Cuban Consulate in Montreal was being used not only for spying but also for the training of spies.

The fourth and most important reason Canadians turned against Cuba was Angola. Even as Pierre Trudeau was cheering "*¡Viva el Primer Ministro Fidel Castro!*" in January 1976, the tide of Canadian public opinion was turning against the Cuban leader. In May of the same year, Fidel Castro announced unexpectedly that he would begin a staged withdrawal of Cuban forces from Angola, at the rate of two hundred troops per week. "I do not wish to become the crusader of the twentieth century," he remarked. Henry Kissinger expressed skepticism about Castro's intentions, noting that the proposed schedule would still leave more than seven thousand Cuban soldiers in Angola at the end of the year. Others gave him the benefit of the doubt. All agreed that Castro was not likely to abandon Neto if this meant placing the MPLA government in jeopardy. Sure enough, in late July 1976, when FNLA guerrillas killed forty-one government troops and captured two cities and an airport in northern Angola, Castro backtracked on the troop withdrawal. Cuban forces would remain in Angola "as long as necessary" to defeat foreign aggressors, he said.

Pierre Trudeau watched Castro's machinations from the sidelines over the summer of 1976. Then he took the virtually unprecedented step of sending the Cuban leader a personal letter. Dated August 10, and hand-delivered to Castro by Ambassador Hyndman, the note expressed in diplomatic language Trudeau's hope that Cuba would keep to the withdrawal schedule announced in May. "I have continued to watch with considerable interest the passage of events in Southern Africa and congratulate you on your program of troop withdrawals from Angola," wrote the prime minister. "I continue to be of the opinion, as I expressed to you in Cuba, that the resolution of the basic political problems of that country, and the achievement of permanent stability, will be hastened by the removal of all elements of foreign involvement. Your commitment to a military disengagement is accordingly welcomed by the Canadian government." The subtext of the letter was not hard to discern, given that it was drafted after Castro's *volte-face* on the troop withdrawal. For what it was worth, the

Canadian prime minister, a man who on principle never interfered in the sovereign affairs of foreign states, was expressing his personal displeasure at Cuba's continuing presence in Angola. Predictably, it had no effect on Castro. When the idea began to circulate that Canada might provide peacekeepers to stand between warring factions in Rhodesia (now Zimbabwe), yet another African trouble spot, Trudeau dropped the tact. "Fidel Castro had made a mistake in sending troops to Africa," he reportedly said, "and Canada would be doing the same thing."

The Canadian press, which had so often extended Fidel Castro the benefit of the doubt in the past, turned resolutely against him as the Cuban presence in Africa expanded. The response of the *Globe and Mail* was typical. It announced in mid-February 1977 that Canadians were fed up. "Cuba has abused the friendship [of Canada] brazenly, outrageously," the paper said. "It has spied on us and our friends from Ottawa, trained spies and mercenaries in Montreal, used Gander as a base for running mercenaries to Angola. It has, in short, got away with murder." Then, one year later, the *Globe* advised the Trudeau Liberals to drop the "developing-country label" that made Cuba eligible for Canadian aid. If the island could afford to send thousands of troops to Angola, said the paper, it could not be all that needy.

In the House of Commons, Opposition MPs escalated their attacks on both Cuba and the Liberal government. Again the charge was led by former prime minister John Diefenbaker, who in the twilight of his life appeared to some Canadians to be atoning for his own government's stand on Cuba in the 1960s. Throughout 1977, Diefenbaker went after the Liberals for appeasing Castro instead of doing anything concrete to punish him for his African policies. "In Great Britain, in the United States, in France and in West Germany I have spoken to the leaders of those countries," he told the House in December 1977. "They cannot understand the close and abiding relationship that prevails between the Prime Minister of Canada and Castro. An international brigand—that is what he is—who has his forces destroying freedom in African countries.

Yet he is Canada's pet. It is beyond my understanding." Twice in 1978, Diefenbaker tabled strongly worded resolutions in the House to force the government's hand. "This House calls on the government," read one of them, "to inform Castro that his deplorable and shocking action is dangerous to world peace and must be discontinued, and, if not, will cause Canada to consider terminating diplomatic relations with Cuba." Other Conservative MPs fell in behind Diefenbaker, demanding that Canada suspend CIDA aid to Cuba and cancel the leases on Air Canada's DC-8s. At one point, Tory MP Lloyd Crouse told that House that "Cuban troops in Angola and elsewhere in Africa" could be the "catalyst" for a third world war.

Pierre Trudeau, whose disdain for parliamentary debate was by the late 1970s more obvious than ever, mostly left it to his ministers to answer such charges. When he finally reappeared in the House to defend his Cuba policy, in May 1978, it was to inform Canadians that the government would be terminating CIDA aid to the island to protest Castro's activities in Africa. Aid projects then on the books, he said, would be funded but no new projects would be launched. "Canada disapproves with horror [of] the participation of Cuban troops in Africa," he told the House.

Estimates of the number of Cuban troops in Angola by this time ranged between twenty and forty thousand. By the mid-1980s, the number was fifty thousand or more. Not until 1991, sixteen years after they had arrived, would Cuban troops leave Angola for good (leaving behind over two thousand dead). Meanwhile, in 1978 Castro sent eighteen thousand troops to help the Soviet-backed regime of Mengistu Haile Mariam in Ethiopia defend itself against the invading Somali army. The Cuban military was also active in as many as eight other African nations in the 1980s, though on a much smaller scale. The number of Cuban civilians in Africa, most of them teachers, doctors and construction workers, numbered in the tens of thousands. Nelson Mandela would later praise Cuba's record in Africa as "selfless," but few in the West saw it this way at the time.

Pierre Trudeau knew that the termination of aid to Cuba marked a milestone. For the first time since the rebel victory in 1959, Canadians had resorted to economic reprisals to punish Fidel Castro. For the remainder of Trudeau's tenure as prime minister and throughout Brian Mulroney's, the ban on aid to Cuba would remain in force. Only humanitarian aid would be exempt (hurricane relief, for example). Not until mid-1994, well after Fidel Castro had pulled his troops out of Angola, would Canada restore aid funding for Cuba. And when it did, all of Trudeau's old arguments about the importance of dialogue were restored along with it. "The isolation of Cuba is unhealthy," said Secretary of State for Latin America and Africa Christine Stewart, "and it's within all of our interests to support change in Cuba that is positive and healthy."

———

The fifth reason for Pierre Trudeau's loss of interest in Cuba was personal. His marriage to Margaret was going down in flames.

It is no easy matter, even now, to discern fact from fantasy in the wreckage of the Trudeau marriage. Margaret bared her soul in two racy autobiographies, *Beyond Reason* (1979) and *Consequences* (1982), omitting nothing of her confused and contradictory experience of the break-up. Pierre said nothing at the time, and little afterwards. "I was a neophyte at both politics and family life at the same time," he recalled in his *Memoirs*. "So perhaps it was a little too much for me and, regrettably, I didn't succeed all that well." That was it.

Margaret and Pierre had always had their vastly different ages and temperaments to navigate. As many Canadians had perceived early on, she was fire, and he was ice. Their marriage became increasingly acrimonious in the mid-1970s, yet it is also true that Margaret's nervous breakdown in 1974 had changed its underlying dynamic. Even as she became an increasingly "hateful person" and "a spoiled little bitch," as she later put it, he came to understand that there was more to her petulance and impulsiveness than youthful exuberance or the stresses of life as the prime minister's wife. He became both more intense in his surveillance of her, which she resented, but also far more solicitous, which she enjoyed—at least for a time. As noted above, Pierre's affection for Margaret was as much on public display in Havana in January 1976 as it had been any time since their wedding. But in the end, the centre could not hold. As Margaret's spirited defence of her song for Señora Pérez demonstrated, after "finding herself" again in Cuba she was no longer prepared to rein herself in.

What followed was not merely the public dissolution of the Trudeaus' marriage but a five-year whirlwind of debauchery and self-indulgence that made Margaret an object of loathing in Canada. "The aftermath of my marriage sent me on a downward spiral of exploration and adventure," she later recalled. "I seized on people, on jobs, on drugs, avidly, with desperation. Each let me down. I seemed to have no sense of the weight or worth of anything. Often, there were days when I truly did not see how I could carry on." Cocaine was one of the things she seized upon. She developed a dependence on the drug that made her "thin and tense," as well as "boastful, obnoxious and argumentative." She also seized on the Rolling Stones, Studio 54, Jack Nicholson and Ryan O'Neal, the sordid details of which she recounted in *Playgirl* and elsewhere. Not until the spring of 1977 would she formally separate from Pierre. Even then, the two would speak intermittently of reconciliation. "Pierre and I had evolved a curious and highly secretive way of life," she recalled. "Every two or three weeks I would disappear to New York or London. Then, after ten days or two weeks, I would become so homesick, so desperate to get back to the boys, that I would return to Canada." Fed up with her antics, many Canadians criticized her mercilessly for abandoning her children, a charge that wounded her deeply. By the summer of 1978, increasingly captive to her own paranoia and rage, she convinced herself that Pierre wanted her dead. In November 1979, they parted for good.

In two important respects, the public record on the demise of the Trudeaus' marriage has been skewed in Pierre's favour. The first concerns Margaret's penchant for publicity and indiscretion. Why, Canadians asked, would she spill her guts in soft-core magazines and ghost-written books about such deeply private matters as her affairs, her drug use and her mental illness? The standard answer was that her craving for the limelight was part and parcel of the "spoiled bitch" persona in which she had straightjacketed herself. The truth is far simpler. She did it because she needed the money. Early on, Pierre Trudeau had imposed two conditions on his wife should they separate or divorce. The first was that he would keep the children. The second was that she would not get a cent from him. Never did he compromise on either demand. He could have made the logistics of their separation easy—at least in the sense that he could well afford to provide for Margaret's financial needs as she tried to establish herself as a newly single young woman. He refused. Resentful and in desperate need of money, she played the only card she was holding. She revealed the deepest and darkest secrets of their lives at 24 Sussex in exchange for a publishing deal and two hefty author's advances.

The second myth about the Trudeau break-up relates to Pierre's own emotional state. His biographers have made much of the toll his dissolving marriage was taking on him, suggesting that the tumult of his home life was bleeding into his life in politics. Without question, he paid a high personal price for all of Margaret's antics and for all of the acrimony they endured together. But throughout the ordeal, he remained utterly in control of his emotions in public, employing the survival skills he had learned as a child and cultivated throughout his adulthood. "I kept a watertight seal between my private life and my public life," Trudeau recalled in his *Memoirs*. "It really was almost schizophrenic—and it helped me a lot."

———

In November 1976, just as Pierre Trudeau and many other Canadians appeared to be writing Fidel Castro off, Jimmy Carter was elected president of the United States on a promise to overhaul American foreign policy. Morality, said Carter, would be the new watchword for America abroad, and it would extend even to Cuba.

Carter had not been in the White House a month before his plan to ease Cuban-American tensions was in full swing. Citing "indirect sources," the president announced in early February 1977 that Fidel Castro intended to make good on his promise of the previous May to withdraw his troops from Angola. "If I can be convinced that Cuba wants to remove their aggravating influence in this hemisphere, will not participate in violence in nations across oceans, will recommit the former relationships which existed in Cuba toward human rights, then I would be willing to move toward normalizing relationships with Cuba," said Carter. Castro was receptive to the president's overtures, but he was not optimistic about the prospect of normalization. George McGovern could not even get a partial lifting of the blockade through Congress, Castro remarked at the time, and without the lifting of the embargo there could be no discussion of setting aside the "differences between the United States and us" or of putting the relationship between the two countries on an "equal footing."

Castro proved correct: normalization would remain out of reach. Even so, his and Carter's unprecedented willingness to negotiate produced some equally unprecedented compromises in 1977. An agreement on fishing rights was negotiated. The United States authorized U.S. citizens to visit Cuba, and Cuba welcomed them—"even though," as Castro put it, "we don't know what inconvenience this may cause us, since we are running the risk of having terrorist elements come here, the risk that CIA elements might come." Cuba and the United States established interests sections in each other's capitals—de facto embassies, though they could not be called that since the two countries had not officially restored diplomatic relations. And thanks to the selfless efforts of Bernardo Benes, a first-generation exile and President Carter's point man for *El Diálogo*, Castro agreed to release thirty-six hundred political prisoners. (For his efforts then and later, Benes was blacklisted in Miami's exile community and denounced as a traitor. His business, a Miami bank, was bombed and picketed, threats were made on his life and his children and friends were harassed.)

In mid-1977, the promise of normalized Cuban-American relations began to go sour. Cuban involvement in Africa proved to be the decisive issue for the Carter administration, just as it had been for the Canadian government. In June, amid rumours that Carter and Castro might be planning to meet in person, U.S. intelligence reported to the White House that Cuba was backing rebels in Zaire. Carter was measured in his public response to this discouraging revelation, saying only that it would now be "inappropriate" for him to meet with the *Comandante*. His attitude continued to cool until finally, in October 1979, he publicly abandoned his policy of dialogue. "I think we've got to have a firm policy on Cuba," he said. "Until Cuba can bring their own troops back from unwarranted involvement in the internal affairs of other countries, until they release the hundreds and hundreds, even thousands of political prisoners they have in jail, we will not recognize Cuba."

The dovish premises of Jimmy Carter's foreign policy came apart at the seams in late 1979. In November of that year, Iranian militants loyal to the Ayatollah Khomeini took more than sixty Americans hostages in Iran, producing a bedevilling 444-day crisis that ended the day Ronald Reagan was sworn in as president. Then, in December 1979, the Soviet Union invaded Afghanistan, vindicating the growing ranks of conservatives in the United States who believed that détente had weakened America's position in the world. In this new atmosphere of international crisis, Castro's status in the West reverted once again to that of a Soviet "puppet," as President Carter himself put it. To the likes of Ronald Reagan, who was then beginning his second run at the U.S. presidency, Castro's interventions in Africa merely confirmed Cuba's key role in the global communist conspiracy. Some hawks in the U.S. Congress demanded a naval blockade of Cuba. "We must not go to war with Cuba," said a beleaguered Carter in mid-January 1980.

The symbolic death of *El Diálogo* with Cuba, the ideal that had inspired not only Pierre Trudeau and Jimmy Carter but Cold War stalwart Henry Kissinger and many others, came at Havana's Mariel Harbour in 1980. When Fidel Castro agreed in 1978 to allow Cuban émigrés back into his country to visit their families, he intended it mainly as a means of raising hard currency. Over the next two years, the number of visits to the island by Cuban-Americans exceeded one million. Far from being the downtrodden *gusanos* described in official propaganda, however, the visitors carried with them food, medicines and the trappings of the good life, fundamentally altering Cubans' perceptions of their own lives. "As soon as people from outside started visiting us, it opened our eyes," recalled one disillusioned resident of Havana. "All the things we were told about the U.S. weren't true. That's when I knew I had to leave." A groundswell of interest in emigration began to build in Cuba. In April 1980, when a dispute with Peru prompted Castro to remove his soldiers from the gates of the Peruvian Embassy in Havana, more than ten thousand desperate Cubans crowded in requesting exit visas. An embarrassed Fidel Castro sought to defuse the crisis as quickly as possible, so he simply opened Cuba's doors to emigration. Anyone who wanted to leave Cuba, he said, was free to go. Such people were not "real Cubans" anyway, he said, but *escoria* (scum). "We don't want them; we don't need them."

Castro's decree set in motion the Mariel boatlift over the summer of 1980. With the help of three thousand private boats from south Florida (dubbed the Freedom Flotilla), over 129,000 Cubans made their way to the United States. (Three hundred *marielitos* were also granted political asylum in Canada by Liberal Immigration Minister Lloyd Axworthy. All were drawn from the first wave of Cubans who had stormed the Peruvian Embassy.) Jimmy Carter initially welcomed the refugees, praising their courage and allocating $10 million in emergency funding. The exodus demonstrated that the Cuban Revolution was a failure, he said. But when it was discovered that Castro had freed some of Cuba's worst criminal offenders from prison so he could dispose of them in the United States, the boatlift turned into a serous political liability for the president. Well before Cuba terminated all emigration in September 1980, the *marielitos* were stigmatized in the United States as deviants and psychopaths—a stereotype that would be immortalized in the character of Tony Montana (played by Al Pacino) in Brian De Palma's 1983 movie *Scarface*.

The Mariel boatlift was, as Fidel Castro put it himself, a deliberate "act of defiance" against the United States. The Cuban leader used the crisis to humiliate President Carter publicly for his adoption of a hardline approach to Cuba after 1978. It was a rash decision on Castro's part, the more so because it came in an election year and gave additional ammunition to Carter's many domestic critics. Mariel marked the lowest point in Cuban-American relations since the missile crisis of 1962 and, along with all of Carter's other foreign policy problems, helped to give Ronald Reagan the White House in 1980. Fidel Castro found himself once again out in the cold, a pariah both to his enemies in the United States and to his friends in Canada.

Alexander Haig, President Reagan's secretary of state, encapsulated this change of heart bluntly in 1980. "Give me the word," he reportedly told his cabinet colleagues, "and I'll make that island a fucking parking lot."

10

"The Idea of Our Time"

The Human Rights Revolution

Pierre Trudeau would not be reunited with Fidel Castro until he was retired from politics and travelling the world once again as a private citizen. Seen in retrospect, his state visit of 1976 represented the high-water mark of Canada's amicable relationship with revolutionary Cuba, at least until Lloyd Axworthy and Jean Chrétien ventured to the island in the late 1990s. No western heads of state would follow Trudeau to Cuba. Certainly, none would cheer "¡*Viva el Primer Ministro Fidel Castro!*" Castro knew in 1975 that his intervention in Angola was risky, but he underestimated the price he would pay in North American disaffection to win the affection of millions of Africans. By 1977, Pierre Trudeau had distanced himself from the Cuban leader because of his African adventure; Jimmy

Carter did so the following year. Well before Ronald Reagan entered the White House, Fidel Castro had become an outcast once again, at least from the North American perspective.

El Diálogo, the mid-1970s idea that Cuba could mend its fences with the United States and re-enter the family of nations, did not collapse only because the Miami exile lobby grew stronger or because President Reagan disliked communism. Dialogue failed as well because the model of international relations that had anchored it—détente—gave way to an entirely new one based on human rights. This turned out to be no minor shift but a full-blown revolution. With the rise to global prominence of advocacy groups like Amnesty International and Human Rights Watch, the standard for acceptable international conduct was no longer confined to relationships between governments. The sovereignty of nations gave way to the sovereignty of individuals. Governments' human rights records became intensely scrutinized. How regimes policed, charged, tried and punished their own citizens, particularly political dissidents, now determined their status on the world stage. The implications of this sea change were nowhere more revolutionary than in the case of Cuba, where Castro's regime had a long record of "meting out" revolutionary justice, as he had himself put it, in a brutal and sometimes careless fashion. To their credit, Cuban émigrés had long sought to draw the world's attention to the regime's record of human-rights abuses. But only in the late 1970s did this record become part of the official rationale for Cuba's continued isolation. By the 1990s, human rights was the driving force behind American and Canadian pressure on Cuba, displacing virtually all other concerns. When Castro finally pulled his troops out of Angola in 1991, Canada did not restore the aid funding it had cut in 1978. Instead, it cited Cuba's human rights abuses as the pretext for maintaining the ban. When Cuba was devastated by the "storm of the century" in 1993, which caused an estimated $1-billion in damage, Ottawa did nothing to help.

The human rights paradigm, in short, eclipsed the Cold War paradigm. All of a sudden, Pierre Trudeau and others who had spent a political lifetime working to ease Cold War tensions found themselves under the gun for cuddling up to Castro while his regime was routinely torturing and killing its own people. It is a charge that Trudeau's detractors continue to level, implying that the prime minister was blind to Cuba's human rights violations or indifferent to the suffering of Cuban dissidents. No book on Pierre Trudeau and Fidel Castro would, therefore, be complete without careful consideration of these accusations. For in the case of Trudeau, a liberal who devoted his life to the cause of extending basic liberties in Canada and worldwide, they call into question the very essence of the man.

———

After losing the 1979 election to Joe Clark's Tories and spending less than a year as leader of the Opposition, Pierre Trudeau was returned to power in February 1980 with a commanding majority. Exactly four years later, he would retire from politics for good.

Preoccupied at home with Quebec and abroad with the nuclear-arms race, the prime minister showed little interest in Cuba in his final term in office. Trudeau was without question uneasy about Ronald Reagan's crusading anti-communism (although he appreciated that the president's senior advisers, most notably Alexander Haig, were far more hawkish than the president himself). Reagan adopted an antagonistic approach toward Castro, reinstating the travel restrictions that Jimmy Carter had loosened, launching Radio Martí and even making veiled threats of invasion from time to time. Like Republican presidents before and after him, Reagan forged strong links within the Cuban-American community. In May 1983, he famously toasted Jorge Mas Canosa and other émigré leaders at Esquina de Tejas in Miami's Little Havana, saying, "*Viva Cuba libre. Cuba Sí, Castro No.*" Trudeau later recalled being "deeply distressed" by the American invasion of Grenada in 1983, and "bemused" by the claims of the Reagan administration that Cuban construction workers were building a runway on that tiny island suitable for Soviet combat aircraft.

Even so, the prime minister did little to warm Canada's frosty relations with Cuba while in office. As one study of Cuban-Canadian relations concluded, "the Trudeau-Castro honeymoon was over."

During the Mulroney years, 1984 to 1992, it was External Affairs Minister Joe Clark and not the prime minister who salvaged what remained of the goodwill between Canada and Cuba that had been built up in the 1970s. Had it not been for Clark's belief in Cuban-Canadian dialogue, Mulroney may well have followed the anti-Castro line of his friend Ronald Reagan, as he did on many other foreign-policy issues. (Secret negotiations between the Reagan administration and Fidel Castro were begun in 1985 but they quickly foundered, on the American side because of Castro's support for the Sandinistas in Nicaragua, and on the Cuban side because of Radio Martí. President Reagan was reportedly indifferent to—and possibly even unaware of—these talks.) The Mulroney years were notable for Canadians' growing involvement in the Cuban economy but this did not change Canada's cool attitude toward Cuba's policies in Africa. The issue of American subsidiaries' trade with Cuba reared its head once again, this time in the guise of the Cuban Democracy Act of 1992 (better known as the Torricelli Act). And once again, the Canadian government registered strong protests against the United States for interfering with Canada's right to set its own trade policy.

By the time Jean Chrétien became prime minister in 1993, the Cold War was no more. The Soviet Union had collapsed, leaving the subsidy-dependent Cuban economy in ruins. And Fidel Castro was sixty-six years of age. In the Chrétien years, Canada and the United States continued to pursue divergent Cuba policies as they had since 1960. Canadian trade, investment and tourists flooded into Cuba, taking full advantage of the regime's "Special Period" economic reforms, while Americans remained on the sidelines. Yet ironically, even as they were squabbling over the Helms-Burton Act and other irritants, Canadians and Americans had begun to position themselves for the same eventuality: the death of Fidel Castro.

It was fitting that Jimmy Carter should win the Nobel Peace Prize in 2002 for his human rights work. For it was Carter who insisted that human rights become "the soul" of U.S. foreign policy, setting in motion the revolution that has made human rights "the idea of our time." As president, he created a special human rights monitor in the State Department and gave his full support to congressional initiatives designed to punish human-rights abuses. Carter corresponded personally with André Sakharov, the Soviet Union's leading dissident. He imposed trade sanctions on Rhodesia and Uganda, and he banned U.S. weapons exports to South Africa. Because of Carter, NGO advocacy organizations like Amnesty International and Human Rights Watch would not only rise to prominence on the world stage but fundamentally change the way people all over the globe understood their status as citizens. Jimmy Carter was not the first U.S. statesperson to link human rights to the U.S. policy of détente, but he was the most important.

The timing of this human-rights revolution had everything to do with the Cold War. Human rights made its first powerful appearance in the international community in 1948, the year the UN adopted the Universal Declaration of Human Rights. But the division of the world into two hostile camps was hardly promising for making human rights the new benchmark for international conduct. For one thing, the Cold War ensured that the rights of nations would trump the rights of individuals. For another, the American strategy of containment meant in practice that the United States would ally itself with oppressive regimes as long as they were anti-communist. At its worst, as in Guatemala in 1954 and Chile in 1973, this meant undermining democratically elected governments that were perceived to lean too far to the left. "There were times," Jimmy Carter himself later observed, "when right-wing monarchs and military dictators were automatically immune from any criticism of their oppressive actions." In February 1999, President Bill Clinton ventured to Latin America to, as he put it himself, "highlight a new era of democratic co-operation in a region in which, not long before, America had supported repressive regimes with horrible human-rights records as long as they were anti-Communist." On that trip he actually apologized to Guatemala for what he called "America's past actions."

Human rights failed to take priority in international affairs before the Carter presidency for the same reason that human rights are controversial in some quarters today. Human rights talk conflicts with the idea of state sovereignty. And sovereignty is something most states do not wish to give up (which explains the Americans' reluctance to sign international human rights covenants). "I hold the strong view that human rights are not appropriate for discussion in a foreign policy context," Henry Kissinger said flatly in 1975. The United Nations itself acknowledged as much. Though armed with the 1948 Declaration, the UN was extremely reluctant to criticize member nations for their human rights abuses because of its "deference to the sovereignty of states." Today, among theorists of human rights, the argument is frequently made that human rights are a Trojan horse for Western liberalism (which, of course, most Western liberals readily accept). "Don't we want human rights to be the slippery slope toward democracy and the rule of law?" asks David A. Hollinger. "Isn't it simply true that human rights abuses are more likely to occur in nations lacking the consent of the governed, lacking democracy?"

Today, it is the policy of the Bush White House to link human rights reforms in Cuba both to regime change and to the overhaul of Cuban life in the American image. In keeping with his 2004 announcement that he is dedicated to the "liberation of Cuba," President Bush has established a Commission for Assistance to a Free Cuba. "The United States," this commission reported in 2004, "is committed to assist a post-Castro transition government in the promotion and consolidation of representative democratic processes and institutions that will respect the human rights and personal freedoms of all Cuban citizens." And what kind of Cuban society does the commission envisage? "Liberated from the rigidities and corruption of Castro's communist system," stated the same report, "[Cubans] will be free to create a private sector capable of providing jobs and opportunity, generating wealth, and spurring diversified growth. Long denied rights available to peoples in nearly every other country of the world, Cubans can be expected to place a high immediate priority on restoring rights to private ownership and the formation of competitive free enterprise." (James Cason, head of the U.S. Interests Section in Havana, has been equally outspoken in linking U.S. support for Cuban dissidents to regime change on the island.) The Castro regime has drawn the obvious conclusion. After decades of terrorism and "incitement to subversion," Cuba's foreign minister Felipe Pérez Roque has charged, "our people have had to contend with the obsession of U.S. governments to fabricate an opposition in Cuba, to fabricate an organized dissidence in Cuba, to foment in Cuba the emergence or strengthening of groups responding to their interests, with an evidently annexationist vision, those who would be responsible some day for propitiating Cuba's annexation to the United States."

Pierre Trudeau cared deeply for human rights. They had been central to his conception of popular democracy since the late 1940s, and they had inspired his work on behalf of the Canadian Civil Liberties Association beginning in the 1950s. While he was prime minister, he discussed human rights regularly with Canada's allies and even with its adversaries. He took great pride in the fact that he had personally persuaded Leonid Brezhnev during their first meeting in 1971 to provide exit visas for the relatives of Soviet citizens who had emigrated to Canada. He spoke of human rights to Castro privately during his 1976 state visit, and publicly during his Cienfuegos speech. And on the same Latin American tour, he and Venezuelan President Carlos Pérez signed a communiqué affirming "their confidence in the future of democratic society and their belief in the need to defend human rights throughout the world." To suggest that Trudeau was indifferent to human rights is simply cant.

But he was also a man of his times. His top priority in international relations was to ease Cold War tensions. This meant supporting human rights initiatives wherever they were consistent with détente and, more important, where they did not unduly antagonize Canada's main ally, the United States. Far from being ineffectual, this attentiveness to the thorny politics of human rights actually gave Canada a leg up in negotiating new multilateral treaties. Canadians played a leading role in the negotiation of the Helsinki Final Act of 1975, for example, which established a quid pro quo with the Soviets on family reunification and other "human contact" issues. Trudeau himself was present at Helsinki, where he again took the opportunity to meet Brezhnev privately. "This conference," Trudeau later recalled, "gave us the opportunity to press the Soviets on human rights and the free movement of peoples."

Canada's leading Cold War historian, Robert Bothwell, makes an extremely important point about Helsinki. "Canada's support for the talks entailed a delicate balancing act," he observes. "The United States (more accurately its secretary of state, Henry Kissinger, who gave more importance to power than to morality in foreign affairs) was more reluctant than the Europeans to engage in the [talks], mostly because of its human rights dimension." This observation strikes right at the heart of Trudeau's circumspect behaviour when it came to Cuba's human rights record. It was not because he was insensitive or oblivious that he refused to criticize Castro's human rights violations openly. He did so because any public discussion of human rights in Cuba would inevitably open up the Pandora's box of America's Cuba policy—including U.S. support for anti-Castro insurgencies, covert operations and assassination plots.

———

In the aftermath of the events of 9/11, Fidel Castro gave a major speech claiming that 3,478 Cubans had perished since 1959 as the direct result of acts of aggression that originated in the United States. "It would be as if 88,434 people had died in that country," he calculated, "that is, a figure almost similar to the number of Americans who died in the Korean and Vietnam wars combined." Whether Castro's figure is inflated is anyone's guess. His regime has been notoriously obstinate when it comes to allowing outside observers to gauge the veracity of its statements about human rights abuses in and against Cuba. But there can be no disputing two claims that Castro has made consistently since the early 1960s. The first is that external violence against Cuba and Cuban targets elsewhere in the world has been extensive and virtually continuous since he took power. The second is that this campaign of violence has contributed directly to the regime's intense distrust of internal dissent in Cuba. This is not to say that the Revolution would have been less repressive in the absence of external threats. As the terror that followed the rebel victory demonstrated, the seeds of violent repression were built into the anti-Batista ideology that originally inspired the *Fidelistas*. More to the point, little of what is known about Fidel Castro suggests that he would have opened Cuba up to political competitors or domestic critics under any circumstances. Nor does the external threat in any way excuse the regime's well-documented human rights abuses. But it does help to place Castro's own position on human rights into perspective. Had the United States (and the CIA in particular) not been so relentless in its efforts to foment counterrevolution within Cuba, he has always said, his government would not have to be so heavy-handed in rooting out and punishing dissent.

American critics of the Castro regime have always taken such statements from Fidel Castro with a grain of salt. As Henry Kissinger and William D. Rogers both said after the collapse of their secret talks with the regime in 1976 (and still say), Castro claims to want peace with the United States but knows the political advantages within Cuba of maintaining the United States as a highly visible enemy. Fair enough. They may well be correct. But this does not change the broader pattern in Cuban-American relations: when Cuba's relations with the United States warm up, as they did in the mid-1970s, the regime tends to be more tolerant of internal dissent, more likely to grant amnesty to political prisoners (usually on condition that they emigrate), and more apt to allow the free movement of people between the United States and Cuba. In July 1964,

Castro put on record an offer to the United States that has stood for four decades: if the United States normalized relations with Cuba, he said, he would release 90 per cent of the political prisoners being held on the island (then estimated at "something under 15,000"). It was not coincidental that Jimmy Carter (via his secret emissary Bernardo Benes) was able to negotiate the release of "almost all of Castro's political prisoners" in the late 1970s Journalist Edward Lawrence Rabel of CBS asked Castro in September 1978 whether the release of so many Cuban politicals was "a gesture toward President Carter and his human rights policy." "The Government of the United States might have had some indirect influence on this," Castro replied, "but not due to its verbal human rights policy, but rather because there's no question that this administration put an end to the policy of supporting terrorist activities against Cuba."

When the Cuban leader was in Canada for the state funeral of Pierre Trudeau, he was asked about the three hundred or so political prisoners known still to be held in Cuban jails. "Three hundred?" he responded. "Listen, if we jailed all of those who receive a salary from the United States to fight against the revolution, there would be a lot more than those three hundred. I do not know the exact number; I am not up to date on it. Let us admit that there are between 200 or 300, 320, or 400. At the beginning of the Revolution, when the United States organized 300 counterrevolutionary and terrorist organizations, and invaded the Bay of Pigs, blockaded this country, and encouraged counterrevolution in every possible way, we ended up with up to 20,000 prisoners, referred to as political, counterrevolutionary prisoners. You call them political prisoners, I am not going to argue about that. Call them whatever you like, we do not call them ordinary prisoners, because they are not ordinary prisoners. We do not call them political prisoners because they are counterrevolutionary prisoners. And the word political has a different, more honourable connotation for us. These are prisoners who have fought against their own country." (Castro has also criticized human rights abuses originating in the United States. He has said that the embargo is a human rights obscenity, and that life in America's prison system violates the country's nominal commitment to human rights.)

Washington's criticisms of Cuban human rights violations have always been mired in politics, and Canadians have always known it. So have some Americans. In 1989, for example, Human Rights Watch opened its annual report on Cuban human rights abuses with a critique of the United States. "The Bush administration's human rights policy toward Cuba," it observed, "has been marked by internal contradiction. The impression that emerges is of an administration that is interested in human rights in Cuba when it serves the purpose of discrediting Fidel Castro, but which quickly loses interest if there is an ideological price to pay." In response to U.S. claims of political executions and torture in Cuba, the UN Human Rights Commission undertook a review of the island's human rights practices in 1989. The commission found "no evidence" to support American allegations, a conclusion that had the unintended effect of exonerating Castro. "U.S. credibility before the Commission," concluded Human Rights Watch the same year, "was hurt by the perception that the administration's single-minded focus on Cuba was to the exclusion of comparable violators who happened to be U.S. friends."

To many outside observers, American claims about Cuba's human rights abuses are inconsistent with Washington's willingness to extend the benefit of the doubt to one-party regimes with horrendous human rights records elsewhere in the world. In 1993, for example, just four years after Tiananmen Square, President Bill Clinton met with China's President Jiang Zemin. "We still had differences over human rights, Tibet, and economics," the president later recalled, "but we had a shared interest in building a relationship that would not isolate but integrate China into the global community." In 1994, Clinton normalized relations with communist Vietnam. And in 2000 he toured Hanoi and Ho Chi Minh City (formerly Saigon) as a guest of Prime Minister Phan Van Khai. Clinton's rationale for extending most-favoured-nation status to China was a textbook case of constructive engagement. "China was extremely sensitive to other nations' 'interfering' in its political affairs," Clinton recalled. "Because our engagement had produced some positive results, I decided, with the unanimous support of my foreign policy and economic advisers, to extend MFN and, for the future, to delink our human rights efforts from trade. The United States had a big stake in bringing China into the global community. Greater trade and involvement would bring more prosperity to Chinese citizens; more contacts with the outside world; more co-operation on problems like North Korea, where we needed it; greater adherence to the rules of international law; and, we hoped, the advance of personal freedom and human rights." This was precisely the rationale for Canada's policy of constructive engagement in Cuba.

There is an even more persistent flaw in the U.S. critique of Castro's human rights record, one that has taken centre stage in the wake of damning revelations from Abu Ghraib and Guantánamo. As even the most reluctant Cold War leaders, including Pierre Trudeau, had always known, human rights violations are never arbitrary. They always arise out of specific political contexts. Human rights violations are the by-products of policies adopted by governments that have specific goals, whether this means the self-preservation of a particular regime or even the preservation of a way of life. As Seymour Hersh has shown in his book *Chain of Command*, the second Bush administration is today mired in a debate about the definition of torture. "To this day," Human Rights Watch executive director Kenneth Roth told Hersh, President Bush and his top aides "cling to the fiction that there is a realm of coercion that does not violate the international prohibition against torture. Until the Administration formally abandons all forms of coercive interrogation, it is inviting the abuse that has become standard fare since September 11th."

American leaders (and citizens) are not indifferent to human rights abuses. But certain U.S. foreign policy objectives—ending terrorism, rooting out al-Qaeda, capturing or killing Osama bin Laden—cannot be achieved, some believe, without bending internationally recognized rules on human rights. Specifically, human rights violations in the context of the War on Terror are legitimized by the idea that this war will be won not by superior force but by superior intelligence. Knowing how and when terrorists will strike is of the essence, which means that obtaining information from captured terrorists is also deemed essential. There is general agreement among experts on intelligence gathering that carrots are more effective than sticks in extracting intelligence from captured enemy soldiers. But when carrots fail, when the only available means of getting information is via coercion, then coercion acquires a political legitimacy that leads directly to state-sanctioned torture. The revelations of human rights abuses at Guantánamo and Abu Ghraib, where captured Muslims were humiliated and abused at the hands of U.S. authorities, shocked the world. But there is another perspective on this issue, as even American liberals like Bill Clinton have acknowledged. If 9/11 could have been prevented by coercive interrogation techniques, would the end have justified the means? In October 2001, President Bush gave the CIA $1 billion to hunt down and assassinate Osama bin Laden—the first open assassination order in the United States since Kennedy told the agency to kill Castro. There was no hue and cry, least of all about human rights.

In the Chrétien years, Canada consistently backed American efforts at the UN to spotlight Cuban human rights abuses. And when Lloyd Axworthy and later Chrétien himself travelled to Cuba, they did so in the hope that Canadian influence might compel Fidel Castro to initiate reforms. "We called our initiative Principled Pragmatism," Axworthy later said. "It involved bilateral engagement with selected countries where the human rights record was poor. Candidates that readily came to mind were China, Cuba and Indonesia. Rather than skirting around the fact that these were places for investment and trade, the idea was to use the access that such contacts afforded to see if we might graft into the relationship an engagement on human rights." In Cuba, this policy plainly failed. But even in countries where the Canadian presence is said to have made a difference, Canada faces many of the same dilemmas in pressing for human rights reforms as the United States. Concerning China in particular, where Prime Minister Chrétien zealously promoted Canadian trade, there was a great outcry against the Liberal government for failing to protest adequately against the regime's policies in Tibet and its jailing of dissidents. Nor does Canada appear to be any less cognizant of U.S. security prerogatives during the War on Terror than it was during the Cold War. There is considerable evidence, now regularly cited by Human Rights Watch, that the Canadian security agency, CSIS, knowingly deported at least one Canadian citizen, Maher Arar, to face torture in Syria because he was suspected of having links to al-Qaeda.

In April 2001, Prime Minister Chrétien defended the exclusion of Cuba from the Third Summit of the Americas, held in Quebec City, on the grounds that the regime had failed to rectify its human rights record. Referring to his own 1998 state visit to Havana, Chrétien said that he had spent several hours trying to persuade Fidel Castro to change his policies. In a lengthy written statement, the outraged Cuban leader dissected what he believed to be the many diplomatic missteps Chrétien had made. Unlike Pierre Trudeau, Castro concluded, Chrétien did not understand Cuba. "I am sure that Trudeau would never have said that he spent four hours giving advice to someone who had not asked for it," railed the Cuban leader, "nor would he seek excuses for excluding an honorable country from a meeting that it did not ask to attend, or ask it to sign an agreement that it would never have signed. History will say who is right."

———

Pierre Trudeau knew something about the complexity of international politics. Much of what he said and did as a Cold War prime minister has since been vindicated by the awkward policy dilemmas in which his successors have found themselves. Although he cared passionately about human rights, Pierre Trudeau knew when he travelled to Havana in 1976 that exposing Castro's record of human rights abuses would simply give the Cuban leader an entree to criticize the United States—the very outcome that he was at pains to avoid. His state visit coincided with the striking revelations of what the CIA had been doing in the name of national security, including plotting the assassination of foreign leaders, spying on U.S. citizens and assisting in the 1973 coup in Chile that brought the brutal dictator Augusto Pinochet to power. It also coincided with a (relative) loosening of Cubans' freedom to express criticism of the regime. The timing was hardly favourable for a Canadian prime minister to pronounce on Cuban human rights violations when its main Cold War ally was awash in allegations of dirty tricks. So Trudeau chose to tread lightly but firmly on human rights, in his private talks with Castro, in his speech to the people of Cienfuegos and in his communiqué with President Pérez of Venezuela. And the Ford administration thanked him for it.

More generally, Trudeau believed that easing international tensions was more likely to advance human freedom in the world, rather than vice versa—a view that continues to colour Canada's policy of principled pragmatism. Human rights were not mentioned in the long list of objectives drafted by External Affairs in late 1975 for Trudeau's state visit to Havana. Nor did human rights appear on the Ford administration's wish list of reforms that William D. Rogers carried with him to his secret negotiations with the Cubans in 1975–76. In those years, Castro's human rights record did not provide a rationale for the U.S. embargo nor did Washington cite it when pressing Canada to cool its trade relations with Cuba. From the American perspective, the only issue preventing normalization in 1975 was that of U.S. claims on confiscated property (and, of course, a more generalized objection to the appearance of communism in the western hemisphere). From the North American perspective more generally, Castro's crime in 1975 was Angola. In the 1970s, in short, the issue was still the Cold War.

—•—

Pierre Trudeau was Canada's first sound-bite prime minister. No one came to the job with a stronger intellectual grounding or with as many published writings to his credit. Yet, ironically, it was the offhand quips that somehow seemed to encapsulate the man's wilful independence— "Fuddle duddle." "Where's Biafra?" "Just watch me."

"*¡Viva el Primer Ministro Fidel Castro!*" was without question one of those defining phrases. In the immediate aftermath of the now-famous cheer, with the world eager to know what exactly was meant by such a spirited statement of camaraderie, Trudeau's aides had immediately moved to downplay it. His "*Vivas*," they said, were nothing more than "conformity to Cuban protocol." But nobody bought it. He had not shouted "*¡Viva!*" in Mexico. And having felt the sting of Charles de Gaulle's famous "*Vive le Québec libre!*" in 1967, Trudeau well understood the power of the phrase. More than this, there could be no mistaking his uncharacteristically exuberant tone, his voice raised to shouting pitch. When Pierre Trudeau cheered "*¡Viva el Primer Ministro Fidel Castro!*" he meant it. He affirmed, in front of Cuba, Canada and the world, that despite their differences, he and Castro had forged a strong personal bond. Trudeau's many critics, then and later, saw his "*¡Viva!*" cheer as a defining moment in his reign as prime minister. They were correct. It was.

Trudeau himself never apologized for the cheer. And despite his aides' attempts to characterize the "*Vivas*" as spontaneous, there can be little doubt that he had calculated beforehand their political costs and benefits. There may well have been something of the devil-may-care Trudeau style in the cheer—as there had been when he pirouetted behind the queen, for example. But everything in Trudeau's political bag of tricks was fastidiously well rehearsed. What Trudeau did say in the aftermath of his "*¡Viva!*" speech is what he had been saying about his state visit to Cuba all along. "Some Americans and some Canadians will feel that we are going a bit far in having this kind of warm relationship with Communist countries. But I repeat, what is happening in Cuba is of great importance to the world."

As it turned out, he was half correct. Most North Americans did indeed think that he had gone "a bit far" in his enthusiasm for Fidel

Castro. But what was happening in Cuba *circa* 1976 turned out to be of little interest to the Western world. Fidel Castro had been a hero to many North Americans in the heady 1960s, but by the late 1970s and well into the 1980s he had again become *persona non grata*—a brigand, in the words of John Diefenbaker, and a Soviet puppet, as Jimmy Carter put it. The Cubans' long and costly intervention in Angola saw to that. "*¡Viva el Primer Ministro Fidel Castro!*" did not, as Pierre Trudeau had hoped, usher in a new rapprochement between Cuba and the West. On the contrary, like so many other sound bites from the Trudeau era, these words had no sooner crossed the prime minister's lips than they became one of the Cold War's most memorable anachronisms.

"Call Me Pedro"

Pierre Trudeau was reunited with Fidel Castro in 1991 when he first journeyed back to Havana. Accompanied by his three sons, the former prime minister went snorkelling with the Cuban leader and the two men quickly rekindled their old friendship. Their advancing age had the effect, especially after Castro turned seventy, of accentuating their essentially philosophical natures and thus of orienting their conversations toward the personal rather than the political. Trudeau would enjoy three more visits as Castro's guest before his failing health curbed his ability to travel in the late 1990s. These were private journeys, undertaken with little fanfare and virtually no official pomp.

Quite often Trudeau could be found poolside at the Canadian ambassador's residence indulging in his favourite pastime, reading. In the evenings he and Castro would engage in free-ranging discussions over meals that sometimes included Cuban officials but more often were small in scale and intimate in tone. Trudeau showed no interest in discussing Canadian foreign policy per se and did not, as some reports have claimed, presume to counsel Fidel Castro on his own policies or on Cuba's future. Former Canadian ambassador to Cuba Mark Entwistle played host to many of these soirees. Entwistle, who estimates that he spent a total of one hundred hours in Fidel Castro's presence between 1993 and 1997, says that he never saw the Cuban leader treat anyone with the attentiveness or respect he accorded Pierre Trudeau. The only other person for whom the *Comandante* demonstrated anything like the same reverence was Pope John Paul II. In marked contrast with his usual conversational style, which meant occupying centre stage and delivering monologues that could last hours on end, Castro *listened* to Trudeau. Theirs was a "mentor-student" relationship, Entwistle recalls, with Trudeau in the senior role.

Trudeau continued in retirement to identify with the social policy achievements of the Revolution, just as he had when he visited Cuba in 1964 and 1976. No longer bound by diplomatic niceties, Trudeau spoke bluntly of the privation he witnessed in Cuba during the Special Period. "What the U.S. is doing is criminal," he told two Canadian friends over lunch in Havana in 1992. "It's a clear violation of international law."

In 1995, Trudeau agreed to promote an investment deal that would see the Canadian firm York Medical become the first company in the West to secure licensing rights to Cuba's drug and medical-device industries. He called himself the éminence grise of the venture, emphasizing that he owned no shares in the company and would not profit from any arrangement with Cuba. Trudeau and David Allen, the head of York Medical, agreed that the deal was important "for compassionate reasons." At the same time, Trudeau helped to launch the Health Partners International of Canada medical-aid program in Cuba, which over the following decade would see roughly $40 million in Canadian medical supplies sent to

Cuba. "Canada's relationship with Cuba is a special and cherished one," Sacha Trudeau said in a rare public appearance in 2005, the tenth anniversary of the program. "I am happy that this program that my father envisioned is continuing to grow and bring healing to many Cubans."

———

Despite the long history of Cuban-Canadian trade relations and occasional diplomatic milestones like Pierre Trudeau's 1976 state visit, only since the end of the Cold War have Canadians begun to loom large in Cuban life. A rising tide of tourists, investors, students, academics, aid workers, journalists, authors and musicians have been making their way to Cuba from Canada since the early 1990s. Their presence can be felt in the streets of Cuba, in its shops and bars, in its oil fields and nickel mines, practically everywhere. On Cuba's white sand beaches, Canadians predominate. Half a million Canadian sun-seekers today descend on the island annually, making Canada the largest single market for the Cuban tourism industry. Canada is now Cuba's second-largest commercial partner, after Spain, while Alberta-based Sherritt International is by far the largest foreign firm doing business there. The Royal Winnipeg Ballet performs regularly in Cuba, as it has done since the 1970s, and its leading male dancers are today Cuban. Collaborative literary projects are nurtured by novelist Margaret Atwood and her husband Graeme Gibson, who are regular guests of Cuban writers. Canadian universities sponsor conferences and student exchanges. Canadian musicians led by saxophonist Jane Bunnett have fashioned award-winning careers recording and touring with Cuban musicians.

Canadians have been the main foreign beneficiaries of Cuba's retreat from a Soviet-styled planned economy over the last fifteen years, and many of the warm relationships they have cultivated there are the natural by-products of this process. Although doing business in Castro's Cuba is still fraught with difficulties, especially for smaller players, Canadian investors, exporters and tour operators admit their good fortune at simply being in the right place at the right time. To judge from Castro's remarks at least, the Cubans are grateful. Canadian and Cuban officials take pains to downplay the success of the bilateral partnership. They know that celebrating it openly would only goad the United States and undercut Canada's condemnation of Castro's human rights record, something both Pierre Trudeau and Jean Chrétien learned the hard way. Off the record, though, they agree that Canada has been essential to Cuba's economic recovery and that Canadians are well positioned to profit from the island's inevitable reintegration into the global economy. Canadian politicians routinely criticize the U.S. embargo but the fact is that, in locking the Americans out of the Cuban market, the sanctions have continued to give Canadians a decisive leg up.

The American government knows all of this, of course, which is why it occasionally opts to play hardball. In March 2002, James Sabzali became the first Canadian businessman to be indicted by the U.S. Justice Department on charges that he had violated the 1919 Trading with the Enemy Act. His crime: selling water-purification equipment to Cuban hospitals and factories under contract to the U.S. chemical company Purolite. (Three American executives were also charged.) Facing a $19-million fine and a 205-year prison sentence, Sabzali pled guilty in 2004 to a single charge of "smuggling" in exchange for one year's probation. After the trial, Assistant U.S. Attorney Joseph Poluka lectured Canadian reporters. "You're not allowed to violate the laws of this country just because you live outside it," he said. "You need to educate your Canadian audience."

Meanwhile, back in Canada, the Castro mystique that had its origins in the Sierra Maestra almost fifty years ago has become a staple of popular culture. Cuba gets more press coverage in Canada than all other Latin American countries combined. Canadian journalists and pundits regularly pronounce on the U.S. embargo and Cuba's human rights record, and so do the many ordinary Canadians who have seen at first-hand their impact on the people of Cuba. Every new twist in the Cuban-American stand-off is grist for the media mill, while sensational human-interest stories like the Elián González saga are front-page news. "Cuba, sí!" shouts one of Toronto's most ubiquitous mid-winter billboard campaigns.

As for Cuba, the world is today watching and waiting. Having tried for half a century to undermine the Revolution with threats and economic sanctions, American hard-liners have resigned themselves to what they crudely called the "biological solution"—the death of Fidel Castro. Whether the Revolution can survive without him is the question on everyone's lips, and these days it is no longer even spoken in whispers.

———

In one of his last trips to Cuba, Pierre Trudeau was accompanied by the Canadian journalist Brian McKenna to film a conversation with *El Comandante* for his *Memoirs* project. "They greeted each other with an embrace," McKenna later recalled, "like two ageing Catholic cardinals."

"What shall I call you on camera?" Castro asked Trudeau.

"Call me Pierre or Pedro," replied Trudeau, "as long as I can call you Fidel."

Notes

PROLOGUE Funeral for a Friend

2   "*The regard I felt*": Fidel Castro, cited in Paule Robitaille, "Feature Interview,"
        CBC (October 2000).

2   "*intellectual soulmates*": Mark Entwistle, cited in Jennifer Ditchburn, "Castro
        Travels to Canada to Mourn Trudeau," CP (October 2, 2000).

2   "*I have come to Canada*": Fidel Castro, "Official Statement" (October 2000).

3   "*one of the most sincere men*": Fidel Castro, cited in Robitaille, "Interview."

4   *"ready to trade Canada's soul"*: Pierre Trudeau, "The Values of a Just Society,"
     Thomas S. Axworthy and Pierre Elliott Trudeau, eds., *Towards a Just Society*
     (Toronto: Penguin, 1992), 427.

5   *"Micha just actually"*: Margaret Trudeau, cited in Dene Moore, "Trudeaus
     Remember Michel and Promote Avalanche Awareness," CP (January 14, 2000).

5   *"We could see him"*: Eric Lemieux, cited in Jeff Adams, "Sliding into Oblivion,"
     SP (spring 1999).

6   *"When you have"*: Margaret Trudeau, cited in Moore, "Trudeaus Remember."

7   *"Presently, I share in the grief"*: Fidel Castro, "Official Statement."

7   *"I met that little baby"*: Fidel Castro, cited in Robitaille, "Interview."

7   *"He was sad"*: Margaret Trudeau, cited in "Margaret Trudeau Reveals the Final
     Days of Ex-Prime Minister's Life," CPN (January 4, 2001).

10   *"The applause"*: Sylvain L'Heureux, cited in "Family Lays Pierre Trudeau to Rest
     after Grand State Funeral," CP (October 3, 2000).

11   *"the most devout of Catholics"*: John English et al., eds., *The Hidden Pierre Elliott
     Trudeau: The Faith behind the Politics* (Toronto: Novalis, 2004).

11   *"Pierre loves ritual"*: Margaret Trudeau, *Beyond Reason* (New York: Simon and
     Schuster, 1979), 50-1.

11   *"Pierre Trudeau was"*: Jean Chrétien, cited in "Family Lays Pierre Trudeau to
     Rest."

15   *"You're a brave girl"*: Jimmy Carter, cited in "Son Remembers Trudeau," CBS
     (October 3, 2000).

16   *"Cuba sends an unfortunate signal"*: Jean Chrétien, cited in Anita Snow, "Cuba
     Sentences 4 Dissidents to Jail," AP (March 15, 1999).

17   *"burned"*: "Powell Takes Tough Line on Castro," BBC (March 14, 2001).

17   *"Of all the presidents"*: Fidel Castro, cited in Robitaille, "Interview."

1   *¡Viva Fidel!*: Castro in Montreal

25   *"The Mounties"*: Fidel Castro, cited in "Feel Like in Havana: Fidel Defies Guards,
     Hailed by Montreal," TS (April 27, 1959), 27.

25   *"revolutionary hero"*: "Castro Hurries Home, Can't Visit Toronto," TS
     (April 23, 1959), 2.

25   *"That's silly"*: Fidel Castro, cited in "Feel Like In Havana," 27.

26   *"a full discussion"*: John G. Diefenbaker, cited in "Castro to Return for Official
     Visit," TS (April 24, 1959), 10.

26   *"My own appraisal"*: Richard Nixon, cited in Robert M. Levine, *Secret Missions
     to Cuba: Fidel Castro, Bernardo Benes and Cuban Miami* (New York: Palgrave
     Macmillan, 2001), 30.

27   *"In Cuba they had tanks"*: Fidel Castro, cited in "Hired Castro Killers on Peaceful
     Pursuits," UPI (April 24, 1959).

28   *"I feel as if"*: Fidel Castro, cited in "Feel Like in Havana," 27.

28   *"visitors from other parts"*: "Castro," *MS* (April 27, 1959), 4.

29   *"Women and teenagers"* to *"There's a Latin atmosphere"*: Fidel Castro, cited in "Feel Like in Havana," 27.

29   *"frightful massacre"*: Monroe Johnston, "Washington Deciding It Likes Fidel Castro," *TS* (April 23, 1959), 7.

31   *"It has reached the point"* to *"I came to this dance"*: Fidel Castro, cited in Michael Johnson, "Cuban Top Problem Claimed Financial," *MS* (April 27, 1959), 1.

31–32 *"I got to know"*: Andy McNaughton, cited in "I Like Life Interesting," CP (January 6, 1959).

32   *"rare gift"*: Boyce Richardson, "Inner Fire Is Mark of Castro," *MS* (April 27, 1959), 1.

32   *"Right now"*: Fidel Castro, cited in "Feel Like in Havana," 27.

35   *"the bitter days"*: Ernesto Che Guevara, cited in Tad Szulc, *Fidel: A Critical Portrait* (New York: Post Road Press, 1986), 415.

35   *"I think highly of you"*: Fidel Castro, cited in ibid., 447.

36   *"He easily reinforced"*: Louis A. Pérez, Jr., *On Becoming Cuban: Identity, Nationality & Culture* (New York: Ecco Press, 1999), 216–17.

39   *"with every facility"*: Douglas Blanchard, "Havana Exciting Town, Meets Steve Allen," *TS* (January 25, 1958), 10.

39   *"more modern"*: "West Indies Tour Mixes Voodoo Europe Flavour," *TS* (August 2, 1958), 26.

39   *"Havana is now"*: Blanchard, "Havana Exciting Town," 10.

40   *"We have been"*: Hector Allard, cited in John M. Kirk and Peter McKenna, *Canada-Cuba Relations: The Other Good Neighbor Policy* (Miami: University Press of Florida, 1997), 28.

40   *"Castro is not"*: G. A. Browne, cited in ibid., 29.

40   *"Concerning Batista's position"*: Hector Allard, cited in ibid., 29.

41   *"a lawyer"*: "Fighting is Fierce in Cuba Revolt," UPI (November 30, 1956).

41   *"We have been fighting"*: Fidel Castro, cited in Pedro Alvarez Tabío and Otto Hernández, "An Interview That Made History," *G* (February 27, 1977), 7.

42   *"Cuba's crack . . . division"*: "Bombers Attack Cuba Insurgents," UP (June 4, 1957).

43   *"intellectual dishonesty"*: Szulc, *Fidel*, 432.

43   *"already had deep"*: Fidel Castro, cited in "An Interview with Fidel by U.S. Journalist Barbara Walters," *G* (July 17, 1977), 4.

44   *"Castro doesn't kick"* to *"Come to think of it"*: Edward Cannon, cited in James Y. Nicol, "Rebels May Win Cuba by Kindness," *TS* (July 3, 1958), 1, 14.

45   *"Robin Hood"*: Carlos Carrillo, cited in editorial "The Free Air," *TS* (January 2, 1959), 6.

45   *"First, I want it known"*: Fulgencio Batista, cited in Lloyd Lockhart, "'I'm No Dictator,' Batista Says Nature on Side of Rebels," *TS* (February 10, 1958), 3.

45–46 *"There is a tendency"*: E. J. Clarke, letter to the editor, "In Favour of Castro," *TS* (July 15, 1958), 6.

46   *"I have recently returned"*: J. Norman, letter to the editor, "Protests Jets to Cuba," *TS* (October 29, 1958), 6.

46   *"We will not interfere"*: Fidel Castro, cited in William Kinmond, "Private Estates Get Castro Axe, Farms for Poor," *TS* (January 7, 1959), 1, 23.

46   *"the desire"*: "Canada Recognizes Castro," *TS* (January 9, 1959), 13.

47   *"Tell the Canadian businessmen"*: Fidel Castro, cited in "RCMP to Be Model for Cuba Mounties," AP (January 21, 1959).

47   *"I am a leftist"*: Ernesto Che Guevara, cited in William Kinmond, "$100,000 for Castro" *TS* (January 10, 1959), 3.

47   *"Every correspondent"*: Ernesto Che Guevara, cited in "Cuban Blueprint," *TS* (February 13, 1959), 7.

47   *"menace"*: "Anti-Castro Group Meeting in Miami," AP (February 18, 1959).

48   *executions were rumoured*: "Castro Firing Squads Busy Day and Night," UPI/AP (January 12, 1959).

48   *"a widespread purge"*: "Birthplace of Castro Scene of Executions," AP (January 7, 1959).

48   *"outstanding, militant revolutionary"*: "Stop 'Suspect-Killing' Castro Tells Army," UPI/AP (January 13, 1959).

48   *"Fidel Castro's uprising"*: Editorial, "Cuba's New Peril," *TS* (January 14, 1959), 6.

48   *"We have given orders"*: Fidel Castro, cited in "'Shoot Murderers,' Castro May Execute 11,000 Batista Men," AP/UPI (January 15, 1959).

48   *"as soon as possible"*: Fidel Castro, cited in "Castro May Seek to Be President," *TS* (January 23, 1959), 3.

49   *"Orwellian"*: Levine, *Secret Missions*, 33.

51   *"most Canadians"*: Barbara Amiel, "Castro: Torturer, Murderer—and Hero of the Liberals," *DT* (January 30, 1997).

2   Paddling to Havana: Canada and the Cuban-American Stand-Off

54   *"If we get there"*: Alphonse Gagnon, cited in Allen Abel, "Trudeau Rows to Cuba," *SN* (July 15, 2000).

54   *Balsero fatalities*: Armando M. Lago estimates that, as of December 2005, 77,833 *balseros* had died attempting to reach the United States. See "Non-combat Victims of the Castro Regime January 1, 1959 to Date," posted at www.CubaArchive.org.

55   *"That would call"*: Don Newlands, cited in Abel, "Trudeau Rows to Cuba."

55   *attracted to fascism*: Max and Monique Nemni, *Young Trudeau 1919–1944: Son of Quebec, Father of Canada* (Toronto: McClelland and Stewart, 2006).

56   *"The view"*: Pierre Trudeau, *Memoirs* (Toronto: McClelland and Stewart, 1993), 40.

56   *"This trip"*: ibid., 48.

57   *"We wanted to unite"*: ibid., 70.

57   *Trudeau's grudge*: Peter C. Newman, *Here Be Dragons: Telling Tales of People, Passions and Power* (Toronto: McClelland and Stewart, 2005), 343.

59   *Trudeau corrected the record*: Carlos Fernández de Cossío, personal interview (June 8, 2004).

59   *"peasants"*: Fidel Castro, "Speech on the Fifteenth Anniversary of the Agrarian Reform Law," *G* (May 26, 1974), 2.

59   *"anti-Cuban rampage"*: Edwin A. Leahy, "Warn Castro, U.S. Buys Cuba Sugar," *TS* (October 15, 1959), 11.

59   *"Our Agrarian Reform"*: Fidel Castro, sound bite from *Fidel* (Estela Bravo director, Bravo Films, 2001).

60   *"Those who talk of war"*: Anastas Mikoyan, cited in "Mikoyan Boasts of Missile Might," AP (February 8, 1960).

60   *"friendly and selfless assistance"*: Nikita Khrushchev, cited in "Khrushchov [sic] in India Offers 'Selfless' Aid to Castro," R (February 11, 1960).

60   *"take it easy"*: Christian Herter, cited in John Brehl, "'Kicked in Teeth' by Castro, U.S. May Soon Get Tough," *TS* (March 10 ,1960), 3.

60–61   *"I don't think"*: Christian Herter, cited in "Herter: Reds in Cuban Regime," AP (March 21, 1960).

61   *Eisenhower administration announcement*: Harold Jones, "Bomb-for-Pay Adventurers and Anti-Castro Pilots Fly out of Florida Airports," UPI (April 4, 1960).

61   *"Our objective"*: Livingston Merchant, National Security Council undersecretary, cited in Piero Gleijeses, *Conflicting Missions: Havana, Washington and Africa, 1959–1976* (Chapel Hill: University of North Carolina Press, 2002), 14.

61   *"thorough consideration"*: J. C. King, head of the CIA's Western Hemisphere Division, cited in *Alleged Assassination Plots Involving Foreign Leaders: An Interim Report of the Select Committee to Study Governmental Operations with Respect to Intelligence Activities* (Washington: United States Senate, 1975), 92.

62   *"harassment"*: Gordon Gray, special assistant for national security affairs, cited in Gleijeses, *Conflicting Missions*, 15.

62   *"challenge to the sovereignty"*: Fidel Castro, cited in "Expect Ike to Hit Cuba Early," UPI (July 4, 1960).

62   *"in a frenzy"*: Fidel Castro, cited in "Castro Condemns 'U.S. Hate Frenzy,'" UPI/AP (July 7, 1960).

62   *"On our part"*: Nikita Khrushchev, cited in "We Will Use Rockets—Nikita," UPI (July 9, 1960).

62–63   *"Hands off Cuba"*: Dwight D. Eisenhower, cited in "Ike Warning: Won't Let K. Take Cuba," UPI/AP (July 11, 1960).

64–65   *"I think it would be"* to *"appreciation of Canada"*: John G. Diefenbaker, *One Canada, Volume II* (Toronto: Macmillan, 1976), 130, 132, 151–2, 175.

65   *"at no time"* to *"prevent Canada"*: Bruce Macdonald, "Canada Plans Cuba Trade Curb," *GM* (October 21, 1960), 23.

65   *"We respect the views"*: Diefenbaker, *One Canada*, 176.

66   *"The effect"*: Editorial, "A Voice of Our Own," *GM* (October 22, 1960), 6.

66   *"I am not satisfied"*: John F. Kennedy, cited in "Kennedy Won't Hide Weaknesses of U.S.," AP (September 21, 1960).

67   *"Canadian policy"*: Diefenbaker, *One Canada*, 173–74.

68   *"There is a limit"*: Dwight D. Eisenhower, cited in E. W. Kenworthy, "U.S. Breaks off Relations with Cuban Government," NYTS (January 4, 1961).

68   *"diplomatic difficulties"*: "Canada Intends to Continue Official Ties," CP (January 4, 1961).

68   *"it is only for Ottawa"* to *"This country"*: Editorial "Washington, Havana and Ottawa," *GM* (January 5, 1961), 6.

69   *"You can't do business"*: George Hees, cited in Peter C. Newman, *Renegade in Power: The Diefenbaker Years* (Toronto: McClelland and Stewart, 1989; originally published in 1963), 352.

69   *"Turkeys, pigs and cows"*: Eldon Stonehouse, "Cuba Seeks More Cattle," *GM* (January 7, 1961), 6.

69   *"bootlegging U.S. goods"*: R. A. Farquharson, cited in "View of Trade with Cubans Called Distorted," AP (January 24, 1961).

70   *"uncomfortable"*: Arnold Heeney, cited in cited in Kirk and McKenna, *Canada-Cuba Relations*, 50.

71   *"We really have no points"*: Fidel Castro, cited in "Castro Speech Seen as Bid for U.S. Deal," AP (January 14, 1961).

71   *"Well, he has indicated"*: John F. Kennedy, News Conference Number 9 (April 12, 1961).

72   *"We knew about 90 per cent"*: Fidel Castro, cited in "Fidel's Interview with Several Cuban Journalists Writing for the Cuban Community Abroad and Several U.S. Journalists," *G* (September 17, 1978), 6.

73   *"soften up"*: Tad Szulc, "Rebels Say Monumental Mismanagement by CIA Wrecked Invasion," *NYT* (April 22, 1961).

73   *"Let the record show"* John F. Kennedy, cited in W.H. Lawrence, "U.S. to Act if Security Endangered," *NYT* (April 20, 1961).

73   *"witch hunt"*: Dwight D. Eisenhower, cited in "Eisenhower's Orders," AP (May 1, 1961).

73   *"We believe the punishment"*: Fidel Castro, cited in "No Mass Executions, Castro Tells Invaders," R (April 28, 1961).

74   *"There is no danger"*: Américo Cruz, cited in Walter Gray, "Sure Canadians in No Peril," *GM* (April 18, 1961), 9.

74   *"Kennedy Doctrine"*: George Bain, "Kennedy Doctrine Applies to Canada," *GM* (April 22, 1961), 1, 2.

74   *"assurances from Washington"*: William MacEachern, "Not Backing Kennedy on Cuba—Ottawa," *TS* (April 24, 1961), 3.

74   *"imperialism's first military defeat"*: Salvador Escalona Virgili, "Three Decisive Days in Cuban History," *G* (April 27, 1975), 4.

75   *Operation Mongoose*: Noam Chomsky, "International Terrorism: Image and Reality," in Alexander George, ed., *Western State Terrorism* (New York: Routledge, 1991).

76   *"President Kennedy"*: Diefenbaker, *One Canada*, 171–2.

76   *"fucker"*: John F. Kennedy, cited in Knowlton Nash, *Kennedy and Diefenbaker: The Feud That Helped Topple a Government* (Toronto: McClelland and Stewart, 1991), 160.

76   *"still agitated"* to *"having decided"*: Diefenbaker, *One Canada*, 170–1.

77   *"break the union"*: Américo Cruz, cited in Kirk and McKenna, *Canada-Cuba Relations*, 53.

77   *"Your Mr. Diefenbaker"*: Cited in Nash, *Kennedy and Diefenbaker*, 151.

77   *"I am a Marxist-Leninist"*: Fidel Castro, cited in "Castro Proposes Communist State," AP (December 4, 1961).

80   *"cessation of all subversive activities"*: Fidel Castro, cited in "Relinquish Base, Halt Arms Buildup, Castro's Demand to Washington" AP (October 29, 1962).

80   *"the big loser"*: Editorial, "The Big Loser," *GM* (October 30, 1962), 6.

81   *"If we go along"*: Howard Green, cited in Jamie Glazov, *Canadian Policy toward Khrushchev's Soviet Union* (Montreal: McGill-Queen's University Press, 2002), 142.

81   *"dumbfounded"*: Robert Kennedy, cited in ibid., 142.

82   *"The Soviet Union"*: John G. Diefenbaker, cited in "Text of Statements by Prime Minister and Liberal Leader on Cuban Crisis," CP (October 26, 1962).

82   *"It seems to me"*: T. C. Douglas, cited in "Douglas Assails U.S.," *GM* (October 23, 1962), 13.

82   *"It is good to know"*: Lester B. Pearson, cited in "Text of Statements" CP (October 26, 1962).

83   *"statesmanlike"*: Editorial, "Canada and the Crisis," *GM* (October 24, 1962), 6. See also editorial, "The Crisis Continues," *GM* (October 25, 1962), 6.

84   *"canoodling with Castro"*: John G. Diefenbaker, *Hansard* (February 9, 1977), 2875.

84   *"Mr. Speaker"*: John G. Diefenbaker, ibid. (February 3, 1976), 10572.

84   *"love affair"*: John G. Diefenbaker, ibid. (May 23, 1978), 5628.

84   *"idiots"*: Pierre Trudeau, cited in J. L. Granatstein and Robert Bothwell, *Pirouette: Pierre Trudeau and Canadian Foreign Policy* (Toronto: University of Toronto Press, 1990), 7.

85   *"Canadian government"*: Pierre Trudeau, paraphrased in "PM Visit to LATAM: Official Talk" (confidential memo from Havana to External Affairs Ottawa, January 28, 1976). LAC, RG25, file 20–CDA–9–Trudeau-Latam, pt. 3.

86   *"continue diplomatic"*: Paul Martin, cited in David van Praagh, "Martin Stands Firm on Trade with Cuba despite OAS Action," *GM* (July 28, 1964), B1.

3   The "Canadian Castro": Pierre Trudeau in Power

89   *"really didn't interest me"*: Trudeau, *Memoirs*, 202.

89   *"I felt it was a duty"*: ibid., 224.

89   *"Canada's Henry Kissinger"*: Trudeau, *Beyond Reason*, 176.

90   *"the brainchild"*: Ron Gostick, cited in Ron Haggart, "Martin Mailing List Used for Smear: Trudeau Aides," *TS* (April 3, 1968), 9.

90   *"pro-Soviet, pro-Castro and pro-Mao"*: Pamphlet, cited in "Anti-Trudeau Hate Campaign Floods Metro," *TS* (June 14, 1968), 4.

90   *"a potential Canadian Castro"*: Edmund Burke Society pamphlet, cited in ibid., 4.

90   *"I've canoed"*: Pierre Trudeau, cited in "Trudeau," *TS* (June 14, 1968), 4.

91   *"Never before"*: Peter C. Newman, "The Facts and Fiction of the Trudeau Smears," *TS* (June 13, 1968), 7.

91   *"We've got a crypto-Communist"*: George Wallace, cited in "Trudeau a
      Communist, Says George Wallace," CP (September 27, 1971).

91   *"Since June of 1968"*: John Birch Society pamphlet, cited in "John Birchers
      Recruit in Canada, Call Trudeau Red," TS (June 17, 1971), 13.

91   *"Red Mike"*: John Birch Society booklet, *Canada: How the Communists Took
      Control*, cited in Fraser Kelly, "Our Latest Import: Anti-Red Smears," TS
      (July 8, 1972), 16.

91   *"virulent collectivism"*: *Baron's* editorial, cited in "'Canada Has a Lot of Fence-
      mending to Do' with Neighbor," GM (July 1,1976), 7.

92   *"orthodox alliance priorities"*: Ivan Head and Pierre Trudeau, *The Canadian Way:
      Shaping Canada's Foreign Policy, 1968–1984* (Toronto: McClelland and Stewart,
      1995), 219.

92   *"I felt that people"*: Pierre Trudeau, cited in John English, *Citizen of the World*
      (Toronto: Knopf, 2006) 268.

93   *international star*: Richard Gwyn, *The Northern Magus: Pierre Trudeau and
      Canadians* (Toronto: PaperJacks, 1981), 295.

94   *"possibility of the two countries"*: Pierre Trudeau, sound bite from "Trudeau's
      Telegram," CBC Radio broadcast (October 1, 1972).

96   *Serious studies of Cuban-Americans*: See, for example, Brett Heindl, "From Miami
      with Love: Transnational Political Activism in the Cuban Exile Community,"
      Michele Zebich-Knos and Heather N. Nicol, eds., *Foreign Policy toward Cuba:
      Isolation or Engagement?* (New York: Lexington, 2005), 161–90.

96   *Cubans in Canada*: Roger E. Hernández, *Cuban Immigration* (Philadelphia:
      Mason Crest, 2004).

96   *"I can no longer defend"*: Luis A. Baralt Mederos, cited in "No Longer Can
      Defend Cuban Policy, Envoy Says," CP (June 16, 1960).

98   *"tame the bear"*: Peter W. Rodman, *More Precious Than Peace: The Cold War and
      the Struggle for the Third World* (New York: Scribner's, 1994), 153.

98–99 *"Differences in ideology"*: *Basic Principles of Relations between the United States of
      America and the Union of Soviet Socialist Republics*, cited in H. W. Brands, *The
      Devil We Knew: Americans and the Cold War* (New York: Oxford University Press,
      1993), 125.

100   *"There will be no change"*: Richard Nixon, cited in Roger Morris, *Uncertain
      Greatness: Henry Kissinger and American Foreign Policy* (New York: Harper and
      Row, 1977), 106.

100   *Kennedy used classified intelligence*: Seymour M. Hersh, *The Dark Side of Camelot*
      (New York: Little Brown, 1997), Chapter 12.

101   *"too many good friends"*: Richard Nixon, cited in Morris, *Uncertain Greatness*, 106.

101   *"stronger than Brazil"*: Richard Nixon, cited in Robert Reguly, "Unsinkable
      Richard Nixon Takes a New Shot at U.S. Presidency," TS (February 5, 1968),
      25.

101   *"The first thing"*: Roy Burleigh, cited in Seymour M. Hersh, *The Price of Power:
      Kissinger in the Nixon White House* (New York: Summit, 1983), 251.

101   *"fifteen years behind the times"*: Fidel Castro, cited in Wayne Edmonstone, "Contemptuous Cubans Call Nixon a Gangster and Await War Cries from the White House," *TS* (January 13, 1969), 7.

102   *"dialogue and détente"*: "Kosygin's Cuba Visit Expected to Explain New Talks with U.S.," R (October 21, 1971).

102   *"inflexibly opposed"*: "Castro Flexible," *GM* (March 3, 1972), B1.

102   *"complex man"*: Trudeau, *Memoirs*, 217.

103   *"It cannot be said"*: Henry Kissinger, *The White House Years* (New York: Little Brown, 1979), 383.

103   *"there was no way"*: Trudeau, *Memoirs*, 218.

103   *"I had been called"*: Ibid., 218.

103   *"I laid the foundations"*: Ibid., 156.

104   *"our Canadian friends"*: Richard Nixon, cited in "Nixon Calls for Tougher Stand against Castro," AP (July 8, 1968).

104   *"Oh yeah"*: Richard Nixon, cited in Hersh, *The Price of Power*, 106.

104   *"This is rather silly"*: Editorial, "The Last Outlaw" *TS* (November 12, 1971), 6.

104   *"It is important to recognize"*: Pierre Trudeau, cited in Terrance Wills, "Trudeau Fields Hawkish Question and Calls for U.S. Dialogue with Cuba," *GM* (March 26, 1969), 1.

104–105 *"Short of being"*: Trudeau, cited in Kirk and McKenna, *Canada-Cuba Relations*, 98.

105   *"stinger"*: Editorial, "Off to an Encouraging Start," *GM* (March 26, 1969), 6.

105   *"a couple of dozen"*: René Lévesque, "For an Independent Quebec," Michael D. Behiels, ed., *Quebec since 1945* (Toronto: Copp Clark Pitman, 1987), 272.

105   *"FLQ suicide commandos"*: "FLQ," *GM* (June 4, 1963), 2.

106   *"Québec separatists"*: Wayne Edmonstone, "Cubans *Are* Interested in Quebec Separatists," *TS* (November 14, 1967), 7.

106   *"undermining the national integrity"*: José Fernández de Cossío, cited in Kirk and McKenna, *Canada-Cuba Relations*, 104.

107   *"If a democratic society"*: Pierre Trudeau, "Notes for a National Broadcast by the Prime Minister," (October 16, 1970).

108   *"jarred by the rigidity"*: Jeremy Kinsman, "Who Is My Neighbour? Trudeau and Foreign Policy," *London Journal of Canadian Studies* 18 (2002–03), 103–20.

109   *"Dear Mr. Prime Minister"*: Pierre Trudeau, letter to Fidel Castro (December 14, 1970). LAC, RG25, file 20–1–2–Cuba, 1.

109–110 *"For visiting Canadians"*: Tom Leach, cited in "Cross Kidnappers Find Few Laughs in Cuba Exile," *TS* (November 6, 1971), 3.

110   *RCMP views of Cuba and the FLQ:* "Russians Hope Trudeau Trip Can Break Arms Deadlock," *TS* (May 15, 1971), 5.

111   *"The stiletto"*: Ambassador W. Walton Butterworth, cited in Gleijeses, *Conflicting Missions*, 223.

111   *"I've always believed"*: Luis Posada Carriles, cited in "U.S. Detains Castro Foe," AP (May 18, 2005).

111   *Cuban allegations against Bosch*: "Orlando Bosch's Terrorist Curriculum Vitae," G (January 31, 2002).

111   *U.S. complicity in emigré terrorism*: Salim Lamrani, ed., *Superpower Principles: U.S. Terrorism against Cuba* (New York: Common Courage Press, 2005).

111–112 *"U.S.-directed international terrorism"*: Chomsky, "International Terrorism."

112   *"aid and trade" letter to Canadian Embassy in Cuba*: Cited in "Threats Sent Canada by Castro Enemies," AP (January 20, 1961).

113   *"because of the insulting"*: Felipe Rivero Díaz, cited in "Anti-Castro Chief Says Followers Planted Cuban Embassy Bomb," *GM* (September 23, 1966), 4.

114–115 *RCMP and the Montreal consulate bombing*: John Sawatsky, *Men in the Shadows: The RCMP Security Service* (Toronto: Doubleday, 1980), 1–6.

116   *"for caring more"*: Gwyn, *Northern Magus*, 139.

116   *"institute policies"*: Trudeau, *Memoirs*, 164–5.

116   *"new nationalism"*: Ryan Edwardson, "'Kicking Uncle Sam out of the Peaceable Kingdom': English-Canadian 'New Nationalism' and Americanization," *Journal of Canadian Studies* 37:4 (winter 2003).

116   *"reduce our economic dependence"*: Trudeau, *Memoirs*, 203–5.

117   *"very buddy-buddy"*: Joey Smallwood, cited in Kildare Dobbs, "Joey Smallwood's Book Going Strong around the Country," *TS* (October 16, 1973), G7.

117   *"What impresses one"*: David Lewis, "The New Cuba: Immense Progress Made in 12 Years," *TS* (March 29, 1975), B3.

117–118 *"It is easy"*: Pierre Trudeau, cited in Ronald Lebel, "New Mideast Turmoil Possible, Trudeau Says," *GM* (September 29, 1970), 2.

119   *"harsh medicine"*: Trudeau, *Memoirs*, 196.

119   *"I found myself"*: Ibid., 198.

119   *"Trudeau is trying"*: Edgar G. Burton, cited in Jack McArthur, "Investors Yawn While Trudeau Threatens Upheaval," *GM* (January 1, 1976), B7.

119   *"confirmed what a lot"*: Peter Bawden, cited in Chris Dennett, "Folks Back Home Give MPs an Earful," *TS* (January 24, 1976), 1–2.

119   *"similarities"*: Jack Horner, cited in "Daniel Stoffman, "Horner Likens Trudeau to Hitler," *TS* (January 14, 1976), A4.

120   *"thinking out loud"*: Richard Gwyn, "Trudeau is Only Thinking Out Loud," *TS* (January 3, 1976), B7.

120   *"heading toward socialism"*: "Gallup Poll: Half of Canadians See Trend towards Socialism," *TS* (January 21, 1976), B5.

120   *"Can you imagine"*: McArthur, "Investors Yawn," B7.

120   *"no plans to subvert"*: Trudeau, *Memoirs*, 198.

4   *El Diálogo*: Thawing the Cold War

121–122 *Venceremos Brigades*: See Sandra Levinson, "The Venceremos Brigades," Aviva
Chomsky et al., eds., *The Cuba Reader: History, Culture Politics* (Durham, NC: Duke
University Press, 2003), 517–20.

122 *"This return"*: Alastair Gillespie, cited in Kirk and McKenna, *Canada-Cuba
Relations*, 100.

122 *"Cuba has a serious shortage"*: Editorial "Cuba, 10 Years after" *GM*
(January 1, 1969), 6.

123 *"The message"*: Paul Gérin-Lajoie, cited in "Delegates from the Canadian
International Development Agency Meet with Carlos Rafael Rodríguez," *G*
(February 17, 1974), 5.

124 *"Castro-land"*: Gerry Hall, "Fly to Cuba," *TS* (February 28, 1970), 3.

124–125 *"Right now"*: Fred Miller, cited in Bob Pennington, "Metro Tourists' Brief
Encounter with New Cuba," *TS* (February 3, 1973), 87.

125 *"a four-by-four-foot cell"*: "Hijackers Will Face Life behind Bars, Pilot Quotes
Castro," R (November 14, 1972).

126 *"equality and strict reciprocity"*: "Cubans to Send Hijackers Back to Their
Countries," *NYT* (September 20, 1969).

127 *"trapped in Cuba"*: "Canadian Pilots Delayed in Cuba," CP (April 19, 1961).

127 *"one more time"*: Genevieve Lippert, cited in "Mother Begs Castro for Last Sight
of Son," *TS* (February 13, 1973), 22.

128 *"Canadian officials"*: Rosemary Lawrence, cited in "Cuba Eases Smuggler's
Detention," *TS* (July 4, 1973), 83.

128 *"This is the most exciting"*: Ruth Ann MacLean, cited in "Cuba to Let Daughter, 19,
Visit Canadian Jailed for Arms Flight," *GM* (March 15, 1973), W6.

128 *"fit and well"*: "Cuba Eases Smuggler's Detention," 83.

128–129 *"There have been many"*: Fidel Castro, cited in "Castro to Review Canadian's Jail
Term," CP (September 18, 1973).

129 *"in the interests"*: Cuban official, cited in "Words Inadequate, Only Tears," *GM*
(November 5, 1973), 1.

129 *"I didn't hear"*: Ronald Lippert, cited in ibid., 1.

130 *"There wasn't a time"*: Ronald Lippert, cited in "Lippert Says He Was Beaten,
Bayoneted by Cubans," *TS* (November 6, 1973), A4.

130 *"If the Cubans"*: Ronald Lippert, cited in ibid., A4.

130 *"compromis[ed] my covert activities"*: Ron Lippert-Jones, *Spy Bate: Memoirs of a
Covert Agent* (Mansfield, Ohio: Bookmasters, 2003), x.

131 *"Castro's Bitch"*: Ibid., 240.

132 *"Cuban-Canadian Relations"*: LAC, RG25 file 20–1–2–CUBA, pt. 28, 2.

132 *"solidify[ing] Canadian-Cuban relations"*: "Prime Minister's Visit: Briefing Books,"
LAC, RG25, file 20–CDA–9–TRUDEAU–LATAM, pt. 1, 3.

133 *"Never before"*: George Lambie, "Western Europe and Cuba's Development
in the 1980s and 1990s," Alistair Hennessy and George Lambie, eds., *The*

Fractured Blockade: West European–Cuban Relations during the Revolution (London: Macmillan, 1993), 291.

133 *"to pre-empt"*: Dan Turner, "Cuba Cool to Canadians Trying to Bolster Trade," *TS* (March 20, 1975), A23.

134 *"We are really not impatient"*: Fidel Castro, cited in Lionel Martin, "Canada Links Sound, Castro Says," *GM* (March 22, 1975), 10.

134 *"Increasingly our sanctions"*: Henry Kissinger, *Years of Renewal* (New York: Simon and Schuster, 1999), 772.

135 *"the death knell"*: Timothy Ross, "OAS Keeps Ban on Trade with Cuba," *TS* (November 13, 1974), B14.

135 *"If Cuba will reevaluate"*: Gerald Ford, cited in Kissinger, *Years of Renewal*, 777.

135 *"We see no virtue"*: Kissinger, ibid., 777.

135 *"A very short time"*: Pierre Trudeau, "Transcript of the Prime Minister's Press Conference, Havana, Cuba, January 29, 1976," LAC, RG25, file 20–CDA–9–TRUDEAU–LATAM pt. 3, 11–12.

135 *"puts a finish"*: Editorial, "Ending the Boycott That Didn't Work," *TS* (August 2, 1975), B2.

136 *"Since the administrators"*: Fidel Castro, cited in "Bureaucratic Bungling Admitted by Castro," *GM* (August 12, 1963), 19.

137 *"economic contribution"*: Susan Eva Eckstein, *Back from the Future: Cuba under Castro* (Princeton, N.J.: Princeton University Press, 1994), 42, 51–2.

138 *The repression of opponents*: See Jorge Dominguez, "Cuba Since 1959," Leslie Bethell, ed., *Cuba: A Short History* (New York: Cambridge University Press, 1993).

138–139 *"Without going beyond"*: Osvaldo Dorticós, Speech of 27 October 1975," *G* (November 9, 1975), 7.

139 *"We must do without"*: Fidel Castro, cited in "PM Visit to Latin America: Official Talks," LAC, RG25, file 20–CDA–9–TRUDEAU–LATAM, pt. 3, 3.

139 *"very strongly"*: George McGovern, cited in "McGovern Seeks End to Cuba Trade Boycott," *R* (May 10, 1975).

139–140 *"There can be no mistake"*: George McGovern, cited in "Ship Food, Drugs to Cuba, U.S. Urged," AP (May 14, 1975).

140 *"The mood has changed"*: Editorial, "From Havana," *GM* (August 16, 1975), 6.

140 *"a deep dark secret"*: William D. Rogers, cited in Ann Louise Bardach, *Cuba Confidential: Love and Vengeance in Miami and Havana* (New York: Random House, 2002), 258.

141 *"It is not that Cuba reject[s]"*: Fidel Castro, cited in Kissinger, *Years of Renewal*, 787.

141 *"Castro needed the United States"*: Kissinger, ibid., 786.

144 *"We are not enemies"*: Fidel Castro, "Angola: African Girón, 19 April 1976," Michael Taber, ed., *Fidel Castro's Speeches: Cuba's Internationalist Foreign Policy 1975–80* (New York: Pathfinder, 1981), 95–6.

5   Trudeau's Gamble: The Angolan Crisis

146 *"The world"*: "1976 . . . Or Is It 1983?" *TS* (January 1, 1976), A8.

147 *"The time has come"*: Pierre Trudeau, cited in "Trudeau Calls on Canadians to 'Do More and Be Better,'" CP (January 1, 1976).

147 *"We now have in Canada"*: Ed Broadbent, cited in "Trudeau Incompetent, NDP Leader Charges," *TS* (January 24, 1976), A2.

148 *"may have been behaving"*: Frank Church, cited in "Senator Believes CIA May Have Behaved Like 'Rogue Elephant,'" *TS* (July 19, 1975), 10.

150 *"I was deeply troubled"*: Jimmy Carter, *Keeping Faith: Memoirs of a President* (New York: Bantam, 1982), 143.

150 *"The intelligence investigations"*: Kissinger, *Years of Renewal*, 343.

150–151 *"The war in Angola"*: Birch Bayh, cited in Brands, *The Devil We Knew*, 136.

151 *"If ever there is"*: Edward Kennedy, cited in ibid., 136.

152 *"an eclectic interpretation"*: Gleijeses, *Conflicting Missions*, 236.

152 *"sympathetic to the West"*: Gerald R. Ford, *A Time to Heal* (New York: Harper and Row, 1979), 345.

153 *"a cockpit of covert operations"*: Murray Harder, "Angola: U.S. Miscalculated in African Struggle," *TS* (January 10, 1976), B6.

154 *"the collaborator"*: Ibid., B6.

154 *"We shall defend"*: Fidel Castro, cited in "Who Needs You? A Defiant Castro Tells Jerry Ford," AP/UPI (December 23, 1975).

155 *"associated with the advent"*: D. Fraser, "Prime Minister's Visit: Briefing Books" (November 6, 1975), LAC, RG 25, file 20–CDA–9–TRUDEAU–LATAM, pt. 1, 2.

156 *"touchy issue"*: External Affairs official, cited in Bruce Garvey, "Trudeau Will Ask Castro to Stay out of Angola Fight," *TS* (January 15, 1976), A8.

156 *"Was Russia behind"* to *"In doing so"*: James Hyndman, personal interviews and correspondence (December 2004–June 2005).

157 *"sharp frictions"*: Editorial, "Trudeau's Cuban Trip Poorly Timed," *TS* (January 22, 1976), B4.

157–158 *Intelligence files on Venceremos Brigades*: Juan Antonio Blanco, personal interview (April 21, 2006).

6   *¡Bienvenido!* Pierre and Margaret in Latin America

161 *"Bloody cold"*: Pierre Trudeau, cited in Bruce Garvey, "Trudeaus Receive Warm Welcome in Sunny Mexico," *TS* (January 24, 1976), A1.

162 *"the year I fell in love"*: Trudeau, *Memoirs*, 156.

162 *"Don't be the mistress"*: Trudeau, *Beyond Reason*, 46.

162 *"student rebellion"*: Ibid., 18.

164 *"square, critical"*: Ibid., 21.

164   *"I was absolutely taboo"*: Ibid., 83.

164   *"I learned far more about him"*: Ibid., 33.

165   *"destined for eternal solitude"*: Ibid., 42.

165   *"I want to be"*: Pierre Trudeau, cited in Gwyn, *Northern Magus*, 31–2.

165   *"I don't even know"*: "Margaret Plans to Take a Job—'Moms Can Have Careers, Too,'" UPI (February 7, 1976).

166   *"arrogant and aloof"*: Trudeau, *Beyond Reason*, 158.

166   *"saddened every time"* to *"I didn't care"*: ibid., 48.

166   *"I would marry Pierre"*: Ibid., 61.

167   *"Tears pouring down my own face"*: Ibid., 58.

167   *"just laughed"*: Ibid., 165.

168–169   *"I was the youngest"*: Ibid., 148.

169   *"What struck me"*: Hyndman, interview.

169–170   *"the most hippy member"*: Trudeau, *Beyond Reason*, 171.

170   *"It was like coming home"*: Ibid., 171.

171   *"a failure to overcome"*: Pierre Trudeau, cited in Bruce Garvey, "Trudeaus Receive Warm Welcome in Sunny Mexico," *TS* (January 24, 1976), A2.

171   *Contrapesos*: "Report on the Prime Minister's Visit to Mexico, Cuba and Venezuela," LAC, RG25, file 20–CDA–9–TRUDEAU–LATAM, pt. 3, 15.

171   *"very strong and friendly relations"*: Pierre Trudeau, cited in Bruce Garvey, "A Brief Rest in Mexico and PM's Off to Cuba," *TS* (January 26, 1976), A1, A9.

172   *"Leave the people"*: Luis Echeverría Álvarez, cited in ibid.

172   *"more advantageous"*: Pierre Trudeau, cited in ibid.

172   *"who was not only charming"*: Trudeau, *Beyond Reason*, 171.

172   *"surprise and delight"*: Pierre Trudeau, cited in "With a Bottle and Burps Baby Michel Steals Show," *TS* (January 26, 1976), A9.

173   *"Thank you so much"*: Trudeau, *Beyond Reason*, 171.

173   *"long-winded answers"*: Garvey, "A Brief Rest," A1.

174   *"exploited"*: Bruce Garvey, "Castro Gives Huge Welcome for Trudeau," *TS* (January 27, 1976), A1.

174   *"You make me so bloody mad"*: Margaret Trudeau, cited in "With a Bottle," A9.

175   *"The category of people"* to *"We'll likely agree to disagree"*: Pierre Trudeau, cited in Bruce Garvey, "Cubans Cheer Trudeau," *TS* (January 27, 1976), A2.

176   *"a stream"*: Trudeau, *Beyond Reason*, 172.

176   *"Hi, Jim"*: Hyndman, interview.

176   *"I am very glad"*: Fidel Castro, cited in Trudeau, *Beyond Reason*, 172.

177   *"treated as junior"*: "PM's Visit to Latin American: Program" (November 19, 1975), LAC, RG25, file 20–CDA–9–TRUDEAU–LATAM pt. 1, 2.

177   *"This is the answer"*: Trudeau, *Beyond Reason*, 173.

178   *"a glittering occasion"*: Garvey, "Castro Gives Huge Welcome," A1.

178   *"You are not only pretty"*: Fidel Castro, cited in Trudeau, *Beyond Reason*, 172.

178   *"a ridiculously romantic man"*: ibid., 177.

178–179 *"It is clear that women"*: Fidel Castro, "Speech before the Federation of Cuban Women," *G* (December 8, 1974), 2.

179 *"he desired from the outset"*: Garvey, "Castro Gives Huge Welcome," A1.

179 *"Trudeau and his wife"*: Garvey, "Cubans Cheer Trudeau," A2.

180 *"continuous dialogue"*: "PM's Visit to Latin American: Program" (November 19, 1975), LAC, RG25, file 20–CDA–9–TRUDEAU–LATAM, pt. 1, 1.

180 *"Prime Minister Castro"*: "Report on the Prime Minister's Visit to Mexico, Cuba and Venezuela" (n.d.), LAC, RG25, file 20–CDA–9–TRUDEAU–LATAM pt. 3, 1.

181 *"worse than Hitler"*, Fidel Castro, cited in "PM Visit to Latin America: Official Talks," LAC, RG25, file 20–CDA–9–TRUDEAU–LATAM, pt. 3, 4.

181 *"It was an example"*: Hyndman, interview.

181 *"He receives aid"*: Pierre Trudeau, "Transcript of the Prime Minister's Press Conference" (January 29, 1976), LAC RG25, file 20-CDA–9–TRUDEAU–LATAM, pt. 3, 7.

182 *"clucking and cooing"*: Photo caption, *TS* (January 28, 1976), A2.

182–183 *"In truth"*: Pierre Trudeau, "Transcript of the Prime Minister's Press Conference," 2.

7   Cayo Largo: The Origins of an Unlikely Friendship

184 *"real home"*: Szulc, *Fidel*, 83.

185 *"We may still have"*: James Hyndman, "PM's Visit to Latin America: SITREP" (December 1, 1975), LAC, RG25, file 20–CDA–9–TRUDEAU–LATAM, pt. 1, 2.

185 *"special program"*: Ibid., 3.

185–186 *"Suddenly"*: Hyndman, interview.

186 *"The rejoinder"*: Ibid.

186 *"I want to be frank"*: Ibid.

187 *"My own feeling"*: Ibid.

187 *"would only embarrass"*: Trudeau, *Beyond Reason*, 175.

187 *"I am not inviting any press"*: Fidel Castro, cited in ibid., 175.

187 *"Pierre is such a pacifist"*: Trudeau, ibid., 176.

188 *"it was as well"*: Ibid., 177.

188 *"You know, my eyes"*: Fidel Castro, cited in ibid., 177.

189 *"insatiable interest"*: Gwyn, *Northern Magus*, 40.

189 *"well-informed"*: Bruce Garvey, "PM Says Cuba Links Will Be Expanded," *TS* (January 29, 1976), A1–2.

189 *"pointed, trenchant questions"*: Hyndman, interview.

190 *"intense rapport"*: Pierre Trudeau, cited in Garvey, "PM Says Cuba Links Will Be Expanded," A1.

190 *"What is happening"*: Pierre Trudeau, cited in ibid., A1–2.

191 *"far less than honest"*: Trudeau, *Beyond Reason*, 175.

191   *"minimized the number"*: Trudeau, *Memoirs*, 212.

191   *"The nature and future"*: Hyndman, interview.

191   *"brutally frank"*: Pierre Trudeau, cited in Peter Lloyd, "Cuban Visit by Trudeau May Do Good: NATO Chief," *TS* (February 5, 1976), A3.

191   *"very, very wide open"*: Hyndman, interview.

192   *"explained that this"*: Trudeau. *Memoirs*, 212.

192   *"The imperialists"*: Fidel Castro, "Closing Speech to First Party Congress, 22 December 1975," Taber, ed., *Fidel Castro's Speeches*, 80.

192   *"He spoke above all"*: René Hernández Gattorno, cited in Gleijeses, *Conflicting Missions*, 300.

193   *"on its own initiative"*: David Binder, "Kissinger Believes Cuba 'Exports' Revolution Again," *NYT* (February 5, 1976), 12.

193–194 *"Ford and Kissinger lie"*: Fidel Castro, "Angola: African Girón, 19 April 1976," Taber, ed., *Fidel Castro's Speeches*, 91–3.

194   *"The Cuban intervention"*: Don Oberdorfer, "Cuban Intervention in Angola Intrigues World Capitals," *WP* (February 18, 1976), A6.

194   *"Something seemed to happen"*: James Ferrabee, "Disturbing Words on Cuba," *WT* (February 5, 1976), 8.

195   *"might have done some good"*: Joseph Luns, cited in Lloyd, "Cuban Visit by Trudeau May Do Good," A3.

195   *"a better insight"*: Pierre Trudeau, cited in "Trudeau Greeted by Venezuelans" *TS* (January 30, 1976), A2.

195   *"There was very extensive exploration"*: Pierre Trudeau, "Transcript of the Prime Minister's Press Conference" (January 29, 1976), LAC, RG25, file 20–CDA–9–TRUDEAU–LATAM, pt. 3, 2–3, 8.

195   *"What happens"*: Ferrabee, "Disturbing Words," 8.

195–196 *"He is certainly a man"*: Pierre Trudeau, "Transcript of the Prime Minister's Press Conference," 2–3, 8.

196   *"unquestionably a leader"*: Pierre Trudeau, cited in Garvey, "PM Says Cuba Links Will Be Expanded," A1–2.

196   *"he and Castro"*: Pierre Trudeau, cited in ibid.

197–198 *"We will never forget"*: Fidel Castro, cited in Garvey, "PM Says Cuba Links Will Be Expanded," A1.

198   *"This record"*: Pierre Trudeau, cited in ibid.

200–201 *"I'd rate him A-1"*: Pierre Trudeau, cited in ibid.

202   *"moved by the enthusiasm"*: Pierre Trudeau, cited in ibid.

202   *"We cannot and will never"*: Fidel Castro, "Speech at Cienfuegos, 28 January 1976," *G* (February 8, 1976), 2.

202–203 *"For Cuba this year"*: Pierre Trudeau, *"Notes pour le Discours du Premier Ministre à Cienfuegos"* (January 28, 1976), LAC, RG25, file 20–CDA–9–TRUDEAU–LATAM, pt. 3, 1.

205   *"almost frantic"*: "PM's Aides Clash with Castro's Guards at Canadian Embassy," *TS* (January 29, 1976), A2.

205   *"You can't really blame them"*: Canadian official, cited in ibid., A2.

205   *"pick and choose"*: Hyndman, interview.

205–206 *"the dogs of war"*: Fidel Castro, cited in Bruce Garvey, "'Dogs of War' Are Driven out, Castro Claims," *TS* (January 29, 1976), A12.

206   *"I'll read all about it"*: Pierre Trudeau, cited in ibid., A12.

206   *"It is a duty practically"*: Fidel Castro, cited in Garvey, "PM Says Cuba Links Will Be Expanded," A1–2.

206–207 *"tearful"*: Trudeau, *Beyond Reason*, 178.

207   *"I'm glad you're still with me"*: Pierre Trudeau, cited in ibid., 179.

8   A Song for Blanquita: Controversy in Caracas

208   *"I don't see why"*: Pierre Trudeau, cited in "PM's Visit to Cuba: General Assessment," LAC, RG25, file 20–CDA–9–TRUDEAU–LATAM, pt. 3, 1.

209   *"This is a historical happening"*: Carlos Andrés Pérez, cited in Bruce Garvey, "PM in Venezuela—Canada Dances to a Latin Beat," *TS* (January 31, 1976), A3.

209   *"Latin connection"*: Pierre Trudeau, cited in Bruce Garvey, "PM Accepts Venezuelan Offer for a New 'Latin Connection,'" *TS* (February 2, 1976), A3.

210   *"not just deaf"*: Trudeau, *Beyond Reason*, 179.

210   *"We weren't destined"*: Trudeau, *Beyond Reason*, 179–80.

211   *"all for it"*: Pierre Trudeau, cited in ibid., 181.

212   *"many of the guests"*: Bruce Garvey, "Tears in Listeners' Eyes at Margaret's Surprise Song," *TS* (February 2, 1976), A1.

212   *"The Canadian delegation"*: Trudeau, *Beyond Reason*, 181.

212   *"just about every Canadian"*: Canadian official, cited in Garvey, "Tears in Listeners' Eyes," A3.

213   *"There has been"*: Pierre Trudeau, cited in "PM's Visit to Cuba: General Assessment," 3.

9   Stranded in Havana: Pierre Trudeau and the New Cold War

219   *"Supporting the bill"*: Bill Clinton, *My Life: The Presidential Years* (New York: Random House, 2005), 310.

219–220 *"In private"*: Trudeau, *Memoirs*, 210–12.

220   *"a significant diplomatic achievement"*: Pierre Trudeau, cited in Bruce Garvey, "PM Accepts Venezuelan Offer," A3.

220   *"contributed significantly"*: Pierre Trudeau, cited in Garvey, "PM Says Cuba Links Will Be Expanded," A1–2.

220   *"He probably does"*: Gwyn, *Northern Magus*, 305.

220–221 *"Prime Minister Trudeau"*: Juana Carrasco, "Trudeau Emphasizes Progress Made by Cuba in Agriculture, Health, Education and Housing," *G* (February 8, 1976), 5.

221   *"The strong handshake"*: Héctor Hernández Pardo, "Warm Send-off for Trudeau and Canadian Delegation," *G* (February 8, 1976), 1.

221   *"extreme gratification"*: Fidel Castro, cited in "Castro's Stopover at Gander," (February 23, 1976), LAC, RG25, file 20–CUBA–9, pt. 3, 1.

221   *"On Angola"*: "Stopover at Gander by Prime Minister Castro," (February 23, 1976), LAC, RG25, file 20–CUBA–9, pt. 3, 2.

221   *"He wanted to assure"*: "Stopover at Gander," 2.

222   *Cossitt on Trudeau's "¡Viva!"*: See *Hansard* (January 29, 1976), 10423.

222   *"the reported invasion"*: Tom Cossitt, ibid. (February 2, 1976), 10522.

223   *"Since there could be"*: Pierre Trudeau, ibid. (February 3, 1976), 10570.

223   *"Why was it not appropriate"*: Robert Stanfield, ibid. (February 3, 1976), 10570.

224   *"That policy was established"*: Pierre Trudeau, ibid. (February 3, 1976), 10570.

224   *"The general perception"*: Robert Stanfield, ibid. (February 3, 1976), 10570.

224–225 *"The Prime Minister mentioned"*: John G. Diefenbaker, ibid. (February 3, 1976), 10572.

225   *"in his childhood"*: Pierre Trudeau, ibid. (February 3, 1976), 10573.

226   *"Viva Canada y Cuba"*: Pierre Trudeau, ibid. (February 3, 1976), 10579.

226   *"I think she is"*: Trudeau, *Beyond Reason*, 182.

226   *"I doubt you are listening"*: Ibid., 183.

226   *"I'm not going"*: Margaret Trudeau, cited in "Won't Be Rose on Pierre's Lapel, Margaret Says on Radio Show," *TS* (February 3, 1976), A1.

227   *"I learned an awful lot"*: Margaret Trudeau, cited in "Margaret on Herself: 'I Just Want to Work,'" *TS* (February 13, 1976), B3.

227   *"I'm talking about the freedom"*: Margaret Trudeau, cited in "Not a Martha Mitchell, Margaret Says on Radio," *TS* (February 6, 1976), A1.

227   *"She really seemed"*: Cited in Bruce Garvey, "Women Applaud as Margaret Sings Again," *TS* (February 4, 1976), A1.

227   *"The infamous escapades"*: Lily Tasso, *"Margaret, vue d'ici : Pour une Fois qu'une Anglaise se Dégèle,"* *LP* (February 6, 1976), A6.

227   *"Fuddle duddle"*: Gerry Gallagher, cited in "Margaret Praised for 'Song of Love' on Her Latin Tour," *TS* (February 5, 1976), A1.

227   *"in great shape"*: Margaret Trudeau, cited in Bruce Garvey, "Love, Life, Loneliness—Margaret Talks on TV," *TS* (February 13, 1976), A1.

228   *"Pierre understands"*: Margaret Trudeau, cited in "Margaret on Herself," B3.

228   *"I always believe"*: Pierre Trudeau, cited in "Margaret's Identity? Trudeau Skirts Issue," UPI (February 11, 1976).

229   *"incensed"*: Trudeau, *Beyond Reason*, 188.

229   *"At this stage"*: Ibid., 189.

229   *"raised eyebrows"*: "Viva Canada, Cuba, Trudeau Repeats," *WP* (February 5, 1976), A15.

229   *"The wonder is"*: William F. Buckley, cited in "Trudeau-Castro Affair Upsets U.S. Columnist," CP (February 7, 1976).

229   *"It seems a pity"*: Editorial, "Canada's Man in Havana," *NYT* (January 31, 1976), 19.

230   *"gone to great lengths"*: Richard D. Vine, cited in "PM's Visit to Cuba and Venezuela" (January 29, 1976), LAC, RG25, file 20–CDA–9–TRUDEAU–LATAM, pt. 3, 1.

230   *"feed in some valuable information"*: Hyndman, interview.

230   *"increasing its political contacts"*: James Reston, "Castro and the Caribbean," *NYT* (March 17, 1976), 41.

231   *"We've been given"*: Henry Kissinger, cited in Richard C. Thornton, *The Nixon-Kissinger Years: Reshaping America's Foreign Policy* (New York: Paragon, 1989), 354.

231   *"I have no question"*: Leonid Brezhnev, cited in Rodman, *More Precious Than Peace*, 163.

231–232 *"unwise for a President"*: Gerald Ford, cited in Thornton, *The Nixon-Kissinger Years*, 354.

232   *"worried about the state"*: "Jimmy Carter's Big Breakthrough," *T* (May 10, 1976).

232   *"the right to sell Pepsi"*: Ronald Reagan, cited in David Broder, "Beware of Détente, Reagan Warns Ford, Kissinger," *TS* (February 11, 1976), A12.

233   *"My administration"*: Gerald Ford, cited in John Picton, "Ford Warns U.S. Will Resist Aggression in West by 'International Outlaw' Castro," *GM* (March 1, 1976), 1.

233   *"we are prepared"*: Kissinger, *Years of Renewal*, 777.

233–234 *Murder of Luciano Nieves*: Bardach, *Cuba Confidential*, 192.

234   *"We have an explosion"*: Cited in ibid., 187

235   *"magnetic bomb"*: "Cuban Jet Crash Kills 78, Officials Fear Sabotage," CP (October 7, 1976).

238   *"loss of interest"*: "Herrara Case" (July 20, 1976), LAC, RG25, file 20–CUBA–9, pt. 3, 1.

238   *"quite concerned and worried"*: James Hyndman, "Canada-Cuba Relations" (September 19, 1977), LAC, RG25, file 200–10–2–CUBA, pt. 28, 2.

239   *Cuban debt*: See Eckstein, *Back from the Future*, 52.

239   *"As a result"*: James Hyndman, "Canada-Cuba Relations," 3.

239   *"It has been determined"*: Cited in "Canada Orders out 5 Cubans after Probe of Spying at Consulate," CP (January 11, 1977).

240   *"I do not wish"*: Fidel Castro, cited in "Cuba Plans to Move Troops from Angola," NYTS (May 26, 1976).

240   *"as long as necessary"*: Fidel Castro, cited in "41 Angolan Troops Are Reported Killed," R (July 27, 1976).

240   *"I have continued"*: Pierre Trudeau, letter to Fidel Castro (August 10, 1976), LAC, RG25, file 20–1–2–Cuba, pt. 28, 1.

241   *"Fidel Castro"*: Pierre Trudeau, paraphrased in "Troops to Rhodesia Would Be Error: PM," CP (June 30, 1977).

241   *"Cuba has abused"*: Editorial, "When Cuba Offends, Say So," *GM* (February 14, 1977), 6.

241   "*developing-country label*": Editorial, "Export: War," GM (April 3, 1978), 6.

241   "*canoodling with Castro*": John G. Diefenbaker, *Hansard* (February 9, 1977), 2875.

241–242 "*In Great Britain*": John G. Diefenbaker, ibid. (December 20, 1977), 2048.

242   "*This House*": John G. Diefenbaker, ibid. (9 March 1978), 3597.

242   "*Cuban troops*": Lloyd Crouse, ibid. (18 April 1978), 4612.

242   "*Canada disapproves*": Pierre Trudeau, ibid. (23 May 1978), 5628.

242   "*selfless*": Nelson Mandela, cited in Gleijeses, *Conflicting Missions*, 394.

243   "*The isolation of Cuba*": Christine Stewart, cited in Gillian McGillivray, "Trading
       with the 'Enemy': Canadian-Cuban Relations in the 1990s," Cuba Briefing Paper
       Series, Georgetown University Caribbean Project XV (December 1997), 1–16.

243   "*I was a neophyte*": Trudeau, *Memoirs*, 179.

244   "*The aftermath*": Margaret Trudeau, *Consequences* (Toronto: McClelland and
       Stewart, 1982), 13.

244   "*She developed*": Ibid., 28.

244   "*Pierre and I*": Ibid., 60.

245   "*I kept a watertight seal*": Trudeau, *Memoirs*, 178–9.

246   "*If I can be convinced*": Jimmy Carter, cited in "Carter Has Data on Cuban Plans,"
       AP (February 17, 1977).

246   "*differences*": Fidel Castro, cited in "An Interview with Fidel," G (July 17, 1977), 2.

246   "*even though we don't know*": Fidel Castro, cited in ibid., 2.

247   "*I think we've got*": Jimmy Carter, cited in "U.S. Switches Policy against Cuba."

247   "*puppet*": Jimmy Carter, *Keeping Faith: Memoirs of a President* (New York: Bantam,
       1982), 479.

247   "*We must not go to war*": Jimmy Carter, cited in "Carter Says Cuba Will Lose
       Backing," R (January 17, 1980).

248   "*As soon as people*": Rafael Gutierez, cited in Ross Laver, "Freedom," GM (April
       30, 1980), 1.

248   "*real Cubans*": Fidel Castro, cited in "Castro Security Agents Attack Crowd of
       Would-Be Refugees," AP/R (May 3, 1980).

249   "*act of defiance*": Fidel Castro, cited in Bardach, *Cuba Confidential*, 262.

249   "*Give me the word*": Alexander Haig, paraphrased by Michael Deaver in Lou
       Cannon, *President Reagan: The Role of a Lifetime* (New York: Public Affairs, 2000),
       163.

10   "The Idea of Our Time": The Human Rights Revolution

252   "*Viva Cuba Libre*": Ronald Reagan, cited in Levine, *Secret Missions*, 157.

252   "*deeply distressed*": Trudeau and Head, *The Canadian Way*, 130-1.

253   "*The Trudeau-Castro honeymoon*": Kirk and McKenna, *Canada-Cuba Relations*, 117.

253   *Reagan and secret negotiations*: See Levine, *Secret Missions*, Chapter 4.

254   "*the idea of our time*": Louis Henkin, cited on the Columbia University Law
       School website, www2.law.columbia.edu/hri/contact.htm.

254   *"There were times"*: Carter, *Keeping Faith*, 142.

254–255 *"highlight a new era"*: Clinton, *My Life*, 508–9.

255   *"America's past actions"*: Ibid., 509.

255   *"I hold the strong view"*: Kissinger, cited in Hersh, *Price of Power*, 137.

255   *"deference to the sovereignty"*: Michael Ignatieff, *Human Rights as Politics and Idolatry* (Princeton, N.J.: Princeton University Press, 2001), 11.

255   *"Don't we want"*: David A. Hollinger, "Debates with the PTA and Others," ibid., 121.

255   *"The United States"*: Office of the White House Press Secretary, *Executive Summary: Report to the President from the Commission for Assistance to a Free Cuba* (May 2004).

256   *"incitement to subversion"*: Felipe Pérez Roque, *We Are Not Prepared to Renounce Our Sovereignty* (Havana: Editora Política, 2003), 1–2.

256   *Pierre Trudeau cared deeply*: English, *Citizen of the World*, 193–4, 302.

256   *"their confidence"*: Joint communiqué, cited in "PM Brutally Frank with Castro," CP (February 3, 1976).

257   *"human contact"*: Thomas Delworth, former ambassador to the Commission on Security and Cooperation in Europe (CSCE), personal interview (December 2005).

257   *"This conference"*: Trudeau, *Memoirs*, 208.

257   *"Canada's support"*: Robert Bothwell, *The Big Chill: Canada and the Cold War* (Toronto: Irwin, 1998), Chapter 5.

257   *"It would be"*: Fidel Castro, speech (October 6, 2001).

259   *"something under 15,000"*: Fidel Castro, cited in Richard Eder, "Cuba Bids to Ease U.S. Relations," NYTS (6 July 1964).

259   *"almost all"*: Levine, *Secret Missions*, 147.

259   *"The Government of the United States"*: Fidel Castro, "Interview," G (September 17, 1978), 5.

259   *"Three hundred?"*: Fidel Castro, cited in Robitaille, "Interview."

260   *"The Bush administration's"*: Human Rights Watch, "Cuba" (1989).

260   *"U.S. credibility"*: Ibid.

260   *"We still had differences"*: Clinton, *My Life*, 125.

260–261 *"China was extremely sensitive"*: Ibid., 174.

261   *"To this day"*: Kenneth Roth, cited in Seymour M. Hersh, *Chain of Command: The Road from 9/11 to Abu Ghraib* (New York: Harper Perennial, 2004), 71.

262   *"We called our initiative"*: Lloyd Axworthy, *Navigating a New World: Canada's Global Future* (Toronto: Vintage Canada, 2004), 68.

263   *"I am sure that Trudeau"*: "Response by President Fidel Castro Ruz to a question posed by the moderator of a round table discussion on a statement made by Canadian Prime Minister Jean Chrétien during the III Summit of the Americas" (April 30, 2001).

265   *"conformity to Cuban protocol"*: Garvey, "PM Says Cuba Links Will Be Expanded, A2.

265   *"Some Americans"*: Pierre Trudeau, "Transcript of the Prime Minister's Press Conference," 13.

EPILOGUE "Call Me Pedro"

268   *"mentor-student"*: Mark Entwistle, interview.

268   *"What the U.S. is doing"*: Pierre Trudeau, cited in Brian McKenna, "Comrades-in-Arms: When Pierre Trudeau and Fidel Castro Met Again Recently, It Was Not as Leaders but as Old Friends" *SN* 108:10 (December 1993).

269   *"Canada's relationship with Cuba"*: Alexandre Trudeau, cited in Health Partners International of Canada press release (March 25, 2005).

270   *"You're not allowed"*: Joseph Poluka, cited in Steve Eckardt, "Canadian Accused of Trading with Cuba Given Fine, Probation for 'Smuggling,'" CP (February 27, 2004).

271   *"biological solution"*: Oscar Corral, "Analyst's New Job: Visualizing Cuba after Castro Dies," *MH* (June 2, 2006)

271   *"Call me Pierre"*: Pierre Trudeau, cited in McKenna, "Comrades-in-Arms."

Select Bibliography/Filmography

Axworthy, Lloyd. *Navigating a New World: Canada's Global Future*. Toronto: Vintage Canada, 2004.

Axworthy, Thomas S. and Pierre Elliott Trudeau, eds. *Towards a Just Society*. Toronto: Penguin, 1992.

Bardach, Ann Louise. *Cuba Confidential: Love and Vengeance in Miami and Havana*. New York: Random House, 2002.

Bartleman, James. *Rollercoaster: My Hectic Years as Jean Chrétien's Diplomatic Adviser, 1994–1998*. Toronto: McClelland and Stewart, 2005.

Bell, Michael, Eugene Rothman, Marvin Schiff, and Christopher Walker. *Back to the Future? Canada's Experience with Constructive Engagement in Cuba*. Ottawa: ICCAS Occasional Paper Series, September 2002.

Bethell, Leslie, ed. *Cuba: A Short History*. New York: Cambridge University Press, 1993.

Bom, Philip C. *Trudeau's Canada: Truth and Consequences*. St. Catharines: Guardian Publishing, 1977.

Bonsal, Philip W. *Cuba, Castro and the United States*. Pittsburgh: University of Pittsburgh Press, 1971.

Bothwell, Robert. *The Big Chill: Canada and the Cold War*. Toronto: Irwin, 1998.

Brands, H.W. *The Devil We Knew: Americans and the Cold War*. New York: Oxford University Press, 1993.

Bravo, Estela, director. *Fidel*. Bravo Films, 2001.

Bundy, William. *A Tangled Web: The Making of Foreign Policy in the Nixon Presidency*. New York: Hill and Wang, 1998.

Cannon, Lou. *President Reagan: The Role of a Lifetime*. New York: Public Affairs, 2000.

Carr, Barry, Pamela Maria Smorkaloff, and Aviva Chomsky, eds. *The Cuba Reader: History, Culture Politics*. Durham: Duke University Press, 2003.

Carter, Jimmy. *Keeping Faith: Memoirs of a President*. New York: Bantam, 1982.

Castañeda, Jorge G. *Compañero: The Life and Death of Che Guevara*. New York: Vintage, 1998.

Castro, Fidel. *Second Period of Sessions of the National Assembly of People's Power*. Havana: Political Publishers, 1977.

Cavell, Richard, ed. *Love, Hate and Fear in Canada's Cold War*. Toronto: University of Toronto Press, 2004.

Chomsky, Noam. "International Terrorism: Image and Reality" in *Western State Terrorism*, Alexander George, ed., Routledge, 1991.

Clinton, Bill. *My Life: The Presidential Years*. New York: Random House, 2005.

Cohen, Andrew and J.L. Granatstein, eds. *Trudeau's Shadow: The Life and Legacy of Pierre Elliott Trudeau*. Toronto: Vintage, 1988.

Cook, Ramsay. *The Teeth of Time: Remembering Pierre Elliott Trudeau*. Montreal: McGill-Queen's University Press, 2006.

Corbett, Ben. *This is Cuba: An Outlaw Culture Survives*. Cambridge: Westview Press, 2004.

Diefenbaker, John. *One Canada*. Toronto: Macmillan, 1976.

Eckstein, Susan Eva. *Back from the Future: Cuba Under Castro*. Princeton: Princeton University Press, 1994.

English, John. *Citizen of the World: The Life of Pierre Elliott Trudeau, Volume One: 1919–1968*. Toronto: Knopf, 2006.

English, John, Richard Gwynn, and P. Whitney Lackenbauer, eds. *The Hidden Pierre Elliott Trudeau: The Faith Behind the Politics*. Toronto: Novalis, 2004.

Erisman, H. Michael. *Cuba's Foreign Relations in a Post-Soviet World*. Gainesville: University Press of Florida, 2000.

Ford, Gerald R. *A Time to Heal*. New York: Harper and Row, 1979.

Fournier, Louis. *FLQ: The Anatomy of an Underground Movement*. Toronto: NC Press, 1984.

Fursenko, Alexandr and Timothy Naftali. *One Hell of a Gamble: Khrushchev, Castro and Kennedy, 1958–1964*. New York: Norton, 1997.

Garthoff, Raymond L. *The Great Transition: American-Soviet Relations and the End of the Cold War*. Washington, D.C.: Brookings Institution Press, 1994.

George, Alexander, ed. *Western State Terrorism*. New York: Routledge, 1991.

Geyer, Georgie Anne. *Guerrilla Prince: The Untold Story of Fidel Castro*. Kansas City: Andrews and McMeel, 1993.

Gillies, David. *Between Principle and Practice: Human Rights in North-South Relations*. Montreal: McGill/Queen's Press, 1996.

Glazov, Jamie. *Canadian Policy toward Khrushchev's Soviet Union*. Montreal: McGill-Queen's University Press, 2002.

Gleijeses, Piero. *Conflicting Missions: Havana, Washington and Africa, 1959–1976*. Chapel Hill, N.C.: University of North Carolina Press, 2002.

Glynn, Patrick. *Closing Pandora's Box: Arms Races, Arms Control and the History of the Cold War*. New York: HarperCollins, 1992.

Granatstein, J.L. and Robert Bothwell. *Pirouette: Pierre Trudeau and Canadian Foreign Policy*. Toronto: University of Toronto Press, 1990.

Guevara, Ernesto Che. *Reminiscences of the Cuban Revolutionary War*. New York: Monthly Review Press, 1968.

Gwyn, Richard. *The Northern Magus: Pierre Trudeau and Canadians*. Toronto: PaperJacks, 1981.

Halperin, Maurice. *Return to Havana: The Decline of Cuban Society under Castro*. Nashville: Vanderbilt University Press, 1994.

Head, Ivan and Pierre Trudeau. *The Canadian Way: Shaping Canada's Foreign Policy, 1968–1984*. Toronto: McClelland and Stewart, 1995.

Hennessy, Alistair and George Lambie, eds. *The Fractured Blockade: West European–Cuban Relations During the Revolution*. London: Macmillan, 1993.

Hernández, Roger E. *Cuban Immigration*. Philadelphia: Mason Crest, 2004.

Hersh, Seymour M. *The Price of Power: Kissinger in the Nixon White House*. New York: Summit, 1983.

_____. *The Dark Side of Camelot*. New York: Little Brown, 1997.

_____. *Chain of Command: The Road from 9/11 to Abu Ghraib*. New York: Harper Perennial, 2004.

Ignatieff, Michael. *Human Rights as Politics and Idolatry.* Princeton: Princeton University Press, 2001.

Kirk, John M. and Peter McKenna. *Canada-Cuba Relations: The Other Good Neighbor Policy.* Miami: University Press of Florida, 1997.

Kissinger, Henry. *The White House Years.* New York: Little Brown, 1979.

_____. *Years of Renewal.* New York: Simon and Schuster, 1999.

Lamrani, Salim, ed. *Superpower Principles: U.S. Terrorism Against Cuba.* New York: Common Courage Press, 2005.

Latell, Brian. *After Fidel: The Inside Story of Castro's Regime and Cuba's Next Leader.* New York: Palgrave MacMillan, 2005.

LeoGrande, William M. *Our Own Backyard: The United States in Central America, 1977–1992.* Chapel Hill, N.C.: University of North Carolina Press, 1998.

Levine, Robert M. *Secret Missions to Cuba: Fidel Castro, Bernardo Benes and Cuban Miami.* New York: Palgrave Macmillan, 2001.

Lippert-Jones, Ron. *Spy Bate: Memoirs of a Covert Agent.* Mansfield, Ohio: Bookmasters, 2003.

McDonald, Kenneth. *His Pride, Our Fall: Recovering from the Trudeau Revolution.* Toronto: Key Porter, 1995.

McNeill, Don, producer. *Viva Cuba: Trudeau Goes Abroad.* Toronto: CBC Television News Special, 3 February 1976.

Mesa-Lago, Carmelo. *Cuba in the 1970s: Pragmatism and Institutionalization.* Albuquerque: University of New Mexico Press, 1974.

Morris, Roger. *Uncertain Greatness: Henry Kissinger and American Foreign Policy.* New York: Harper and Row, 1977.

Nash, Knowlton. *Kennedy and Diefenbaker: The Feud that Helped Topple a Government.* Toronto: McClelland and Stewart, 1991.

Nemni, Max, and Monique Nemni. *Young Trudeau 1919–1944: Son of Quebec, Father of Canada.* Toronto: McClelland and Stewart, 1963.

Newman, Peter C. *Renegade in Power: The Diefenbaker Years.* Toronto: McClelland and Stewart, 1963.

_____. *Here Be Dragons: Telling Tales of People, Passions and Power.* Toronto: McClelland and Stewart, 2005.

Nixon, Richard M. *The Memoirs of Richard Nixon.* New York: Grosset & Dunlap, 1978.

Office of the White House Press Secretary. *Executive Summary: Report to the President from the Commission for Assistance to a Free Cuba.* Washington: 2004.

Paterson, Thomas G. *Contesting Castro: The United States and the Triumph of the Cuban Revolution.* New York: Oxford University Press, 1994.

Pérez, Jr., Louis A. *On Becoming Cuban: Identity, Nationality & Culture.* New York: Ecco Press, 1999.

Pons, Eugene. *Castro and Terrorism: A Chronology.* Miami: Institute for Cuban & Cuban-American Studies, 2001.

Rodman, Peter W. *More Precious Than Peace: The Cold War and the Struggle for the Third World.* New York: Scribner's, 1994.

Rogoziński, Jan. *A Brief History of the Caribbean.* New York: Plume, 1999.

Roque, Felipe Pérez. *We Are Not Prepared to Renounce Our Sovereignty*. Havana: Editora Política, 2003.

Sawatsky, John. *Men in the Shadows: The RCMP Security Service*. Toronto: Doubleday, 1980.

Schwab, Peter. *Cuba: Confronting the U.S. Embargo*. New York: St. Martin's, 1999.

Select Committee to Study Governmental Operations with Respect to Intelligence Activities (Church Committee). *Alleged Assassination Plots Involving Foreign Leaders: Interim Report*. Washington: United States Senate, 1975.

Sharp, Mitchell. *Which Reminds Me: A Memoir*. Toronto: University of Toronto Press, 1994.

Smith, Wayne S. *The Closest of Enemies: A Personal and Diplomatic History of the Castro Years*. New York: Norton, 1987.

Southam, Nancy, ed. *Pierre: Colleagues and Friends Talk about the Trudeau They Knew*. Toronto: McClelland and Stewart, 2005.

Stevenson, Brian J.R. *Canada, Latin America and the New Internationalism: A Foreign Policy Analysis, 1968–1990*. Montreal: McGill-Queens University Press, 2000.

Sulzberger, C.L. *The World and Richard Nixon*. New York: Prentice Hall 1987.

Szulc, Tad. *Fidel: A Critical Portrait*. New York: Post Road Press, 1986.

Taber, Michael, ed. *Fidel Castro's Speeches: Cuba's Internationalist Foreign Policy, 1975–80*. New York: Pathfinder, 1981.

Thornton, Richard C. *The Nixon-Kissinger Years: Reshaping America's Foreign Policy*. New York: Paragon, 1989.

Torres, Maria de los Angeles. *In the Land of Mirrors: Cuban Exile Politics in the United States*. Ann Arbor, Mich.: University of Michigan Press, 1991.

Trudeau, Margaret. *Beyond Reason*. New York: Simon & Schuster, 1979.

_____. *Consequences*. Toronto: McClelland and Stewart, 1982.

Trudeau, Pierre. *Memoirs*. Toronto: McClelland and Stewart, 1993.

Valladares, Armando. *Against All Hope: The Prison Memoirs of Armando Valladares*. New York: Knopf, 1986.

Welch, Richard E., Jr. *Response to Revolution: The United States and the Cuban Revolution, 1959–1961*. Chapel Hill, N.C.: University of North Carolina Press, 1985.

Weldes, Jutta. *Constructing National Interests: The United States and the Cuban Missile Crisis*. Minneapolis: University of Minnesota Press, 1999.

Zebich-Knos, Michele and Heather N. Nicol, eds. *Foreign Policy Toward Cuba: Isolation or Engagement?* New York: Lexington, 2005.

Index